# IKEA

## HOW TO BECOME THE WORLD'S RICHEST PERSON

Johan Stenebo

GIBSON SQUARE

This edition first published by Gibson Square

USA    Tel:    +1 646 216 9813
UK     Tel:    +44 (0)20 7096 1100

rights@gibsonsquare.com
www.gibsonsquare.com

ISBN        9781783341726

*Papers used by Gibson Square are natural, recyclable products made from wood grown in sustainable forests; inks used are vegetable based. Manufacturing conforms to ISO 14001, and is accredited to FSC and PEFC chain of custody schemes. Colour-printing is through a certified CarbonNeutral® company that offsets its CO2 emissions.*

# Contents

# What (not) to do in an **IKEA** store

1. *Never use the blue shopping bags*
IKEA's famous yellow and blue bags are there to entice you to shop more than you need. Never, ever pick one up.

2. *Beware of open-the-wallet items*
Who doesn't need a toilet brush or a nightlight? These are the kinds of items that appear as soon as you walk into most IKEA stores. They have a price that no one can withstand. Once you buy one, you have opened your wallet and are more likely to buy more.

3. *The cheap, end-of-display item*
This could be a cheap sofa too tacky to put in your home, so you choose the more expensive sofa right next to it instead, believing you did so independently. The price impression of the first sofa contaminates your view on the product you bought. You walk away thinking the store is still cheap.

4. *Spot the hot-hot-hot spot*
This is the most frequented area in each part of the store. In IKEA, it's likely to be a comfortable open corner where customers have space to rest. That's
where products are put they are desperate to get rid of – for a reason.

5. *Get a grip on why you shop*
Think of all the stuff you bought within the last 24-month period that you haven't used in the last year, and calculate the amount of money you spent on them. That will be a sobering exercise.

# 'The will of a furniture seller'

1. The product range – our identity

We shall offer a wide range of well-designed, functional home furnishing products at prices so low that as many people as possible will be able to afford them.

### *Range*

The objective **must be** to encompass the total home environment, i.e. to offer furnishings and fittings for every part of the home whether indoors or outdoors. The range **may** also include tools, utensils and ornaments for the home as well as more or less advanced components for do-it-yourself furnishing and interior decoration. It **may** also contain a smaller number of articles for public buildings. The range must always be limited to avoid any adverse effect on the overall price picture. The main effort must always be concentrated on the essential products in each product area.

### *Profile*

The main emphasis must always be on our basic range – on the part that is 'typically IKEA'. Our basic range must have its own profile. It must reflect our way of thinking by being as simple and straightforward as we are ourselves. It must be hard-wearing and easy to live with. It must reflect an easier, more natural and unconstrained way of life. It must express form, and be colourful and cheerful, with a youthful accent that appeals to the young at heart of all ages.

In Scandinavia, people should perceive our basic range as typically IKEA. Elsewhere, they should perceive it as typically Swedish.

Alongside the basic product range, we may have a smaller range in a more traditional style which appeals to most people and which may be combined with our basic range. This part of the range must be **strictly limited** outside Scandinavia.

### *Function and technical quality*

'Throw-away' products are not IKEA. Whatever the consumer purchases shall give long-term enjoyment. That is why our products must be functional and well-made. But quality must never be an end in itself: it must be adjusted to the consumer's needs. A tabletop, for example, needs a harder-wearing surface than a shelf in a bookcase. In the first example, a more expensive finish offers the consumer long-lasting utility, whereas in the latter it just hurts the customer by adding to the price. Quality must always be adapted to the consumer's interests in the long-term. Our benchmarks should be the basic Swedish Möbelfakta requirements or other sensible norms.

### *Low price with a meaning*

The many usually have limited financial resources. It is the many whom we aim to serve. The first rule is to maintain an extremely low level of prices. But they must be low prices with a meaning. We must not compromise either functionality or technical quality.

No effort must be spared to ensure our prices are perceived to be low. There shall always be a substantial price difference compared to our competitors, and we shall always have the best value-for-money offers for every function. Every product area must include 'breath-taking offers', and our range must never grow so large as to jeopardise our price picture. The concept of a low price with a meaning makes enormous demands on all our co-workers. That includes product developers, designers, buyers, office and warehouse staff, sales people and all other cost bearers who are in a position to influence our purchase prices and **all our other costs** – in short, every single one of us! Without low costs, we can never accomplish our purpose.

*Changes in our range policy*

Our basic policy of serving the many people can never be changed. Changes in the guidelines given here concerning the composition of our product range can be made only by joint decision of the Boards of Ingka Holding B.V. and Inter IKEA Systems B.V.


2. The IKEA® spirit – a strong and living reality

You have certainly experienced it. You may even have given it our own interpretation on it. Obviously it was easier to keep alive in the old days when there were not so many of us, when we were all within reach of each other and could talk to each other. It is naturally harder now that the individual has gradually been lost in the grey conformity of collective bargaining and the numbered files of the personnel department.

Things were more concrete in those days – the readiness to give each other a helping hand with everything; the art of managing on small means, of making the best of what we had; cost-consciousness to the point of being stingy; humbleness, undying enthusiasm and the wonderful sense of community through thick and thin. But both IKEA and society have changed since then.

But the spirit is still to be found in every one of our workplaces. Among old co-workers and new ones. Heroic efforts are still being made – daily – and there are many, many people who still feel the same way. Not everybody in a large group like ours can feel the same sense of responsibility and enthusiasm. Some undoubtedly regard the job simply as a means of livelihood – a job like any other.

Sometimes you and I must share the blame for failing to keep the flame alight, maybe for faltering in our own commitment at times, for simply not having the energy to infuse life and warmth into an apparently monotonous task.

The true IKEA spirit is still built on our enthusiasm, from our constant striving for renewal, from our cost- consciousness, from our readiness to take responsibility and help out, from our humbleness in approaching our task and from the simplicity of our way of doing things. We must look after each other and inspire each other. Those who cannot or will not join us are to be pitied.

A job must never be just a livelihood. If you are not enthusiastic about your job, a third of your life goes to waste, and a magazine in your desk drawer can never make up for that.

For those of you who bear any kind of leadership responsibility, it is crucially important to motivate and develop your co-workers. A team spirit is a fine thing, but it requires everybody in the team to be dedicated to their tasks. You, as the captain, make the decisions after consulting the team. There is no time for argument afterwards. Take a football team as your model!

Be thankful to those who are the pillars of our society! Those simple, quiet, taken-for-granted people who always are willing to lend a helping hand. They do their duty and shoulder their responsibility without being noticed. To them, a defined area of responsibility is a necessary but distasteful word. To them, the whole is just as self-evident as always helping and always sharing. I call them stalwarts simply because every system needs them. They are to be found everywhere – in our warehouses, in our offices, among our sales force.

They are the very embodiment of the IKEA spirit.

Yes, the IKEA spirit still lives, but it too must be cultivated and developed to keep pace with the times. **Development is not always the same thing as progress.** It is often up to you, as the leader and bearer of responsibility, to make development progressive.

3. Profit gives us resources

A better everyday life for the many people! To achieve our aim, we must have resources – especially in the area of finance. We do not believe in waiting for ripe plums to fall into our mouths. We believe in hard, committed work that brings results.

Profit is a wonderful word! Let us start by stripping the word profit of its dramatic overtones. It is a word that politicians often use and abuse. Profit gives us resources. There are two ways to get resources: either through our own profit, or through subsidy. All state subsidies are paid for either out of the state's profit on operations of some kind, or from taxes of some kind that you and I have to pay.

Let us be self-reliant in the matter of building up financial resources too.

The aim of our effort to build up financial resources **is to reach a good result in the long term.** You know what it takes to do that: we must offer the lowest prices, and we must combine them with good quality. If we charge too much, we will not be able to offer the lowest prices. If we charge too little, we will not be able to build up resources. A wonderful problem! It forces us to develop products more economically, to purchase more efficiently and to be constantly stubborn in cost savings of all kinds. That is our secret. That is the foundation of our success.

4. Reaching good results with small means

That is an old IKEA idea that is more relevant than ever. Time after time we have proved that we can get good results with small means or very limited resources. Wasting resources is a mortal sin at IKEA. It is not all that difficult to reach set targets if you do not have to count the cost. Any designer can design a desk that will cost 5,000 kronor. But only the most highly skilled can design a good, functional desk that will cost 100 kronor. **Expensive solutions to any kind of problem are usually the work of mediocrity.**

We have no respect for a solution until we know what it costs. An IKEA product without a price tag is always wrong! It is just as wrong as when a government does not tell the taxpayers what a 'free' school lunch costs per portion.

Before you choose a solution, set it in relation to the cost. Only then can you fully determine its worth.

Waste of resources is one of the greatest diseases of mankind. Many modern buildings are more like monuments to human stupidity than rational answers to needs. But waste costs us even more in little everyday things: filing papers that you will never need again; spending time proving that you were right anyway; postponing a decision to the next meeting because you do not want to take the responsibility now; telephoning when you could just as easily write a note or send a fax. The list is endless.

Use your resources the IKEA Way. Then you will achieve good results with small means.

5. Simplicity is a virtue

There have to be rules to enable a lot of people to function together in a community or a company. But the more complicated the rules are, the harder they are to comply with. Complicated rules paralyse!

Historical baggage, fear and unwillingness to take responsibility are the breeding ground for bureaucracy. Indecisiveness generates more statistics, more studies, more committees, more bureaucracy. Bureaucracy complicates and paralyses!

Planning is often synonymous with bureaucracy. Planning is, of course, needed to lay out guidelines for your work and to enable a company to function in the long term. But do not forget that **exaggerated planning is the most common cause of corporate death.** Exaggerated planning constrains your freedom of action and leaves you less time to get things done. Complicated planning paralyses. So let simplicity and common sense guide your planning.

Simplicity is a fine tradition among us. Simple routines mean greater impact. Simplicity in our behaviour gives us strength. Simplicity and humbleness characterise us in our relations with each other, with our suppliers and with our customers. It is not just to cut costs that we avoid luxury hotels. We do not need fancy cars, posh titles, tailor-made uniforms or other status symbols. We rely on our own strength and our own will!

6. Doing it a different way

If we from the start had consulted experts about whether a little community like Älmhult could support a company like IKEA, they would have undoubtedly advised against it. Nevertheless, Älmhult is now home to one of the world's biggest operations in the home furnishings business.

**By always asking why we are doing this or that**, we can find new paths. By refusing to accept a pattern simply because it is well established, we make progress. We dare to do things differently! Not just in large matters, but in solving small everyday problems too.

It is no coincidence that our buyers go to a window factory for table legs and a shirt factory for cushions. It is quite simply the answer to the question 'why'.

Our protest against convention is not protest for its own sake: it is a deliberate expression of our constant search for development and improvement.

Maintaining and developing the dynamism of our business is one of our most important tasks. That is why I hope, for example, that we will never have two identical stores. We know that the latest one is bound to have several things wrong with it, but, all things considered, it will still be the best yet. Dynamism and the desire to experiment must continually lead us forward. 'Why' will remain an important key word.

7. Concentration – important to our success

The general who divides his resources will invariably be defeated. Even a multitalented athlete has problems.

For us too, it is a matter of concentration – focusing our resources.

We can never do everything, everywhere, all at the same time.

Our range cannot be allowed to overflow. We will never be able to satisfy all tastes anyway. We must concentrate on our own profile. We can never promote the whole of our range at once. We must concentrate. We cannot conquer every market at once. We must concentrate for maximum impact, often with small means.

While we are concentrating on important areas, we must learn to do what people in Småland call 'lista'. 'Lista' is common term in Småland; it means 'making do', doing what you have to do with an absolute minimum of resources.

When we are building up a new market, we concentrate on marketing. Concentration means that at certain vital stages we are forced to neglect otherwise important aspects such as security systems. That is why we have to make extra special demands on the honesty and loyalty of every co-worker.

Concentration – the very word implies strength. Use it in your daily work. It will give you results.

8. Taking responsibility – a privilege

There are people at all levels in every type of company and community who would rather make their own decisions than hide behind those made by others. People who dare to take responsibility. The fewer such responsibility-takers a ompany or a community has, the more bureaucratic it is. Constant meetings and group discussions are often the result of unwillingness or inability on the part of the person in charge to make decisions. Democracy or the obligations for consultation are sometimes cited as excuses. Taking responsibility has nothing to do with education, financial position or rank. Responsibility-takers can be found in the warehouse, among the buyers, sales force and office staff – in short, everywhere. They are necessary in every system.

They are essential for all progress. They are the ones who keep the wheels turning.

In our IKEA family we want to keep the focus on the individual and support each other. We all have our rights, but we also have our duties. Freedom with responsibility. Your initiative and mine are decisive. Our ability to take responsibility and make decisions.

**Only while sleeping one makes no mistakes.** Making mistakes is the privilege of the active – of those who can correct their mistakes and put them right.

Our objectives require us to constantly practise making decisions and taking responsibility, to constantly overcome our fear of making mistakes. **The fear of making mistakes is the root of bureaucracy and the enemy of development.**

No decision can claim to be the only right one; it is the energy that is put into the decision that determines whether it is right. It must be allowed to make mistakes. It is always the mediocre people who are negative, who spend their time proving that they were not wrong. The strong person is always positive and looks forward.

It is always the positive people who win. They are always a joy to their colleagues and to themselves. But winning does not mean that someone else has to lose. The finest victories are those without losers. If somebody steals a model from us, we do not sue them, because a lawsuit is always negative. We solve the problem instead by developing a new and even better model.

Exercise your privilege – your right and your duty to make decisions and take responsibility.

9. Most things still remain to be done – A glorious future!
The feeling of having finished something is an effective sleeping pill. A person who retires feeling that he has done his bit will quickly wither away. A company which feels that it has reached its goal will quickly stagnate and lose its vitality.

Happiness is not reaching your goal. Happiness is being on the way. It is our wonderful fate to be just at the beginning. In all areas. We will move ahead only by constantly asking ourselves how what we are doing today can be done better tomorrow. The positive joy of discovery must be our inspiration in the future too. The word impossible has been deleted from our dictionary and must remain so. Experience is a word to be handled carefully.

Experience is a brake on all development. Many people cite experience as an excuse for not trying anything new. Still, it can be wise to rely on experience at times. But if you do so, you should preferably rely on your own. That is usually more valuable than lengthy investigations.

Our ambition to develop ourselves as human beings and co-workers must remain high. Humbleness is the key word. Being humble means so much to us in our work and in our leisure. It is even decisive for us as human beings. It means not just consideration and respect for our fellow men and women, but also kindness and generosity. Will-power and strength without humbleness often lead to conflict. Together with humbleness, will-power and strength are your secret weapons for development as an individual and fellow
human being.

Bear in mind that **time is your most important resource**. You can do so much in 10 minutes. Ten minutes, once gone, are gone for good. You can never get them back.

Ten minutes are not just a sixth of your hourly pay. Ten minutes are a piece of yourself. Divide your life into 10-minute units and sacrifice as few of them as possible in meaningless activity.

Most of the job remains to be done. Let us continue to be a group of positive fanatics who stubbornly and persistently refuse to accept the impossible, the negative. What we want to do, we can do and will do together. A glorious future!

# Introduction

The small man from the personnel department in Älmhult who greeted me confirmed all my prejudices about IKEA-people. A large lump of chewing tobacco of the type the Swedes call *snus* hid the bulk of his upper teeth and coloured the rest of them brown, a pair of black clogs, a navy blue shirt with an enormous collar, shoulder-straps and a pair of ill-fitting tobacco-brown corduroy trousers. In the middle of the yuppie-frenzy at the end of the eighties he was certainly an unusual sight. In those days double-breasted suits with a sheen, broad lapels and a colourful tie were a must for any company employee, almost irrespective of position. But obviously not at IKEA, I concluded as I sat down in the room.

The job of the IKEA-man was to make me fill out a form, take a Polaroid picture and ask me a couple of standard questions. The latter possibly to eliminate the worst ruffians at an early stage. Apparently I passed, as a couple of weeks later I was summoned to the IKEA headquarters in Helsingborg. I was, to say the least, surprised. I admit that I left my double-breasted suit at home and wore something much more plain, but compared to the personnel person opposite me I was still hopelessly over-dressed.

I was not at all happy with my job at Åhléns. My fiancée at the time, Eva, had seen the IKEA-ad looking for 'key people of the nineties' in the *Dagens Nyheter* newspaper. After which she ceaselessly reminded me of it in her sing-song Swedish Dalarna dialect until I rather reluctantly sent in my application written on my dad's IBM typewriter.

Role models amongst the Uppsala economists of my generation were people in the mould of the character Gordon Gekko from the movie *Wall Street*, and certainly not the founder of IKEA Ingvar Kamprad. Entrepreneurship seemed like being a green-grocer. Attractive company cars and sharp suits attracted us more than clogs and *snus*. In other words I was in two minds about IKEA even after I had put my job application in the post.

'How the hell can you write that?' Anders slapped his knees with laughter while he sat opposite me with my application in front of him.

'I was amongst the absolute top in my economy class, but I am at the same time a humble person', he quoted and continued laughing with *snus* all over his mouth dismissing any attempt of explanation. You should just know that I got in as twenty-fifth reserve, I bitterly thought to myself.

Anders Moberg was the chief executive at IKEA. Naturally I was somewhat surprised when he came into the room and introduced himself. But it occurred so suddenly that I never had time to get nervous. A tall athletic man, a bit over thirty, strikingly good-looking, with a contagious smile, his charisma filled the room. He put some questions to me of which 'What makes a retail business successful?' was the hardest.

My reply then was that a company's competitive power was a function of its logistics. Jan-Eric Engqvist, personnel manager for the company, who was also present at the interview, told me how Anders had handpicked me from amongst thousands of applicants.

Anders suddenly starts talking again, puts his head a bit to the side, leans forward and points at me. The whole time with the broad tobacco-coloured smile on his face.

'Damn it, you are so bloody cocky, we'll send you to Germany.'

Whether this was good or bad news I did not know at the time. However I did understand that I had just been taken on.

'Anyway Jan-Eric', Moberg said to Engqvist, 'could Anders not be sponsor for Johan?' This Anders was Anders Dahlvig who at the time was assistant to both Moberg and Ingvar Kamprad. (He was after that chief executive for ten years and resigned on the 31 August 2009.)

The fact that this was the beginning of a 20 year long journey during which I would be able to – from the inside – experience the fantastic success of IKEA I did not know at the time. During my time with the company it went from a turnover of SEK 25 billion to 250 billion, from 30,000 to 150,000 employees, from around 70 stores mainly concentrated in Northern Europe to 250 with global coverage. This was an unparalleled expansion and achievement, and IKEA has undoubtedly become the biggest Swedish business story of modern times.

I was able to follow and, I hope, contribute to this unique success in various positions within the company: manager for furniture at the store in Wallau, Germany, head of sales for living rooms at the sales office in Helsingborg, project manager and later manager of the store in Leeds, England, responsible for storage, media and dining room furniture at IKEA of Sweden AB (IOS) in Älmhult and managing director for IKEA GreenTech AB in Lund. I was to shadow my sponsor Anders Dahlvig and was during three years in the mid nineties assistant to Ingvar Kamprad and the chief executive Anders Moberg and worked closely with both, sometimes around the clock. During this period I was also responsible for environmental issues, PR and communication within the group.

During these years I obtained a good insight into IKEA and the character of its founder. I was able to follow the rise of the company at close quarters until IKEA was the brightest star in the global home furnishing market. This book is about my impressions during these twenty years.

Why does one write a book about one's ex-employer? The question is valid. Because of bitterness as one feels wrongly done by? Because of greed because one realizes that gossip sells?

In my case none of these.

Why don't I just leave IKEA behind me and get on with my life? Simply because certain things about the company keep nagging me.

After having left IKEA I started considering the journey I had undertaken. All the successes and the set-backs, the colleagues and the trips to destinations nobody knew even existed. Gradually I began to see the company with different eyes from when I was part of the 'IKEA-family', as Ingvar calls it. The image of IKEA that now emerged was distinctly different from the image I had earlier. I understood that I needed to put down my experiences on paper.

What I describe in the book are events that I myself have experienced or situations trustworthy colleagues have witnessed.

The world looks at IKEA with admiration. The successes of the company for many years and in many areas are amazing. IKEA is the kind of company that is never in trouble and always puts the environment and social concerns at the forefront of its policies. It is never caught red-handed when the environmental groups growl and the media bites. It has a brilliant founder who has become a Swedish national icon, and the fifth richest man in the world. It has a solid company culture that has been absorbed completely by its 150,000 co-workers. In short IKEA is a shining sun in the corporate sky that, especially of late, has too often been lined by greyish clouds.

I know that this sunny image does not entirely correspond to the truth. The IKEA-sun is beautiful and marvellous in many ways but it has blind spots.

This book is about those blind spots. In order to understand one first needs an insight into how the company works behind the scenes. To understand the mechanism that has made the success of IKEA possible. To understand what attitudes and values of the decision makers have created such a strong corporate culture.

It is important that we understand large corporations and their actions, just as we try to understand other important powerful factors in our society. The fact that they may be difficult to penetrate or that such an operation may have its perils is no reason to hold back. Without transparency of the powerful factors that influence society, impenetrable colossuses soon appear, giants that have completely different agendas and goals to the rest of society. It is part of the nature of a market economy that, by definition, a company only looks to its own interests. This is maybe the single most important rule in any industry. The only thing that deters companies from losing their way completely in pure narcissism, however, is on the one hand legislation and on the other, equally importantly, scrutiny by media. Just like other companies IKEA has always its own interests at heart. That is in itself not strange, but when the IKEA agenda influences its surrounding in a negative way we need to know. What makes it worse is that the company is perhaps the most closed in the world given its size. This means that no journalist has ever managed to penetrate the massive blue and yellow façade. This is also why any well-informed discussion around the activities and future of IKEA is missing: IKEA staff are sworn to silence.

I mean to say that the image of IKEA of today is oversimplified. The company spends large amounts of resources in order to maintain its rosy image. I know this to be the case as I have myself been part of this work. During the nineties when IKEA went from one media crises to another, I was responsible for PR and communications as well as environmental issues in the company. At the same time I was Ingvar's assistant who was also chief executive of the group at the time. The formidable capacity that IKEA has to paint an appealing picture of itself is in a way impressive in our media controlled society, but also foreboding. Financial journalists have during all these years swallowed the image manufactured by IKEA itself. Perhaps because they were impressed by the colossus Kamprad. Perhaps because they misunderstood the truth. I am really not certain which.

I am well aware that Ingvar Kamprad and IKEA are among Sweden's most important national icons. We are talking about a brand that is so strong it has placed little Sweden on the map the world over. Therefore some people in Sweden become indignant about arguments like mine, not to say angry. Stop talking as Ingvar has meant so much; not just for one of the country's biggest companies but for the country as a whole. My view is that success comes with obligations rather than providing you an alibi. At the end of the nineties I, together with two colleagues, drew up a new strategy: 'Everything that IKEA does must stand up to scrutiny'. Within IKEA this was at the time ground-breaking. It meant for example that the three of us took an active and uncompromising stand against child labour, something that at the time was not widespread within IKEA. 'Children are better off working than going into prostitution', was a common view at INGKA Holding BV, the highest board of directors at IKEA. What they were talking about were children, of which many were young, who worked in slave-like conditions on the Indian peninsula with amongst other things production for IKEA.

I wish to point out that the information and environmental strategy of IKEA, later called 'Teflon IKEA' in *Newsweek* (2001), came about as a direct result of the only serious study of IKEA which was ever made. It was led by SVT's (Swedish Television) Mikael Ohlsson, called 'The Workshop of Father Christmas – IKEA's Backyard' and was broadcast in 1997. These extremely able investigative journalists were hated by the whole of IKEA's cadre of managers, but the outcome of their work on the environment and delivery strategies became fundamental.

Today most of the IKEA strategies regarding purchase and the environment are based on a thinking characterized by care and consideration for our fellow human beings and the world around us, but far from all as we shall see. The transparency which is expected of other companies of the same size ought to be applicable also to Ingvar Kamprad and his IKEA. He who has nothing to hide has nothing to fear.

Or does he?

# 1

## The Secret Behind IKEA

Pages upon pages have been written about IKEA and its extraordinary success in newspapers and books. At universities it has almost become a must to bring up the company as a text-book example for further inspection. Many have tried to answer the question why IKEA has been so successful. Obviously I also have an idea of what has made the company go from strength to strength. My view is informed by the decades I have worked for the company in all its departments. I have experienced great progress, but also terrible failures.

Simplicity is a virtue

The familiar quotation by Ingvar that 'simplicity is a virtue' is central to the success story. Only mediocre people propose complicated solutions, he preaches. With this approach I shall also consider the IKEA phenomenon. What single factors have had the strongest influence on IKEA?

First and foremost, the genius Ingvar Kamprad himself since he is the father of most things, albeit not everything, within IKEA. After that the IKEA-machinery, the global value chain from forest to customer, that Ingvar and his team have built and tuned to perfection. Last but not least the IKEA-culture that Ingvar has created and which makes the IKEA-machinery function precisely and constantly at maximum speed.

Let us examine them one by one and begin with the phenomenon of Ingvar Kamprad, IKEA's billionaire founder and owner.

# 2

# The Man and the Myth

In order to understand IKEA one has to understand its founder Ingvar Kamprad, the world's most reclusive billionaire. Where did he come from?

The palace coup

*November 1994, Kölles Gård, Humblebæk, South of Helsingör in Denmark*
Kölles Gård is a charming building similar to a guest-house in just as charming surroundings a stone's throw from Öresund. Kamprad bought the property in the seventies when he abandoned Sweden for Denmark in order to avoid Swedish taxes. Today, it has housed the board of directors of the IKEA group for over a decade.

Daylight was fading slowly turning afternoon into evening. Cold winds from the sea lashed the property and its surrounding parkland. It was late Autumn and piles of shrivelled beech leaves happily whirled around in the wind. The only thing out of the ordinary were rows of parked cars outside the hedge that surrounded the house. Reporters stood around in groups outside and keenly watched any sign of activity from inside the house. Photographers with camera lenses as long as your arm were gazing at the building window by window. Flashes now and then lit up the apricot coloured façade. The building seemed dark and abandoned with the exception of a few lit up windows.

In the warmth inside was, amongst others, IKEA's chief executive Anders Moberg, serenely calm as usual but showing the seriousness of the situation on his pale face. The group around the table had to take a stand on how to handle the situation that had arisen, and that none of them had been able to imagine only a few days earlier.

The unthinkable had happened. The founder and owner of IKEA had been denounced as a Nazi sympathizer and a member of the Swedish neo-Nazi movement during the forties and the fifties. Ingvar and his assistant Staffan Jeppsson were working feverishly in another room in order to try and find a way out of the dark clouds that had now descended on the old man. The tabloid *Expressen* had released the scoop at full force and the news was spreading like wildfire across the world.

'If the worst comes to the worst, if Ingvar is not be able to handle the situation, there remains only one solution for us.' The words were hovering in the stifling air in the room where Anders Moberg and the top leadership of IKEA were sitting.

'If Ingvar does not find a solution soon and the situation does not calm down, then IKEA will once and for all have to distance itself from Ingvar.'

Thus it had been said. The genie was out of the bottle.

Consider the last paragraph again and its significance. Exactly who said what, I do not know. But the incident was relayed and interpreted for me by Anders Moberg. Could it be said clearer? Ingvar Kamprad is not synonymous with the company IKEA. IKEA is larger than its founder, despite his enormous importance for the development of the company. Ingvar may, in fact, be deposed or rather put aside if he seriously threatens to harm his company.

At this point Ingvar did a complete turnaround and put all his cards on the table, confessed everything and asked his co-workers, not least those of Jewish decent, for forgiveness. With this the story was, in the main, finished with. This rhetoric feat was brilliantly carried out by a man of whom one does not expect anything less. It was used as a text-book example by media educators the world over for a long time.

## The driving force

A lot of people have wondered, what is it that spurs Ingvar on? What is it that makes him drive himself so very hard? Because that is what he does.

To suggest as is done in the official version that he is obsessed with proving 'to people that beautiful furniture does not have to be expensive' is at best a serious misunderstanding and at its worst a conscious falsification. Basically, he is driven by an enormous need to be validated and nothing else. He wants to show the world around him and himself that the impossible is possible. This becomes very obvious when one works with him, as he over and over again adopts the persona of the underdog. It is this way of doing things that first becomes obvious in Ingvar. He may say something depreciatory about some respected and distinguished design critic for one of the big newspaper barons in Stockholm. He formulates strategies and the IKEA-culture from a down-up perspective: IKEA should never boast, but let the results tell their story. He tries hard to cast himself as the underdog by describing himself as a somewhat dim, alcoholic dyslexic. We will come back to this.

Once Ingvar told me that he only has one close friend. A Swiss man whom he now and then goes on trips with. To my mind and to most people of my generation this sounds rather as if 'the friend' was more of a pal or an acquaintance, since the relationship was not more frequent or closer. Other people he socialises with are usually colleagues, apart from his family. So people he pays to work for him. Consequently, their friendship is directly connected to their pay packet. In this place of loneliness the outlook of the underdog can only strengthen.

When Ingvar is able to rub shoulders with the establishment particularly in Sweden, the Wallenbergs, the media and the politicians, through honours and doctorates, then he feels special. Chosen. His need for validation is so great that he resents his company directors being seen in the media limelight. Anders Moberg often asked my advice about whether he should dare accept an interview lest he stole the attention from

Kamprad, and what Ingvar thought about it. If there was the slightest hesitation, he would rather decline than risk provoking the wrath of Kamprad.

Conscious leadership

On one of my first days at work at the group's head office in Humlebæk, Ingvar was in the office. Normally he is either travelling, at home in Switzerland or, occasionally, on a working holiday at his vineyard in France for a couple of weeks. Ingvar and Anders Moberg met just by my desk. Anders went to say hello when something strange happened to his expression. The self-confidence, the assurance and resoluteness disappeared. Instead he had that staring, almost mouth-open gaze that signals fear, which was further accentuated by the strained smile. I felt pure fear rush through my body. If Anders Moberg, the paragon of a strong leader, had such towering respect for Kamprad what should I, a simple assistant, feel? This encounter shaped my behaviour towards Ingvar for well over a year, until I slowly began to realize that he was not that dangerous after all. Quite the contrary.

*Range week, the so called IK-days, at the IKEA of Sweden AB head-office Blåsippan in Älmhult, early Autumn 1996.*
As Ingvar's assistant I follow him closely from one range presentation to another. The week is the culmination of one year's work that concludes in two to three hours together with the founder. During these hours one's work is presented, judged and either given the go-ahead, or rejected.

'This is the worst rubbish I have seen in a long while. How fucking silly can it possibly get? What a disappointment, Johan.'

Ingvar and I had just been witnessing the biggest fiasco of the week. The group had been given the task to develop an outline for home recycling. Their solution was a green tub and a white tub. In plastic. The presentation was deplorable and the excuses during the rather short discussion afterwards even worse. Ingvar asked some questions and took a view on the proposed materials. Afterwards he said thank you in a friendly way and carried on. Only as we were in the car on the way home did he reveal his true feelings.

It is precisely in situations like this that Ingvar's talent for leadership becomes most obvious. I have never met a man with more patience. I have also never met a person who is more aware how he is considered by his surrounding and who uses it as an important tool to obtain power. He is brilliant at standing in the background and allowing others to speak, even if he dislikes what he sees. He sometimes discusses his views, sometimes he lets go. At times, days may pass between the proposals. Sometimes years. But he seems to know exactly when and how he must intervene in the decision process in order for the correct path to be maintained. One good example is the so called the Multipurpose system (later called MPS), which took 30 years of nagging punctuated by years of silence.

This system was an idea for an integrated standard of measurements for kitchens, bathrooms, bedrooms and living rooms that Ingvar hatched in the seventies and that he kept coming back to with ever greater intensity in 1996 than before. Why? IKEA had just undergone a major restructuring where IKEA of Sweden AB (IoS), the range- and purchase corporation, had become the power hub of the company. Being business area manager at IoS became the new position of power. A number of less successful managers had been removed and new ones – long serving managers within IKEA – had replaced them. He probably wanted to try to present the idea again in order to see what happened. More about the Multipurpose system later on in the book.

The same thing happened in 1995 when he was bouncing around ideas about a completely new range of lighting from China and encouraged his men (as they were only men) to search more actively for really cheap energy-saving bulbs there. It ended with them finding a bulb that was 90 per cent cheaper than those of competitors and so made history on a small scale. What Ingvar had done was to place himself in the circle of his men and discuss, ask and listen, and sometimes plead: 'Please you clever lighting guys, would it not be possible to...'

I am pretty certain that Ingvar knew or at least suspected the answer to many of his questions. He probably already knew exactly which suppliers they ought to go to. But his poker face is impenetrable. One year on, the same men stand around him almost bursting with pride over having managed to solve all the challenges. Because they them- selves have solved the problems, the prestige and, with that, the confidence in the product is theirs. At a first glance this generosity towards his co-workers may seem strange coming as it does from a man who demands to have all the attention himself, especially when it comes to the media. But Ingvar is an extremely complex person, full of contradictions and difficult to really understand.

Often Ingvar does not do much more than bounce ideas around and inspire other people in the important range work at IKEA . He knows that if only the right people are in the room at least some ideas will eventually become reality.

Another thing he often does a lot of – especially when ranges are being examined; he jokes frequently in a shrewd and deeply sarcastic way. He himself is more often than not the target of his own jokes. Most of the time he manages to stay on the correct side of rudeness and creates a jolly atmosphere. Not everyone always understands the crushing irony, perhaps, but many see him as a man with a great sense of humour.

Ingvar is in the middle of the group of some twenty people. He wants to ask some specialist a question in order to carry the discussion forward.

'Bosse, where is Bosse?' Ingvar intones.

Before anybody has time to answer, including Bosse, he continues: 'Has he already gone home then? Well, that is not very clever'.

The commotion that follows is just as funny every time and so is the haunted expression on the face of the main character before he makes himself known.

'I see, you're still here, dear Bosse. How nice that you have a moment for us. We are looking at your range you see', Ingvar continues with exaggerated emphasis.

His sense of humour becomes even more tart when there is only the two of you.

An experienced product developer had just presented his – in his own opinion – ingenious coffee table to me and Ingvar. The meeting ended and the colleague had left us. 'Well, well Johan, the only big thing there was his moustache', Ingvar said with regret in his voice about the slender and short product developer with a large beard.

This sense of humour is yet another dimension of Kamprad's leadership. He will only joke in the presence of a chosen few, meaning the usual gang at Blåsippan in Älmhult, but never at a strategic purchase meeting with more important managers. It is cunningly clever.

Sometimes when representatives of one part of the business have been lured into, in the heat of the moment, promising Ingvar too much and the consequences start to become clear to the group of product developers, managers and purchase strategists, Ingvar suddenly comes out with: 'When before Christmas can you be ready with this new range?'

Without fail everybody present is immediately taken aback before they realize the sarcastic undertone in his unreasonable demand. A new range takes two to three years to develop, and range week is at the beginning of September. That would in other words give the team a couple of months to manage several years of development work. The observant participant at the same time realizes that this is not drollness but Ingvar's way of expressing that he is keen.

Should the IKEA range team, on the other hand, try to get out of Ingvar's demand for the quick delivery of a product, they will invariably get the sarcastic answer in a grumpy Småland dialect: 'I see, well, man is nowadays capable of flying to the moon, but a coffee cup for less than 5 kronor (£.50 / $.70) you cannot do...'

When it comes to discussing, twisting and turning arguments Ingvar is just as untiring and brilliant. He knows most about most things to do with IKEA, down to the smallest detail: materials, prices, production, raw materials, range, design, commercial handling. He moves brilliantly from the tiniest detail down to quality of glass, to raw materials, prices and to group strategies that determine the range and purchases and back again. Ingvar is capable of moving back and forth between details and guiding principals like no one else. By debating in a vague, almost tentative way, with his enormous knowledge and 70 years experience, he always gets a discussion going. Sometimes he chooses to argue for a standpoint that he knows will provoke the participants. At the next meeting he may without warning suddenly have changed positions. That's when he wants to hear the arguments against to the solution he himself, secretly, favours.

If someone sits tight and is difficult to convince he puts the questions directly to different people, depending on area of responsibility. Once he gets going Ingvar can keep a discussion going for hours. People look as if they are about to faint, need to go to the bathroom, perhaps want to eat. Not Ingvar. He stands in the middle of the group of people, with his hands together under his stomach and with an unmistakable smell of *snus* around him. Only his thumbs move in circles. He listens, asks, argues, turns things around. If the discussion becomes heated or if he is opposed he never loses his temper. Neither does he lose the thread of the discussion. His brilliant memory stores discussions, people and developments. Often verbatim. Business sector by business sector. The fact that he knows the names of each and every person he is in contact with during for example a range week is a given. Ingvar also knows their background, and if someone has a bad reputation.

Several times I have heard him quote a statement from a meeting held several years earlier word for word. In Ingvar-time that means thousands of meetings ago.

This is the leadership genius of Kamprad. Thus he controls IKEA. Despite the fact that for a whole year he for example only meets the majority of the people during range week, the company moves in the direction he wants it to. Not exactly as he wants. But in the right direction.

He controls the IKEA purchase organization. He travels around to the most important regions and sees IKEA workers and suppliers directly on the factory floor. After which the decisions for strategic buying are made a couple of times a year. This is where decisions about purchasing strategies, and purchasing decisions and invest-ments in products are made. The group's chief executive is chair, Ingvar and his three sons Peter, Jonas and Mathias are present, as well as Torbjörn Lööf, managing director for IKEA of Sweden AB (IoS) and (in practice) number two in the group after the chair. The present head buyer for IKEA, Henrik Elm, is obviously present as is his boss, Göran Stark, who is responsible for the whole IKEA value chain and Bruno Winborg, chairman of the board of IKEA's industrial group Swedwood AB. Ingvar and the group's managing director's assistants are also present. All issues regarding pur-chasing are looked at: prices of raw materials and development, production, large movements of range from region to region and so on. Presentations are made by buyers, purchase strategists or someone responsible for a trading office somewhere. The meeting is thus not reserved for people at director level, but open to the most knowledgeable wood buyers or similar experts who explain their views and suggestions on whiteboards, flipcharts or simple power-point presentations.

In this particular group Ingvar is often more dominant than in other meetings. His excellent memory spits out prices of raw materials and exchange rates at an incredible speed and converts units of timber to cubic metres sawed up into glue joints and exchange rates such as Zloty to USD or SEK even faster. For example, how much Russian pine sawed on location, glued and refined in Poland, would cost in a Swedish store. Within seconds, he will tell you from memory. For the reader's information: a conversion of at least three currencies (at today's rate) requires knowledge of transportation routes and prices over four borders, labour and cost of labour in two countries for three different production operations as well as cost for each stage of the refinement process. Ask a clever forest officer for the same calculation and he will need hours to work it out. I want to point out that the same proficiency applies whether we are talking about glass, cotton, plastic granules, price of oil or silver. Ingvar seems to have knowledge of all raw materials and processes as well as market structures that directly or indirectly have a bearing on his company. Each time I see this I remain just as amazed. But this skill is not used in order to show off but in order to carry the intense discussion forward or to keep it on the right track.

Furthermore he has certain rules of thumb (as he calls them) about everything that can be useful for purchasing, logistics and production. Ingvar likes to turn to experts who he intuitively trusts. Often because they have profound knowledge, are straight-forward, have the integrity and the courage to oppose him. These relationships usually result in new rules of thumb for Ingvar, as for example how many trees there are in one acre in the Ukraine or similar. Another example of a rule of thumb is how many square metres of seamed beech veneer you can get out of one beech log. Further examples are the so-called hot dogs in the range, i.e. products that can be sold impossibly cheaply for 5-10 kronor(£.50-£1.00 / $.75-$1.50). To be able to sell a coffee cup for 5 kronor you have to calculate '1.50 to the factory, 1.50 to IKEA and 1.50 to the tax man'. This rule of thumb is actually more than that. It is the strategy how IKEA brings out these hot dogs and is the basis for design, production and purchase of hundreds of different products from IKEA at prices the competitors cannot manage. IKEA really only covers the cost and does not make any profit in the store. (On the other hand they do that in the purchase and distribution stages.)

It is true that Ingvar can be more direct and more critical at strategic purchase meetings than at other types of meetings. Yet it is extremely rare that he slams his fist on the table and decides how things shall be. He has that presence, that influence, that is needed for most things go in the direction he wants anyway. Perhaps not exactly how he wants, but in the right direction.

Ingvar's factory-floor strategy

What most people find hard to understand is how Ingvar manages to keep such a large company together. The answer is simple. Through his actions he lets good examples speak for themselves. Everywhere he goes he over and over again refers back to discussions he has had with a head of department at a store in Germany or with the boss of a factory at a supplier's or with a colleague at a store in China. He is capable of quoting his co-workers' thoughts and ideas as well as problems in a concrete way.

This factory-floor strategy, travelling around in the real world, is rhetorically brilliant. How can a product developer in Älmhult ever express disapproval of a discussion where all the arguments are taken from reality? Or for that matter a retail manager in Spain. It doesn't matter whether it is about the price of a product, its quality or functionality or a complete range of products or a logistical dilemma.

Moreover what makes this factory-floor strategy so surprisingly efficient is that it provides Ingvar with a detailed general view over the whole value chain. The majority of his travels literally takes him up- and downstream along the company's value chain, from the forest to the store and back. He is therefore able to see problems at an early stage, strategic or in detail, and nip them in the bud. Since by acting at an early stage the problems need not grow and become really costly. Through this behaviour he has always the upper hand over the rest of the organization, from chief executive downwards.

## When he has made up his mind

There are of course also many instances when Ingvar already has made his mind up. His methods for getting what he wants however vary. A very good recent example is a store in Haparanda on the border between Sweden and Finland. The way Ingvar himself told me this story is that he was contacted by an enterprising social-democratic local government councillor from Haparanda and he immediately liked the idea. But in the main nobody else in IKEA wanted a store in Haparanda. Especially not anybody at IKEA Sweden, and it is each individual country's organization that normally takes decisions about location.

Ingvar met with the executive group of IKEA Sweden a few times in order to lobby for his idea. Instead they lectured the 80-year old man about his crazy ideas and that it was really in Luleå, further away from the Finnish border, that the store should be. You may think that this was both clumsy as well as thoughtless, but the whole thing was just as stupid as he told me. I know of no other example from IKEA of Sweden AB or the purchasing organization or of anywhere else in the world where people so openly have opposed the wish of the founder.

Moreover, the sales forecast at the Luleå store was less than at the standard concept stores that IKEA typically builds. Wise after years of under-scaled construction of stores around the world and the extremely costly investments of several billion in order to expand them to meet demand, Ingvar obviously became even more irritated on hearing this – but he did not show anything during the meeting. If Ingvar were to start roaring against the executive group in one particular country it might have unknown repercussions. On the one hand fear could spread like rings in the water throughout the organization and hamper initiatives. It would also demonstrate to the workforce that an outburst by the founder and an aggressive style of management is permitted at IKEA.

'Please, dear friends, do an old man a favour and build the store in Haparanda. And please build it at full size', were the words he left at the executive group.

A plea referring to his advanced age. Implicitly suggesting – possibly – I have not got that long to go, do me this last favour. Knowing Ingvar he would also have pulled a few strings in order to ensure that his 'last will' would be heeded.

Normally he would then meet a number of key people one by one on different levels in the organisation to discuss the decision he wants. 'Can you promise me, dear...' he will plead with each one of them. And a promise to the founder is a promise. As soon as Ingvar has spat out the tobacco in the waste paper basket and gone off, many of the people he approached throw themselves on the phone to the poor guys who are stalling the question (i.e. those who have not followed Ingvar's plea). After each telephone call from these people, often in superior positions, the pressure on the sinners to make the 'right' decision increases. But few of the people who are exerting pressure will mention the fact that Ingvar has contacted them. It is considered inappropriate by managers at IKEA to refer to such pressure. Obviously exactly this is what happened in the case of the slightly narrow-minded Swedish executive group.

And so what was the result? A store in Haparanda was built. In full size. And naturally Haparanda became a success. What Ingvar but nobody else had realized, was that the customer base for a Haparanda store could be counted in millions. Apart from all the Swedes in northern Sweden there were Russians, Finns and Norwegians within (un)likely distances from the store.

It is important to note that Ingvar did not ever mention his loss of prestige after the first meeting where the executives flatly refused to even consider his wish. Instead he was the whole time focused on the matter in hand, the best alternative for IKEA. After that he chose the tactic that would give the best result. Prestige is, in any case, something that Ingvar does not worry about much. If he comes across better and more solid arguments he immediately changes his mind with quizzical eyes and a sly smile on his lips, and with sincere curiosity about the person who has outwitted him and made him see something new. Surprised him even. This is one of the few things that really impresses Ingvar. The other is ability to carry things through – to be able to make things happen.

Ingvar has taken it upon himself to visit as many stores as possible. A normal number has for many years been 45, but as I am writing this book there will be from what I understand fewer, since he after all is 83 years old and every visit takes a whole working day – or thereabouts. The purpose is of course to get a good feel for how ranges perform in different markets, but also to be able to see how different stores handle the ranges. But he also sees it as his task to spread good commercial ideas. Not just 'good' perhaps, but 'the best' judging by the results.

Since he has spent a large part of his working life doing this, he has also seen how stores time and time again have sinned against and ignored the 'best' commercial ideas. At the beginning of the nineties he had had enough. He approached the chief executive at the time Anders Moberg and made him issue a decree: 'The Moberg Musts'. This happened reluctantly on Ander's part. By tradition the stores in different countries until then had, on the whole, had complete freedom. As I don't really know I can only guess, that it was this change of direction that Moberg was opposed to. He nevertheless chose to give in to Kamprad's persistence. The result was what was to become known as Moberg Musts, all in all around 50 clauses on an A4 page.

With constant increasing number of stores and a cadre of store managers with, to put it mildly, varying capability, improvements using the musts of Moberg became more a difference in nuance than a totally radical change. In Northern Europe the stores were given a more open and lighter layout with the possibility for customers to find their way more easily, and a greater number of shortcuts in order to be able to find the department they actually came to visit quicker. For the first time they were also given the choice not to have to walk through the whole furniture display only to buy a couple of coffee cups.

In Germany, which at the beginning of the nineties contributed one third of IKEA's turnover, all displays and market places looked like the catacombs of Rome. High walls along endless narrow aisles. On a normal Saturday the stores were literally packed with people, men, women, children and elderly people, hungry, thirsty, exhausted and dying to go to the loo, who slowly dragged themselves along the 1.4 km long aisles through the furniture exhibition area. Hysterical outbursts bordering on scuffles occurred every time there was a big sale on. In pure desperation these poor wretches would push open the emergency exits in order to flee out into the fresh air whilst the alarm was going off throughout the store.

In the middle of the nineties Ingvar issued a veto on the freedom of the retail stores in different countries. The IKEA-stores should become conceptualized. Ready-made concepts should become established for store buildings with surrounding areas following what had worked best throughout the years. The restaurants should become conceptualized in a way that was rather similar to McDonalds. And all the IKEA-worlds' furniture displays and store buildings should be conceptualized down to the level of price tags and knobs on the furniture. This is also what happened during the rest of the nineties. Many were horrified, including myself, about the limitation of freedom but Ingvar turned out to be right. Again.

Today IKEA's stores are controlled by so called Commercial Reviews which is an audit of all relevant parts of a store: furniture exhibition, market places, communication, control of costs, security, logistics. Everything is compared to best practice, i.e. the concepts. The audit that is done over many days is carried out by the best men and women within each sector, meaning that all auditors have real and hard work experience as their main job. I have never heard a bad word being uttered about these audits. On the contrary I was one of the people who cheered when the Kållered store in Sweden had achieved the highest total score ever – from a few years earlier having been classed as very poor.

## IKEA Home Shopping

In 2008 Ingvar again issued a veto. This time he opposed a venture into web-based shopping. The size of the range in the stores is a big problem for the company. IKEA's range of a few thousand articles is not much compared to its main competitors who normally have twice or three times as many. The bottleneck is the flow of many cubic metres of goods through the store paths. Practically the whole of IKEA was looking forward to a functioning IKEA internet home-shopping concept. You would even be able to show products in the store that would be sent home via a new and more flexible distribution chain. In many overstrained stores around the world capacity would be freed up. Many were optimistic about the possibilities of this new technology.

Ideas were brought forward. Large sums of money were invested in pilot studies. Competitors like Target in the US were looming on the horizon, tempting buyers with their home pages. But when Anders Dahlvig put the proposal to the board the portcullis came down immediately. Kamprad said, eagerly cheered on by his sons, no to an internet venture. A home page where you could do your purchases would decrease the visitors to the stores and thereby you would lose the extra sales – all those items you pick up that you hardly knew you needed. Sixties' truths regarding mail order were applied to the new millenium.

Lennart Ekmark, the man who in 1965 put the IVAR shelving unit (pine shelves for the garage) in the living room, always used to say: 'The worst thing is that Ingvar is almost always right.' It is possible that Ingvar sees something the rest of us do not, but I have not met a colleague who agrees with him this time. Sadly I suspect that his 'no' to the idea depends on his age. Ingvar is perhaps not as up-to-date in the present as he was earlier. After all he is advanced in age. The stakes will however be very high and the losses likewise, if he is wrong. No other sector is growing as rapidly today as internet shopping.

Four years ago IKEA opened a store in Minneapolis, Minnesota. But the American IKEA retail organization did not appear to have checked out where the enormous Target Corporation had its head office. It is, in fact, in Minneapolis. Furthermore, Target is many times larger than IKEA. And they had a bus. The whole head office went by shuttle service to the IKEA store every day for a couple of weeks. More or less every Target-employee bought something from IKEA. A stool of each kind. A glass of each kind. An Oriental rug of each kind. And so on until they had everything.

Six months later Target launched an excellent range at extremely good prices, on the internet (target.com) as their main outlet and not through their one thousand stores. The strength of Target has also always been their skilful designers. Today this range is well established and a very successful part of what they offer. IKEA USA has on the other hand been going backwards during the last 3–4 years.

Conscious or manipulating?

Ingvar Kamprad is a social and verbal phenomenon, an excellent communicator who cannot be overestimated. He never utters a word or shows an expression without having a well considered reason for it. Each question, each plea, each admonition and each comment is a completely conscious act with a specific goal. Some might call it manipulation.

Let's just use as an example a couple of Sweden's most able journalists: K-G Bergström and Lennart Ekdal. Both probably thought it a great privilege to be able to visit Ingvar on his farm Böllsö in Småland an afternoon in late summer. When Lennart Ekdal was there during the summer the other year Kamprad suggested an outing by rowing-boat on lake Möckeln so they could to get to know each other. Ingvar rowed and was as jovial as only he can be. Ekdal, on the stern, was enjoying the lake landscape robed in its beautiful summery foliage. Perhaps he thought: 'Here I am together with the richest man in the world in a rowing boat and he is capable of rowing too! And how pleasant he is!'

I don't blame him, because Ingvar has that effect on people. I can think of only one exception. It was when Ingvar, me and the MD for IKEA Sweden at the time Göran Ydstrand were at the Uppsala store together with a TV-crew that was filming Ingvar and his work. At the checkout he wanted to show off and obligingly packed the bags for the customers. Everyone was grateful apart from an elderly lady with a fierce look who thought this old man was trying to steal her things. 'Do you work here or what?' she yelled so that it could be heard over the entire queue. Not even Ingvar found his feet that time but mumbled almost shyly: 'Yes I do.'

Now back to Ekdal on the stern of the old rowing-boat. Suddenly another boat appears with an engine chugging and breaking the calm on the smooth and shiny lake. With a stylish swerve it stops next to Ingvar and the journalist.

'Hi. Are you out rowing, Dad?'

'But hello, my dear Peter. What are you doing out here?'

'I have been putting out the crayfish pots. Anyway hello Lennart, my name is Peter'.

The fact that Peter Kamprad, Ingvar's oldest son and heir to IKEA, was out on the lake at the same time as his father and one of the most important financial journalists in the country was no coincidence if anybody thought so. Ingvar told me the story when I visited Böllsö a few days later.

Coincidences are not Ingvar's thing. And absolutely never when journalists are involved. The result of Ekdal's visit in Småland was a journalistic failure. Possibly it was charming TV-entertainment, but there were no new revelations. Who dares nail Kamprad with difficult questions after having enjoyed a meal with wonderful homemade hamburgers that the world's richest man himself has himself prepared? Because he is an excellent cook – as well.

Ekdal himself describes his visit like this in an interview about people in power he has met[1]: 'Ingvar Kamprad is also a fascinating man. For a programme I was making with him we spent a few days together in order to get to know each other. Amongst other things we were out laying nets in his old rowing-boat that leaked like a sieve – as did the wellington boots he lent me. Afterwards we were sitting in his 'boathouse' which was nothing but a shack, and ate pike and I drank medium-strong beer whilst he drank Coca-Cola Light.'

A more recent example is given by one of the country's journalistic heavyweights K-G Bergström from SVT (Swedish Television). A more mediocre interview than the one Bergström made with Kamprad in the summer of 2008 would be hard to find. Ingvar was allowed to freely and without interruptions go into great detail about his murky past, his dyslexia and his alcoholism – and to cry crocodile tears over his Nazi sins.

Ingvar is unusually competent when journalists let him loose in this way. All answers are standard answers, carefully formulated and stored away in his excellent memory. There is no hesitation or a moment of spontaneity anywhere. And if someone happens to get too close to him he is extremely clever at furtively changing the subject.

What is worse for Bergström and Ekdal and other colleagues from the media who have been shown Kamprad's charm is that they are handpicked. Ingvar meets with especially chosen, kindly disposed Swedish journalists once a year in late summer, other than that he seldom gives interviews. TV-journalists are chosen with great care in order to pick out the kindly disposed ones. The fact that he agrees to do the summer radio chat programme 'Sommar' has two reasons. Partly it is completely free of charge and therefore great publicity for his company. Partly because he can talk about this and that without being challenged. His capability to communicate, or really dupe or manipulate, when he is allowed to talk without interruptions is matchless.

Now, the truth is that Ingvar does not need a rowing-boat or even a summery meadow in order to mislead Swedish journalists. In connection with the launch of Bertil Torekull's book on Ingvar, *The Story of IKEA*, that was written on Ingvar's commission, there was an important press conference at the Kungens Kurva store. Ingvar later told me how he had arrived with underground-tickets in his hand and immediately began talking about public transport. He had been in a brilliant mood and filled the room with his down-to-earth reflections about the price of *snus* and such like.

Precisely, as in the two previous examples the effect is priceless. On one hand Ingvar firmly and charmingly took command of the situation and set the tone as well as the agenda. And he carried on with this for rather a long while. Without fail the questioners will follow his agenda. Add to that the fact that he exploits his age fully and plays the friendly patriarch who refuses to confess to being the richest man in the world and a living legend. Very few journalists have it in them to give an old man the third degree. We hardly provoke our own grandfather. Thus the press conference falls flatly on its feet and the room is filled with deep admiration for the old man who is standing in the middle of the room with hands folded under his stomach twiddling his thumbs. And he talks continuously. For Ingvar suffers from, according to himself, 'diarrhoea of the mouth' of the worst kind. As entertainment this is very enjoyable, but journalistically not very professional in view of all the pressing questions that ought to be asked.

There is however one wonderful exception in the line of poor journalism, shown by Sweden's TV4 the other year. It was when journalist Bim Enström followed Ingvar and Russian manager Lennart Dahlgren (previously fired by Kamprad but taken on again later). Bim did not have the same urge to shine brightly next to a legend that her male colleagues had. On the contrary she did not say a word during the whole film. But the main protagonists did speak, and a better and more intimate portrait of Ingvar I at any rate have ever seen. He was exactly as much hard work, as hilarious, as sarcastic, jovial, delightful, foul-mouthed, super knowledgeable, tough in business and warm towards close associates that only Ingvar can be.

Ingvar the dyslexic

Back to Ingvar's 'faults and shortcomings'. I am not the only ex-assistant who has realized that much of these are untrue – or in any case hugely exaggerated. A dyslexic can hardly read and/or write. Words tend to be misspelt the whole time. Ingvar, who communicates with his managers around the IKEA-world via hundreds of handwritten letters and faxes, always misspells the same word and always in the same way. For example he writes 'artickle' instead of article. If one has difficulties with spelling this is, as a rule, a chronic and irregular phenomena. And it is not often so incorrect that the message becomes incomprehensible. Ingvar's letters and faxes are completely different from those written by a dyslexic as they are always as correctly spelt as they are well-formulated – apart from a few dozen words.

Another example that perhaps only foreign journalists are exposed to is his poor English. During a stay at home with Ingvar in Switzerland I was surprised when I heard him think aloud in fluent English with a highly advanced English vocabulary. It only lasted a short moment but it made a deep impression on me, as I earlier had thought that his knowledge of languages began and ended with Swenglish (a mixture of Swedish and English).

This was the first time it dawned on me that many of his shortcomings are a front used to manipulate journalists and employees. The journalists by attracting their attention and fascinate them with the many shortcomings of this extremely successful and rich man. Moreover, if the journalists are not Scandinavians Kamprad is able to avoid any awkward question with the help of his poor English. Who wants to round on an old man who cannot speak a foreign language? IKEA colleagues are taken in by him playing the role of the ordinary man, albeit the boss of their world but with all the faults and defects one can think of: meaning someone who 'lowers' himself to their level and becomes a normal mortal just like them. It arouses a lot of sympathy in most people.

Ingvar the alcoholic

An alcoholic is an alcoholic because he or she can no longer control their drinking. Kamprad has regular, carefully scheduled, dry periods. In between that he never becomes blindingly drunk. To have one whisky and soda or two in the evening does not make you an alcoholic. Ask the women and men who attend AA meetings about what alcoholism is. An alcoholic is someone totally different from a person who enjoys a drink in the evening.

The only time I have seen Ingvar drunk was in 1995 at an office party in Poland, when I and other colleagues were at least as inebriated. I have, apart from then, neither seen nor heard that Ingvar is a secret drinker or indeed drinks in any other way either. Or that he has ever acted incorrectly or made a mistake as a result of his drinking. I have in other words never noticed anything about this so widely discussed alcoholism other than from his late summer interviews with gullible journalists. On the contrary I would guess that what Ingvar means is that he feels that he drinks too much because he likes drinking. I know that his family doctor in Switzerland has suggested that he ought to have a certain amount of dry periods if he thinks he is drinking a bit too much or too often in order to save his liver and the rest of his body. My doctor also thinks that I drink a bit too much. Nonetheless, neither I nor Kamprad are alcoholics.

My impression is that Kamprad is extremely clever at using exaggerations that border on lies in order to create an image of himself and IKEA that benefits the company. The world's richest man becomes a much more exciting person as a drunkard, dyslexic, useless at English and to cap it all 'slightly stupid' which is how he describes himself in the company of journalists. If anybody ever wonders, Ingvar Kamprad has certainly one of the sharpest brains of our time. He is just bloody good at hiding it. And he knows exactly why he does it.

When I was visiting Ingvar at home in Switzerland the deputy chief executive and ex-assistant Hans Gydell, who Ingvar considered 'the second most intelligent person he had ever met' telephoned. Ingvar had an idea about 'joint funds' where the liquidity of all three companies, IKEA, Inter-IKEA and IKANO should be amalgamated and managed together. Don't ask me how this should happen as I don't know. Nevertheless, 'Gydde' calls with questions and ideas on how this was to be arranged. Ingvar sounded mighty irritated whilst he in great detail explained what needed to be done. He then threw down the receiver and turned to me. 'Johan, is it necessary to get an old lumberjack in order to make these guys understand how money should be handled?'

What Kamprad in fact does when he is being interviewed, since outside the world of the media he never talks about all his problems, is to put out smoke screens with his alleged weaknesses. They are simply a diversion. His remarkable honesty never fails to intrigue journalists. Thus the focus of the interview moves away from all the delicate IKEA-questions that ought to be highlighted and on to the personal weaknesses of the founder. This has two results. Partly the weaknesses take time and attention as Ingvar really knows how to play the part, show off and put it on when needed. Partly the atmosphere between the reporter and Ingvar becomes affected. Not even the most hardened journalist can remain unmoved when the old man, with tears in his eyes, 'bares his soul'. He thus imperceptibly takes the sting out of the journalistic intention of the reporter. Before the journalist breathes a word the interview is over, as Ingvar without hesitation will fill a whole hour with his long-winded accounts about mainly nothing.

## Ingvar, the WWII past

As far as I am aware, two books have been written about Ingvar and his life-work. *Ingvar Kamprad och hans IKEA: en svensk saga (Ingvar Kamprad and his IKEA: A Swedish Saga)* by Thomas Sjöberg talks largely about Ingvar's earlier sympathy for the Nazis and attempts to prove that he was active for much longer than he cares to admit. Torekull's book, commissioned by IKEA, also covers the Nazi episode. It is possible that Sjöberg is correct and Kamprad hides behind the fact that he can't remember. At the same time he has, as I already have said, an incredible memory that stretches far back in time. My guess is that it is shame that makes him avoid this issue.

When Ingvar was attacked most forcefully after the publication of Sjöberg's book, the so-called second Nazi wave, he was thoroughly shaken. He had retracted and apologized six years earlier when his Nazi sympathies were first exposed. He had made an honest attempt to open the archives and to put all his cards on the table. Still it was not enough. During this onset he often called and we saw each other on a couple of occasions. Ingvar was near to tears as he had been affected on a deeply personal level. Abuse was flying around and people in his immediate vicinity turned their backs on him, as if they could not cope with sharing the shame he once more had to shoulder.

I am convinced of a couple of things in this sad story. Ingvar has today no neo-Nazi or fascist sympathies whatsoever. I have never even heard vague allusions to this. Ingvar is absolutely no anti-Semite. I would say the contrary. He has told many anecdotes from the early sixties when he helped Polish Jews or Jewish groups in need of money or support in other ways. He has a soft spot for colleagues of this religion. Some of them are amongst Ingvar's favourites. Why this is so I do not know, perhaps he wishes to compensate for his earlier sins.

Ingvar grew up in an extremely authoritarian family of German origin. His paternal grandmother was more than pro-German, a matriarch who set the agenda in the Kamprad home. The fact that Ingvar's father Feodor was a confirmed Nazi was, according to the now dead colleague Leif Sjöö, known all around the district. Beatings and indoctrination were part of everyday life on their farm, Elmtaryd, as in so many other homes during the twenties and thirties. To be able to escape from this emotional desert as a child without lasting damage must have been difficult. The fact that Ingvar, as Sjöberg perhaps correctly points out, was a Nazi, or in any case a fascist, at the end of the fifties is decidedly bad. But my assessment is that those acts of folly stopped, in order to never return.

As a final line on the subject, Ingvar's father Teodor was active within IKEA far into the sixties and sacked people left, right and centre depending on his moods. Not even Ingvar could influence him. Remember this as history will repeat itself.

## Ingvar the miser

Yet Kamprad is probably most famous for his extreme tight-fistedness. Who has not heard how Ingvar fills his pockets with portions of salt and pepper in self-service restaurants despite the fact that he is one of the world's richest men? Or how Ingvar's nearest co-workers forced him to stop driving the old Volvo as it was a danger to traffic? Even if the level of truth is low, not to say non-existent, in these stories, this is not the important bit. The point is that Ingvar has succeeded in creating such a swell of stories around his person and his most important personality traits.

If one were to instead talk about Ingvar's stinginess in a more well-informed way a few lines will be enough. He is so stingy with IKEA money that all extravagance is banned, even when it comes to tiny sums of money. Few things can make Ingvar more hopping mad than mindless, unnecessary waste. To forget to turn off the lights when leaving the room can make him mighty irritated as I, when I became his new assistant, was to experience on Böllsö. It was six o'clock in the morning and we were just about to go out into the darkness to the car in order to start our working day, when Ingvar discovered that the lights were still on in my room. A proper telling-off followed which questioned both my talent and my judgement.

At the same time, he does not hesitate to in a meeting open up his wallet in order to finance a new risky project with hundreds of millions of kronor (£9/$14 million) if he believes in the colleague and the idea.

The persona he cultivates around his stinginess is, as far as I can judge, genuine.

Privately he does not allow himself much in the way of luxuries. He wears very basic clothes: a shirt, trousers and a plain jacket, and nothing is designer made. He does not own a luxurious car. The story that Ingvar drove around an old Volvo banger was true. The house where he and his wife Margaretha live is as ordinary as it can be. The Swedish tabloid press has on a couple of occasions reported that the Kamprad family is padded in luxury at their house in Switzerland. It is true that it is situated in a nice neighbourhood but as a home it is very modest. The furnishing is typical of the eighties, and rather simpler than Böllsö seventies style. Size-wise it is like a sizeable family home. The 300 square metres that the papers have quoted must include both a separate flat and a garage. His holiday trips are far and few between as Ingvar hates holidays as much as he hates going to the cinema. Margaretha sometimes has to twist his arm to see a new movie. The vineyard in France is also not extravagant, as a colleague who has worked there told me. Amongst other things it has a couple of rooms that are let out to tourists. For a long time it was Ingvar's problem child rather than his relaxation, as it showed a financial loss despite the fact that the IKEA stores were obliged to sell the sour wine produced there as IKEA-wine. Nowadays it seems that both the wine and the financials are better. And so Ingvar is happier.

However, Ingvar is a very generous host. Whenever I visited him the gifts have been many and always in the form of delicacies like Raclette-cheese, chocolates, wine, cooked and cured meats and many other Swiss goodies. He prepares one delicious dish after another and really takes great pains in order for you to be happy. He even schedules an afternoon nap for his guests to feel at home.

## Apologies and excuses

Looking back I begin to see what a master Ingvar Kamprad is at apologies and excuses. Often when IKEA has been called into question Ingvar came up with and communicated the excuses that calmed co-workers and silenced the media. He realized early on that he does not actually have to solve the problem at hand nor reveal the whole truth. Half truths and halfway solutions will do just as well. Just long enough to allow things to go quiet and to allow the media spotlight to be directed elsewhere.

One store (the one in Kungens Kurva) had for a long time a female store manager called Iréne – a talented and capable woman. She was also the first and only female store manager in IKEA-world at the time. Her boss was the Swedish MD, Bengt Larsson. Bengt did not seem to favour female managers in general and Iréne in particular. Ingvar said that by hook or by crook he tried to make Bengt become kinder. In the end Iréne as far as I can remember was sent to North America and ended her IKEA-days there. According to Ingvar anyway. But his addendum is extremely ingenious: 'Johan, it was really hard for Iréne with Bengt as her boss. I have never had anything against female managers or Iréne, who apart from anything else is very capable.' Note how he channels the responsibility away from himself as chief executive at the time, and on to Bengt Larsson whom Ingvar cordially disliked, as well as had the power to give instructions to. Furthermore Ingvar, at the time, had the right of veto regarding all appointments of store managers. In other words Ingvar was the only one who could really have done something about gender equality at IKEA. But he ignored it and does so still. Furthermore he is clever enough to use a concrete example, Iréne, in order to illustrate his message: this thing with female managers is difficult and there will always be problems, but am decent, and like the idea of female managers.

IKEA has during the years often been accused of copying well-known designer products and selling them much more cheaply under its own name. This is in itself completely true and was for a long time a successful strategy at IKEA. Nowadays direct plagiarism is rare, though products that have been inspired by competitors are fairly common. A logical answer to the question by a journalist about IKEA and imitation one would have thought the obvious reply from Ingvar would have been something along these lines: 'Sure, earlier it unfortunately happened that IKEA copied other people's work. Nowadays, I dare say, it never happens and we have invested a lot of resources in order to tie our own designers to IKEA.'

But no. Instead Ingvar replies: 'Listen, I'm telling you that proper unique new design is a rare thing. Everybody copies one another in this world.' To maintain that there is no unique design today is pure drivel. Still this statement was never questioned by anybody from the media. Possibly because the respect for Kamprad and IKEA is so great in Sweden. He becomes tactical when he blames 'everybody'. The pattern repeats itself, the excuse – the lack of unique design – and then blaming 'everybody' which then in some way would justify IKEA's actions. Cleverly done but hardly honourable.

The Kremlinologists

Ingvar however does not reserve his manipulative vein for the benefit of the media. It is an aid for exercising his power within IKEA and the Kamprad-sphere as well.

One of the more central unofficial mantras within IKEA goes: 'It is not what Ingvar says that is important. It is what he means.'

This term in other words means that each word, sentence and nuance uttered by Ingvar has to be interpreted. And this cult does really exist. A cult which is not far away from the old Soviet researchers, the Kremlin scholars. From each word and clause, from each syllable and comma they tried to decipher the will of the Kremlin rulers. And Ingvar really understands how to exploit the power of the word in all the faxes with which he bombards his subordinates. A few examples:

If he starts with 'Dear' it is neutral. If he starts with only your first name it is a sharp request. If the fax starts with 'Dearest' you are in his good books. The same applies to the ending. A 'With best wishes' is dangerously neutral and he is distancing himself. A simple 'Hugs' on the other hand calms the anxious. At times he will change beginning and end in order to signal to the recipient whether he is pleased or displeased. And believe you me, even a calm and cool person like the chief executive Anders Dahlvig can become stressed by Ingvar's bombardment of Kremlin-style words.

Furthermore, he spices up faxes and letters with innuendos about who is a hero and why or who is not and why. To put people at the bottom of the pecking order and to choose his favourites has become a well developed skill.

The same thing happens when Ingvar meets people. Especially men. A handshake is completely neutral, really nothing. If he gives you a hug you are OK. If you get a hug and a kiss on the cheek you are part of the trusted few. And if you get no kiss next time you obviously wonder why. But Ingvar knows why, you can be sure of that.

Ingvar functions exactly in the same way as a speech writer. He writes his Christmas and autumn speeches by hand with a thin felt-tip pen and with his typical upper-case letters in straight lines, line by line. There is no doubt that he is a good writer. Deliberately he brings up subjects that he feels are topical. The autumn speech that he holds at the end of August each year may take several days to complete and is often written at the dining-table at Böllsö. In the late summer heat he sits there by himself writing away, dressed in just his underpants. Obviously everybody quickly understands who should feel shame and who are the heroes of the day. Slightly disguised personal attacks are an everyday occurrence at IKEA.

The real Kamprad-cult exists among all the inhabitants of Älmhult who work at different levels and areas within the IKEA hierarchy. The most hardened crowd is made up of greying men who have long passed their sell-by date. They study every word and every syllable in Ingvar's various speeches and afterwards make predictions about what will happen in the company in great as in small ways.

Why Ingvar devotes himself to this is rather obvious. By constantly changing moods in his faxes and changing between praise and condemnation in his speeches, his co-workers always feel insecure, are kept on their toes while eagerly divining whatever Ingvar wants. If you aren't able to interpret Ingvar's signals in meetings or faxes, you will soon have reached the zenith of your IKEA-career, irrespective of how good you are. To be able to decipher and interpret Ingvar is essential in order to survive in the company.

Mistrust and spies

Behind Ingvar's charmingly ageing front hides a man who has mistrusted all and everyone during his whole career. He has built IKEA with mistrust. Since he does not trust anybody, or that things will get done, he has for many years been surrounding himself with spies. Experienced, loyal collaborators at all levels in the company, who by fax or telephone or whenever he appears in person disclose their observations to him.

I well remember when Mikael Ohlsson, who was manager of IKEA of Sweden towards the end of the nineties (and who took over as chief executive from September 2009), was attacked like this by Ingvar. Mikael was an extremely knowledgeable MD for IoS, perhaps the most competent one to date. But he was also a man of immense integrity. When he tried to gather the organization around his ideas that may not have corresponded with Kamprad's in all respects, Ingvar knew this before most of the rest of the co-workers. He would then send faxes or make telephone calls in order to get Ohlsson to change his mind. The spies intervened actively in order to make colleagues pass over to the faithful Kamprad-side. The conflict went so far that it for a while felt as if the whole of IoS was divided into camps for and against Ingvar.

Well-informed colleagues say that Ingvar really despises his fifth columnists and exploits them ruthlessly and that deep down it is only co-workers with integrity and with the good sense to shut up that he respects.

The chameleon look

There is one more striking personality trait Ingvar has, which on the surface can be interpreted as hesitation or indecision. In reality it has more to do with his way of looking at things and people. He often sees two sides, one that he likes and one he is less keen on, perhaps detests even. Obviously he can become very enthusiastic about one thing. But often he sees two entirely different sides.

As an example Ingvar has agonised over many new stores abroad. He was completely opposed to Japan, but chose not to use his veto. He thought that to tackle China on a massive scale would have been a wiser investment. It is true that the Japanese market has enormous potential, but IKEA is completely unknown in Japan and to establish the brand there would cost a lot of money. He endlessly listens to arguments. Asks people he has confidence in. Dwells on things, has a rest and comes back to the issue. And then after a long and no doubt frustrating thought-process, he reaches a decision.

*Böllsö farm outside Älmhult, early September 1997*

The working day had as usual been long, as unbearably tedious for me as it had been exciting for the unflagging Ingvar. During the IK-days, the yearly range week, Ingvar and I went from meeting to meeting on the third floor in the faded office-block Blåsippan, or the 'third loft' as Ingvar preferred to call this newly-built complex. As always uncertain about new things he still had a hate/love relationship with the enormous areas that showed his entire company's range including price tags and the lot.

The IK-days were surrounded by unspoken traditions. The assistants must live with Ingvar at Böllsö and closely follow him by day. Neither me nor any of my predecessors had ever worked in buying, development of range or packaging before taking on the assistant's position. The long discussions about these subjects became not merely impossible to understand. They became unbearably boring. But if your task is to write the all important minutes, it means you are in trouble. My dozing-off process went from alert the first five minutes, to listless after twenty. After half an hour I had managed to find a place to sit in a corner within listening distance. After forty-five minutes sleep liberated me.

'Do not sleep, take notes.'

Only seconds at a time, but valuable seconds. During critical moments in the distant discussion, for example if someone had to promise Ingvar improvements, I would stab my pencil deep into my thigh over and over in order to stay awake. In fact, a sleeping assistant is part of the IK tradition, senior colleagues have confirmed. Anders Dahlvig is said to have fallen asleep on several occasions during the IK-days when he was assistant in the eighties. Poor consolation, but still. I was told off every year by Ingvar on account of my useless notes. Years later when I was working on the same issues I benefitted from what I had learnt during the painfully boring range weeks, despite the fact that I was drowsy most of the time.

Dinner had been cleared away and Ingvar and I were filling the dishwasher in the tiny kitchen. Ingvar had, following his traditions, fried chanterelles for a starter and then laid on crayfish from lake Möckeln. A dinner that had been rinsed down with beer.

'Now I'll show you something, Johan. I have something that may interest a friend of the environment like yourself.'

Ingvar sat down at the kitchen table with a cotton bag on his lap and started rummaging around amongst the paper folders held together with rubber bands that contained a large part of his current archive. I think it said COOP on the grubby yellowy bag.

'Here it is. It is a letter, well, a few lines I have written about my views on the forest', he said after about ten minutes.

'Please read this and tell me what you think. Forests are not an easy problem, Johan.'

As usual it was a couple of A4-pages written by hand with a felt-tip pen: observations and sharply formulated thoughts about the forest noted in his usual capital letters. All words were correctly spelled apart from a few. Everything was surprisingly accessible considering the complexity of the problem.

In essence it was simple. The forest is IKEA's most important raw material. The forest is a renewable resource and therefore environmentally ok. The deforestation mainly caused by the population explosion threatens enormous areas. How can we with simple means make our forests will last into the future? IKEA has to after all be able to help the development in the right direction?

'Can't you talk to these tree huggers in order to see if we can do something together', he said.

The 'tree huggers' were Greenpeace, whom Ingvar preferred to the WWF with their headquarters in Switzerland which he considered extravagant and sloppy. I flew to Amsterdam where Greenpeace International has its headquarters. I met with their person responsible for forests, the German Christoph Thies, on a couple of occasions and tried to convince him that on the one hand our intentions were honourable despite the fact that IKEA is multinational, and on the other that we wanted to find a project to work together.

Thies was part of the more pragmatic faction of Greenpeace who recommended cooperation rather than confrontation. Being German he was naturally extremely knowledgeable in his field, but also straight, to the point and open to new and different approaches. After each Amsterdam meeting new supporters joined in, all equally devoted to their cause and with a good knowledge about environmental matters.

Part of this procedure was the fact that Greenpeace had just left the trees in as much as the pragmatic faction of the organization had become more influential. Not that the idea of classic Greenpeace actions had been abandoned. It had been supplemented with opening up different ways to cooperate with, for example, large companies.

Meeting followed meeting. Time went by but no results were achieved. But just as I started to feel it was all pointless Thies turned up with a whole group of colleagues. He asked me to explain IKEA's point of view and suggestions to the others. 'IKEA is very keen on cooperating with Greenpeace. We mean that you are close to our own values and that your problems, chiefly the forest, concerns us to a large extent. To be completely frank we are prepared to join with a large sum of money.'

'I believe we have an idea for cooperation', said Christoph Thies suddenly.

Obviously it was against Greenpeace regulations to receive money from a corporation. On the other hand the organization had found a commendable project within its network that would be able to do so. An American environmental group of good repute had formed Global Forest Watch. The project was to finance the mapping of the world's last vast and continuous intact natural forest, the so-called frontier forests, via satellite photography. The photographs were to be compiled country by country, continent by continent with on-site random samples as well as other scientific data where available.

By publishing the maps on the Internet on their home page *globalforestwatch.org* authorities around the world would be able to keep illegal logging under control in a more efficient way. Companies like IKEA, which cuts down trees on a large scale, could, with the help of the maps, avoid sensitive regions. (This has actually happened, lately in Russian Karelia. The Review Commission cited IKEA as a good example and the paper maker Stora Enso as a bad one.)

I left Amsterdam feeling optimistic. Now we had something concrete and extremely worthwhile to channel money into. That is where my feeling pleased came to an end.

Back at Kölles Farm I was met by a not at all pleased Ingvar. Indeed both the choice of Greenpeace and donating to charity had been his idea, and I had only carried out his wishes. But now he dug his heels in while prevaricating. Charity has never been Ingvar's best side and it still isn't. At the time, at the end of the nineties, all charitable donations, and it was a ridiculously small sum, went to a cancer charity dedicated to Ingvar's mother. To give away 60 million kronor (£4/$8 million), as in the Greenpeace-example, really went against the grain. He enlisted his oldest son Peter to put a stop to the idea, but the questions Peter raised were irrelevant, such as: 'How do you know where the money will go?'

The fact that charitable organizations in the Anglo-Saxon world are very closely monitored by the authorities, was obviously something the young man misunderstood. The chief executive Anders Moberg and I met with a couple of Global Forest Watch representatives and they fully met our expectations. At the same time, Ingvar, who was travelling or in Switzerland at the time, changed between saying absolutely no to co-operation to ultimately demand that IKEA should also gain something from the project. Towards the end an agreement began to take form where IKEA's money should largely be ear-marked for areas that were of interest to us. The sixty million had also shrunk considerably along the way.

Ingvar's irritation had only to do with the charity part of it. The closer to the finalisation of a philanthropic project paid for by IKEA we get, the more irritated he becomes. And the more indecisive. As if he time and time again keeps asking himself how he could ever have said yes to something so absurd.

Some time afterwards I was the project leader for the Ingvar Kamprad Design Centre in Lund, a design school offering designer training and a professorship paid for by IKEA. In the media it was called the biggest privately financed education-venture within the Swedish university-world. Preparations were going ahead six months before the inauguration. Ingvar at the time changed from enthusiastic to expectant to grumpy to rude. At the inauguration he was restless and ill-tempered and barked at me like a watchdog. Again and again he was asked by the board members of INGKA to stop complaining. The inauguration was, just as they were trying to tell him, in effect, extremely successful.

I am not writing this in order to complain: as his assistant I had to make allowances for his moods. Shortly afterwards I moved on (as planned) to a position at IKEA of Sweden AB in Älmhult. It may have been three months when I met Ingvar again and at that time it was over a cup of coffee in the Älmhult office. He was overjoyed and chatting away about the design school and the marvellous inauguration.

At the bottom and the top of the pecking order

Ingvar's view of the world is far from simple or black-and-white. He, if anybody, sees the whole gamut of greys, he mulls over problems, digests new information, discusses issues with his friends and with people in the know before finally making up his mind. Apart from in one respect – when it comes to people. Because people who are able and loyal and who get things done, are quickly noted by Ingvar and end up on his list of favourites. In Ingvar's mind that is when you receive the informal honour of being 'a proper IKEA-guy'. If you do end up on Ingvar's list he will almost always overlook any mistakes and blunders in the future. You become such a favourite that you can make a career far above your actual capability. The IKEA-companies in Älmhult house a number of colleagues whose careers long since should have expired, since their incapacity to cope with their tasks without a doubt harms IKEA. In other words, nowadays the potential and the performance of a person mean very little in Ingvar's judgement of him or her. I write nowadays, as I perceive this blindness of a person's competence or incompetence has become more pronounced during the last ten years.

'What the hell is this?' The outburst started with a rhetorical question made in normal conversational tone in creaking dialect from the Småland region. 'What in hell is this, really? Someone please, Hans-Göran or some other sensible person, what does this mean?'

The voice quickly increased in intensity, but none of the dozen people around Ingvar answered. Not Hans-Göran Stennert, Ingvar's brother-in-law and chairman of the board at INGKA, either. 'Don't you dare? Or you don't want to tell me what kind of rubbish this is!'

At this point something very curious happened. In front of a group of colleagues Ingvar worked himself into such uncontrollable rage that he became deep red in the face, shouted incomprehensibly and was extremely rude to the co-workers whose work he was considering. By the minute he became more and more rude as he rubbished the new bathroom collection and more and more ruthless, mainly towards Julie Desrosiers, the woman behind the collection. Hans-Göran tried to take Ingvar to one side in order for him to calm down but completely to no avail.

But was this just an old man who momentarily had become unhinged? Well, if you run a billion kroner company with plenty of agreeable ideas of which 'the power of the good example' is just one, you have an enormous responsibility towards your co-workers. Then it is never OK to destroy a subordinate – neither in private nor in front of colleagues. At least not if you are Ingvar, since you personally have formulated every syllable in the philosophy of the company. That is why I can't see Ingvar as a victim of any sort. He is very much present, an extremely talented and perceptive person of 83.

I ought to mention that French-Canadian Julie Desrosiers was perhaps the most talented product developer that IKEA has ever had. Everything she touched (the PAX wardrobes, bed- and mattress-ranges) turned into gold. Still as I am writing this, despite the fact that Julie left IKEA six months ago in 2009, her previous ranges of bedrooms are still best-sellers at IKEA. In view of the time needed for product development this is nothing her successors have anything to do with. Bedrooms are growing despite the fact that the world around is in the worst crises since the thirties. And the bathroom range that made Ingvar lose control had furthermore been given standing ovations by all those who know these things at IoS AB, including myself. But Ingvar was allowed to decide and it was all scrapped. Bathrooms are still IKEA's weakest range because Kamprad could not cope with a woman being more talented than himself in the product development area.

'Thomas Rask (false name)? Is that fucking incompetent guy still working here?' Ingvar protests in a loud voice. Just before lunch a winter's day at Blåsippan Ingvar pops into my office. We talk about this and that. On our way out we pass the notice board with pictures and names of all the co-workers. In a flash his eyes stop on Thomas Rask. 'Rask is completely useless, Johan. How the hell can he still be here? And they did promise me they would sack that daft idiot.'

Ingvar's angry statement hit me like a knife in the diaphragm when two thoughts crossed my mind: Had anybody heard the outburst? The office would normally be full of people at this time of the day. Had the poor, but useless guy, Thomas Rask, heard the depreciatory words? I took Ingvar carefully by the arm and led him outside. Despite the fact that a few years had past since I was his assistant, I clearly felt that it was still my duty to protect Ingvar both from himself as well as from his own co-workers. A rumour about him having had an outburst against Thomas Rask was the last thing he needed.

The worst thing about Ingvar's aggressive side is that he consciously chooses who he will use it against, exactly as he chooses who to show pleasure. Chance has no place on his agenda. I have never heard that Ingvar has ever lost it at an INGKA board meeting or at a visit to a store. When he finally lets out his devilish wrath the effect is devastating. The people around him become rigid and the victims of his anger are completely crushed by pure and utter fear.

I know because I have also been the target of his sulphurous aggression. At the time when IKEA was hit by one child labour scandal after the other, I was in a car late at night together with Anders Moberg on our way to a Swedish TV studio in Växjö. As I was responsible for PR and communications of the group as well as assistant to both of them, I was also Anders' closest advisor in a messy situation we never could win. Hardly even reduce the damage. Suddenly my mobile phone rings. Ingvar is bellowing abuse at me. I had forgotten to inform him about an article that Anders had published in a newspaper the same day. Clearly a mistake but hardly a reason to give me the sack there and then, which is what Kamprad wanted to do. Anders looked calmly at me trembling in the car.

'Then he will have to sack us both', he said and just carried on driving.

Up to one million people the world over are dependent on IKEA for their survival. Ultimately Ingvar himself decides over IKEA and so also over their destiny. Soon his sons will have the same power.

# 3

# The IKEA-machine

In order to understand IKEA one has to understand *what* the company really does. And understand *how* IKEA does it. I call this enormous organization of some 150,000 co-workers in a large number of countries across the world who cooperate around the clock throughout the year in order to produce what the IKEA customers want, the IKEA-machine. Everything is connected, coordinated and efficient as clockwork.

'The pipeline'

Every company organizes itself around the activity that produces its goods or services. The IKEA-machine, the IKEA organization, can therefore simply be described as a flow of different activities throughout the whole process, where each activity bit by bit further increases the value of the product on its journey to the customer. Once in the hands of the customer in the shop the product has reached its selling price, that is its value. In the case of IKEA it may, for example, be about the product's journey from a pine to coffee table. If the value of this pine in the forest is 50 Euro (£40/$65), the value of the same pine further up in the process in the form of coffee tables will be considerably higher.

In business analysis, a process of activities that constantly increases the value of a product is the value chain. Each link in this chain corresponds to a key activity that transforms the original pine to a piece of furniture. The value at each stage by which the value of the product is increased is called the surplus value of the activity. At the beginning of the chain/flow the activity would normally be to procure raw materials. After that follows production, product development, logistics and sales.

Now imagine that all companies within the same line of business organized themselves around their value chains. How can one company become more competitive than the other? In reality there are only three ways for a company, irrespective of its product, to compete. Either you make your products more cheaply than the competitors or you make them better (different in some respect) or you make them both more cheaply and better. IKEA decided to concentrate on the last strategy right from its inception.

As we shall see the value chain is only one of three key ingredients in IKEA's secret dispensary. By secret I mean that it is little known outside IKEA's blue and yellow façade. The other two are on one hand the genius of Ingvar who manages the whole organization, on the other hand the so called IKEA-culture which makes the work in the whole value chain flow relatively smoothly.

The value chain and how it over the years has been developed and adjusted, has had an important significance in creating the IKEA we see today. In IKEA-speak it is called 'the pipeline'. In other words imagine how a pine is put in at the forest end and a flat-pack with a coffee table at the consumer end. Let us follow the process from forest to customer. During this journey we will come across some big and serious challenges that IKEA has had to deal with during the last 10–20 years, some of them have been resolved others are still live. All of them have however remained unknown outside the walls of the company.

Forests

Try to imagine a stack of pine- or spruce logs comprising almost 200,000,000 logs. That is how immense IKEA's need for forest raw material is per year. Then consider that the company doubles its size – and its need for pine and spruce – every four years.

In other words IKEA clear-fells hundreds of thousands hectares of forest each year down to the last tree. There is nothing terribly wrong in that. Timber is an environmentally friendly and renewable raw material. That is to say, if it is correctly managed. Provided the forest is looked after, felling is done in the correct way and the production likewise, the impact on the environment is considerably less than for example cultivation of cotton, both when it comes to depletion of water resources, impact of carbon monoxide and emissions. Obviously, the assumption here is that it is cultivated forest and not the last primeval forest that is being cut.

IKEA has been far-sighted in its endeavour to secure its need for timber, not least thanks to Ingvar Kamprad's complete understanding of how things might look in the future. When the Berlin wall fell in 1989 and the map of Eastern Europe changed overnight, IKEA's best buyers had already left the starting blocks. One of the first deals that was made was the purchase of sawmills with enormous forest acreage in Siberia. The man on the ground who fixed it all was the legendary Bernard Furrer, one of the very few non-Swedes in the IKEA leadership. Unfortunately it did not quite work out as the Russian Mafia got their hands on the deal. All in all IKEA had put in 50 million kroner (£4.5/$7.2 million) in money value at the time. Not surprisingly that Bernard was worried when he came to Kölles Farm in Humlebæk.

In the conference room this morning were Ingvar, the chief executive Anders Moberg and a line of other IKEA barons. When the agenda reached the Siberian adventure Bernard Furrer was called in. He told us his bad news objectively but as positively as possible, the whole time ready for the tirade of invectives that he thought he deserved. After all he had lost several billion of Swedish money (which is IKEA-speak for Swedish kronor) from the company's funds. The telling-off did not happen. Ingvar asked a few questions and then remained quiet, seemingly pleased with the answers.

Having been through this point on the agenda we were able to stretch our legs, have a pee, a coffee and a change of *snus* (even if Ingvar always takes care of that during the meetings by confiscating the nearest bin and putting it next to himself). Ingvar approached Bernard with a grim expression and asked: 'Where did you stay last night?' Bernard told him that he had stayed at the local hotel. The proper telling-off that followed was according to witnesses, nasty. To stay anywhere else than at the small and simple overnight rooms at the Kölle farm when you had business there or were passing, was an enormous waste of IKEA's limited resources according to Ingvar who was bright red with anger.

This incidence is interesting from a number of perspectives when one tries to understand IKEA and Ingvar Kamprad. Of course Ingvar realized that the company's fast and daring advances towards the east, both regarding forests as well as factories, would cost a lot in failure and hard cash before any success could be reaped. But this was money in order to learn, i.e. a pure investment in knowledge and not losses. Without colleagues like Bernard, who were prepared to take risks, the breakthrough in new markets would never succeed. If Bernard Furrer was to be sacrificed over the Siberian adventure the fear it induced in his colleagues would put at risk the whole eastern expansion. Seen from that point of view the 50 million was mere change compared to what would be the strategic cost if the main competitors won the race to the forests and factories of eastern Europe and Siberia.

Moreover Ingvar was more than aware of how the costs of the company could run away if managers were allowed a spend-thrift behaviour – even on a small scale. Managers are models. The power of the good example, as he himself calls it. Soon enough all co-workers would start to choose anywhere but IKEA-authorized hotels and so it would be impossible to know where it would end up if you changed these rules even slightly. That is how he reasoned then and that is how he reasons today.

The Siberian flop and many other similar learning curves made way for a fast expansion in Eastern Europe for IKEA. The company learnt one step at a time, bit by bit from all its mistakes. The 'learning organization' has been an abused buzzword in business books for many years now. A better example of what it means in practice than IKEA's eastern expansion is hard to find. And Ingvar used learning as a strategy more than ten years before the learning organization had even been invented as a concept.

The company has for many years had enormous forest franchises (the felling right in a certain forest area), at present hundreds of thousands of hectares of forest in countries like Russia, the Ukraine and Belarus. The strategy is as simple as it is brilliant. Timber is a renewable resource. Nonetheless, if demand goes up substantially then supply will partly become a bottle-neck, and prices will run away from you. Therefore forest areas must be secured at the same pace as the company's insatiable needs.

IKEA has been facing two challenges in recent years. Both still lack a solution as far as I know, and are closely connected. One is what to do in case the market price of pine and spruce increases a lot. As it has done during the last years, being pushed up by the increasing price of oil. The more expensive oil becomes, the more attractive it becomes for timber to be used as well as an alternative source of energy. Even if the price of oil is back to a somewhat lower level for a time one hardly needs to be a rocket scientist to see where the trend is leading to. Despite cyclic movement, the rising prices of oil and timber appears clear.

But one would think that IKEA is able to control the price of Russian and Ukrainian timber for themselves? Not quite. IKEA has indeed constructed some fantastic sawmills and factories near its forests in the east. But to build a sawmill is one thing, to fell and saw the timber another; and that has gone from bad to worse. The explanations and excuses for this have been piling on top of each other. Mild winters and poor ground frost made felling impossible since the forest machinery could not get out and the timber lorries could not get through forests without roads. Without timber the factories were nowhere near their production target, and to send unsawn stock bought on the spot market of raw materials in Russia and to transport it over the borders with Finland, the Baltic or Poland did not work either. More or less at the same time, Russia had imposed unreasonably high tolls on all exports of Russian timber, since they understandably wanted to keep the processing of their own raw materials within the country.

The inevitable result was too little timber for the enormous needs of IKEA and, just as bad, far too expensive timber. Since they had not managed to exploit the competitive advantages they had earlier established in the form of forests and sawmills, the raw materials had to be procured on the open market. Not even in Poland, IKEA's oldest and preferred market of purchase with perhaps the best managed forest in Europe, did the buyers manage to secure cheap timber.

As the new, higher prices started being fed into IKEA's calculation system CALC, the whole value system from purchase to store was substantially shaken. IKEA profit calculations are based on the principle that each link in the chain must be profitable. The problem now was that IKEA's most important raw material, around 60% of all its purchases, was hit by a galloping increase in price.

When the timber price rises pushed prices up through the 'pipeline', they came to a halt at the retailers (IKEA's word for stores) for two reasons. This was in part because the retailers had frozen the price on the 4,000 articles in the catalogue for a year and could that way not compensate for any purchase price rises with higher retail prices. A considerable part of these articles in spruce or pine are furthermore best-sellers such as the IVAR bookshelf, the GORM storage, LEKSVIK storage system and a large number of coffee tables, bed frames, wardrobes and dining tables. The IKEA retail pricing method, which is based on CALC increases in the pipeline, is thus challenged by reality in the form of customers and competitors. If competitors decide to absorb the price increase in timber, that is to accept a lower profit, then IKEA would have to be forced to follow suit as the policy of the company is to have the lowest price in each market. The rule of thumb for IKEA's pricing and profit margins is one third to the supplier, one third to IOS AB (purchasing and logistics), and as much to the stores. To be more exact IKEA makes up on an average 40 per cent compared with the purchasing price and the store nearly 35. You don't need a lot of imagination to see that large and growing price increases will wipe out a sensible profit margin.

I was part of the project that in 2005 aimed to lay the foundation for a massive investment in revolutionary wooden furniture in all ranges – obviously at incredibly competitive prices. Within IKEA, price levels that persistently are 30–50 per cent below those of competitors, are called 'advantage'. The idea was to let our own suppliers put together a well-balanced range of products. We are here talking about dozens of inde-pendent factories placed next to modern sawmills together with an advanced glue board plant and at times perhaps even an assembly factory. Unfortunately the majority of these ideas only lived on paper. As far as I know this magnificent project fell through.

A couple of things about this timber adventure strike me now, after the fact. How was it possible that IKEA was taken by surprise by price increases relating to its most important raw material? We have earlier seen how the company expanded into Eastern Europe at a formidable pace and bought up factories and forests on a large scale in order to have a long-term plan. But when things didn't quite go accordingly to plan, the entire long-term plan seemed to run aground. A multi-billion company that blames its lack of timber on mild weather seems incompetent. Why did they, for one, not construct forest roads in time?

IKEA was taken by surprise. Plan B did not exist. One clumsy rescue plan after the other was put forward – and obviously accepted – by Strategic Purchasing, the IKEA board dealing with all central purchases. Contrary to better judgement, I would argue. Of course, Ingvar had anticipated the looming crisis a long time beforehand. He certainly had ideas about what could have been done. But nothing was done. I watched my colleagues who had been given the task of solving the timber crises with increasing astonishment when we met in order to talk through the decisions taken by strategic purchasing. To me it became obvious that IKEA for the first time did not have clue.

Swedwood – The Industrial Group

IKEA's factory group, Swedwood AB, had originally brought forward the ambitious idea of making sawmills and factories neighbours of the forest. They had acquired enormous areas of forest and were fine-tuning the schedule in order to implement the idea. But now when timber was needed practically nothing arrived. Not just because the weather had been mild and that they had forgotten to build the forest roads. But due to reasons that have remained unknown, even to most people within IKEA, furniture never even left Russia. In most cases it was not even produced. To pointed questions vague replies about delays were given. To me it was incomprehensible how this mess had been allowed to develop. As a former store manager in the UK, I built and led the first store in Leeds, I knew that if I had opened one day too late I would have been fired. There is nothing strange about that. But now Swedwood could – obviously due to incompetence - fail one factory project after the other without anybody reacting or having been made responsible.

It was actually even worse than that. Swedwood saw itself as a completely separate company and prided itself on being independent. The fact that their only customer happened to be called IKEA and that they delivered one tenth of IKEA's total volume appeared irrelevant to them. Swedwood considered itself to be its own 'pipeline' alongside IKEA. To me and to other ex-colleagues it is incomprehensible that neither Ingvar Kamprad nor Anders Dahlvig ever wanted to incorporate the activities of Swedwood into the rest of IKEA. Ingvar most probably understands the problem better than any of us but he chose to remain quiet. I assumed that he perceived a danger in integrating the factory group within the rest of IKEA and rather prefers short-term losses in the form of costly friction than suffer the effects of sub-optimization (overall loss of efficiency) following total integration of the IKEA industries in the long term. The reason was that Swedwood already had a position of monopoly in relation to IKEA. For one line of IKEA's best selling products Swedwood is the sole supplier. They can in other words dictate price and other conditions to their only customer, as IKEA in reality cannot get rid of the company as a supplier. Each attempt at criticizing one part of IKEA would cause reprisals both from Ingvar as well as the rest at Strategic Purchasing. I can personally testify to the fact that Swedwood use this technique. During my years as store director I more than once got it in the neck because I refused to accept missing deliveries and weak pricing.

One thing is absolutely certain. Ten years ago the way the problem with raw materials was handled would have been totally different. A complete lack of several materials would never have been accepted. The only explanation of the current situation is to be found among the people who took the decisions. Josephine Rydberg-Dumont was the overall responsible for the whole of IKEA's value chain with the exception of the stores. Her strengths were in totally different areas and her lack of interest when it came to purchasing was apparent. Her predecessor on the other hand, Mikael Ohlsson, was her complete opposite in this respect and pushed a number of important purchasing questions. Göran Stark, the purchasing manager who reported to Josephine, was rather new when production was interrupted. His predecessor, Sven-Olof Kulldorff, who during a decade made the IKEA purchasing group the most important competitive tool in the company, had been far more energetic. Anders Moberg had, during his time as chief executive, a far better insight into purchasing than the present CEO Anders Dahlvig. The new Swedwood manager Gunnar Korsell lacked the experience within the organization and IKEA. And Ingvar Kamprad and his advisor in industrial questions, Bruno Winborg, chairman of the board at Swedwood, had both become ten years older. On the other hand the Kamprad sons had joined.

There is a common theme in all this shambles. Hans Gydell, 'almost the most intelligent man Ingvar ever met', just before the purchase of Swedwood, let escape the important words: 'IKEA will never own their suppliers.' For those who are wondering, Ingvar considers Hans Skallin, lawyer and the architect behind the Kamprad-sphere and its enormously complex but ingenious company structure, by far the most intelligent of all. I would put my money on Gydell, however. He was financial director and assistant chief executive first under Moberg and now under Dahlvig. The formidable growth and increased profits during these two decades are largely due to him.

And because Gydell was right. IKEA should not own its suppliers involving large investments without pay off, risk sub-optimization, where too much time and effort is taken up by one supplier in a monopoly position. An independent supplier is subject to competition and has to produce better prices, more secure supplies and a higher quality compared with the competitors in order to get an order from IKEA at all. With Swedwood, the situation is the reverse. Swedwood can never be sacked despite obscenely high prices and years of missed deliveries. The fact is that if Swedwood had been independent they would have been dismissed a long time ago. Obviously not the part of the company which produces board-on-frame for the LACK tables and BESTÅ, but definitely the part that deals with timber.

Purely from a business-strategy point of view, nonetheless, the task of Swedwood is really interesting. The company's board is headed by Bruno Winborg. Apart from that there are the IoS Manager Torbjörn Lööf, the purchasing manager Göran Stark and Peter Kamprad. The mission of the company is to create the highest possible profit, a profit which would make any listed company green with envy. Each single factory should also generate the highest possible profit. This for IKEA means that the Swedwood board demands that they sub-optimize not just once, but twice. Partly at the local level where they push their prices up for their only customer, partly at an aggregated level where only a total profit far above what one would expect from a company in a competitive situation. The architect behind this whole arrangement is the previous financial manager Hans Gydell. That is the very same Gydell who did not think IKEA should own any suppliers. I assume his reasoning to have been that if IKEA now has to own a factory, it should in any case give a good profit. Perhaps what happened was that Strategic Purchasing was now largely made up of people who did not understand the policy, or simply could not be bothered to understand, or as in Ingvar's case, chose to close their eyes.

Obviously blunders like this can be absorbed by a large company like IKEA. Even if the losses are in their billions they won't show or be known, either outside the meeting rooms and even less so outside the walls of the company. And on the inside they will soon be forgotten. The problem with mistakes that you just forget about is that you don't learn anything from them. The complete opposite of the goals of a learning organization in other words.

I can only conclude that all the forests that IKEA so wisely invested in after lessons were learnt from the Siberian factory and the Mafia incident do not seem to have been of much use. If neither logs, sawn timber nor as much as a piece of chipboard reaches the IKEA store in the form of flat-packs, the investment was a fiasco.

# 4

# The Suppliers

IKEA has suppliers in around 70 countries in all parts of the world, except South America, consisting of around 1,400 companies. Purchases are dealt with through a network of purchasing offices. Ongoing questions like product quality and constancy of orders are frequently checked. These companies are linked to IKEA through more or less long-term agreements which stipulate volume and cost price per unit. Normally it is precisely the large volumes that IKEA orders that gives the company a price advantage over its competitors, since the home furnishing market is fragmented in most markets and only global in the case of IKEA. Even big US companies like Target and Home Depot, which dwarf IKEA, are essentially national or regional.

Price and volume are at the core of the IKEA machinery. This is the very part of the machinery which makes everything else happen. It is as simple as brilliant in its structure. Start by asking for a considerable volume from a supplier and get the offered price down in exchange for a promise that the agreement will last a few years. To sell the volume will not be a problem since lower cost prices mean lower retail prices. Next year the order is increased again, against the promise of a substantially lower price. And so the wheel goes round year in and year out. The momentum of the wheel is mainly decided by the negotiation skills of the buyers. Naturally this price- and volume-wheel like so many other things at IKEA originated with Ingvar Kamprad.

IKEA has at times been criticized for being too severe a negotiator and for pushing suppliers into bankruptcy. During my years of dealing with suppliers I have never noticed this apart from in one example. It was when IKEA began its globalization in the nineties and large volumes of production was moved from the West to the East that a number of long-lasting relationships were ended. I myself for example decided to move from Swedish supplier Recta in Tibro and Samhall in Visby on the isle of Gotland to China and Eastern Europe, but we made enormous efforts in order to make these decisions in an appropriate fashion. They weren't easy decisions to make: what new jobs can one get on Gotland if one is suffering from a mental or physical handicap? But the price-and volume-wheel had to carry on turning. In this case towards the East.

The Giant in the East

In China the problem is the opposite in nature. The Chinese are far more shrewd businessmen than we Scandinavians. The IKEA purchasing group has for years been making more or less half-hearted attempts to get stuck into the Chinese interior without success. You will find similar excuses here as in Russia: 'Access is difficult and complicated', 'Whatever they say, prices are no better there.' Consequently IKEA's purchasing group and buyers have focused on the Chinese coastline and the volume of the purchases in China have remained around 18–19 per cent. Ingvar's appeal to the buyers in low cost countries to 'forget icy drinks at the coastal hotels and cycle further inland than the competitors' has, until now, not been heeded in China.

In the eighties, before the purchase departments were created, when considerably smaller volumes were bought from Asia, this trade was carried out by agents. The agents were as unreliable as they were expensive, which is why IKEA at the beginning of the nineties started to open up its own purchase departments in all the important places on the Asian continent. One of these agents, a Chinese man, got himself a factory and carried on delivering material for furniture to IKEA. When our own buyers failed regarding cost price, quality or technical problems this ex-agent always managed to solve the problem. He was sitting on a network of spinning and weaving mills, and factories for dyeing and sewing. The normal procedure for IKEA would have been to agree to each stage in the operation separately in order to gain better control over the price and the flow of products. The prices of this agent were never very good but the quality was acceptable and the deliveries arrived on time so they let him carry on: for 20 years! One hardly dares think about how much money IKEA must have lost to this talented businessman.

The situation is really far more serious than that. The price for most things of interest to IKEA and their competitors is at its lowest in the world in the Chinese interior. So far nobody seems to have been able to exploit these enormous possibilities. The one who manages this first will get a price advantage on key products that will be impossible to beat for the competitors. Home Depot some years ago bought B&Q from the British Kingfisher Group. It meant that suddenly an America DIY chain, through B&Q, had thousands of Chinese suppliers in the portfolio that they could easily and cheaply expand in order to supply Home Depot's market in North America. The problem for IKEA is twofold. Home Depot is a very able retailer. In forty years its activity has grown from nothing to the third biggest retailer in the world. Furthermore, they are more than three times the size of IKEA with a purchase volume that, correctly used, could thoroughly shake the foundation of IKEA[2]. What is it that stops Home Depot from making a proper push into China's interior? Are they content with having bought an already existing chain of stores? Have they not realized what a gold mine they are sitting on and what it would mean for IKEA?

It is interesting to note that retailers such as British B&Q and French Carrefour have succeeded very well with this exercise. Nonetheless, these giant chains have still not fully exploited these advantages, but use the suppliers more for the local market where they also have stores. The successful B&Q expansion into the Chinese interior depended on their strategy of putting Chinese people in high positions – IKEA has on principle only Europeans in important posts – and that B&Q, therefore, with the help of these local co-workers, were able to liaise with local governments and councillors in order to get help. If they had had bigger plans and organized purchases for the sales in their domestic markets they would have caused IKEA immense problems.

The IKEA principle only to let Europeans manage the purchase offices in Asia is in itself interesting. I have never heard an explanation for this. Possibly it is an atavism that lives on from the seventies and the eighties, when only Swedes and possibly Danes could be trusted. This viewpoint recently returned with force, which I will deal with further on. However, these expats cost a lot of money to move since they normally move with a family. They want to live in a nice area, the children must go to an English private school, the joining husband/wife must have a job and apart from that their wages are far higher than in their home country.

One wonders, are there really no Chinese or Indians or Vietnamese who can do these jobs just as well or better? Yes, of course, there are. Many other western companies in these countries recruit locally. Why cannot IKEA do the same? Is it in order to maintain the strong Swedish IKEA-culture? Up until the middle of the nineties each IKEA unit had a so called cultural ambassador – Swedish and guaranteed loyal to IKEA. To have several hundred cultural ambassadors, as is the case with China, seems excessive. The Shanghai office today alone has little under a thousand co-workers of which around half are expats. A well-known fact within IKEA is that the Chinese purchasing organization has for a long time been used as a dumping ground for useless managers from the West. That doesn't meant that all managers within purchasing in China are not useless. Far from it. But many of IKEA's less able managers have been put in quarantine there.

Back to the separate career paths: there is a superior one for Westerners and an inferior one for locals at each purchasing office. There are also two wage structures. One for the expats and one local one for the others. IKEA as always pays wages as determined by the local market, which means that the locally employed person only gets a fraction of what the Swede at the next desk gets – for the same job. IKEA is known as one of the worst paying companies from the West. And the Chinese people do not have the social benefits the same Swede has. Often the Asian employee has a better education and has as much experience as well as his invaluable local knowledge and the local language as mother tongue. The IKEA managers will have, at best, Swenglish. The explanation for this curious policy lies in the IKEA-culture in general, and in the Purchasing Group in particular. From a pure cost-effective point of view it would make more sense to have as many locally employed and as few expats as possible. But a deeply rooted suspicion of the unknown makes IKEA choose the opposite route.

Naturally you want to keep the wages and so the costs down. But you can hardly attract the local elite of buyers or technicians with a tactic that underpays. The sum of it all is that you have lower competence in local workers and enormous costs for expats. Why? It is all about trust or rather the lack of trust. The managers of the IKEA Purchasing Group appear not to have faith in people with a different skin colour, with a different culture and who speak a different language. I am not saying that the IKEA purchasing managers are crude racists, but rather that they are unaware of and uninterested in diversification (something in itself bad enough), which kindles the persistent mistrust in locally employed colleagues. Despite things being this bad in the purchasing offices today, things have despite it all, improved. The purchasing managers for Asia who left IKEA at the end of the nineties exercised a neo-colonial regime where human dignity and environmental considerations were of little consequence. They left the company after these questions were given more space on the IKEA agenda and they themselves considered the subject not being of any relevance at all in business.

Success or failure?

With a rare determination IKEA moved their purchase volumes from the West to Eastern Europe and Asia during the nineties. The energy and the attention that purchasing manager and commander Sven-Olof Kulldorff and his colleagues showed, then, are a million miles away from today's situation. Today, few and insignificant changes in the supply chain and how the volumes are distributed are happening. Just as striking, then, a decrease in cost price by minus five per cent compared to previous year was delivered year in and year out. Today the group has to absorb increases in cost price each year sometimes in double figures in many areas.

As I have said earlier the most important and decisive competitive advantage that IKEA has is the ability to exchange increasing purchase volumes at decreasing cost prices. But that is not all. Just as important is to be able to pass these low cost prices on to lower retail prices. As a consequence sales in the stores increase and thereby demand for volumes.

But each strength also has its weakness. In the case with China we have seen how the company tries, but fails, to find new competitive advantages since they have not managed to find the right people to work with in the country's interior. Their own industrial group Swedwood and its complete inability to do anything useful and permanent with all the money IKEA has pumped into Russia during the last years is another example. Sure, the Russian adventure is explicitly long-term, but it is de facto ten years ago that Swedwood launched their venture there.

There are, however, glimpses of hope. One person alone and his capacity and energy may mean the difference between success and failure. Håkan Eriksson, an experienced IKEA-worker living in Poland since the eighties, quickly became an important figure when Swedwood AB was bought at the beginning of the nineties. Håkan is a sympathetic and extremely capable man who looks more Polish than most Poles including the drooping moustache. But his Polish wife has despite all these years never managed to teach her husband anything but the most basic phrases from his new homeland. No problem for Håkan – his Swenglish is impeccable. Well, painful to listen to for any properly English-speaking person, but perfect for his Polish colleagues.

Just a few words about IKEA-language. This type of pidgin English, IKEA-Swenglish, is a must for anybody who wants to make a career in IKEA. Pidgin is a much simplified version of a language that arises out of the necessities of a group of people. The vocabulary is for example very limited and the grammar fluid. The main thing is to be able to communicate in a practical way, not that everything should be the same as the original language. In addition the pidgin version is characterized by a pronunciation that is far removed from the basic language. All these are characteristics of the IKEA-Swenglish – a living and developing language, that has its drawbacks. During my time in England there were not very many Scandinavians who worked there. On the other hand we were probably rather good at setting the tone and, I guess, loud. On the train back after an IKEA-conference in Poland all the British colleagues suddenly got up and left us five Scandinavians and took their own compartment. Afterwards we understood that they could not cope with any more Swenglish. Using pidgin the pronunciation becomes painful, the context vague, the reasoning unclear and the nuances absent to anybody who has the original language as his native tongue.

Back to Håkan Eriksson. Håkan and Ingvar were old chums. Håkan's task was to be responsible for the Swedwood factories in Poland that should make the old material board-on-frame into IKEA's most important competitive advantage – i.e. their 'advantage' in IKEA-language. Board-on-Frame (BOF) was used during the second world war in the aircraft industry, but since then it is most common in the manufacture of doors. It simply consists of a top board made from masonite, paper strips that have been glued together in a honeycomb pattern put on its side, a bottom board of masonite identical to the top one, and frames of masonite or wood along the bottom and top plank edges. The frames keep the whole structure together and it becomes extremely strong and sturdy even compared to solid wood or chipboard yet it is a lot lighter – and considerably cheaper in material. Picture any ordinary internal door in most houses and you will know what BOF is.

LACK coffee table 55x55 cm is probably IKEA's most important product. The table in itself is a model that was sold by all home furnishing players in the eighties. One could easily sum it up as modern but generic design. During the nineties the table was being used as the engine in what was to become known as 'advantage' planning. Ingvar Kamprad and Håkan Eriksson redesigned a number of old furniture factories in order to become the very best at BOF in general and the LACK-table in particular. No detail was too small and no question too big for Håkan and his gang of Polish factory managers and production technicians. New ways of producing the table legs in which the masonite literally folded. They found new ways of treating the surface in order to keep the production speed as high as possible. They found new ways of cutting the bought masonite board in order to exploit the material better. In a couple of years the retail price (at the time) could be decreased from 200 to 99 kronor (£18/$28 to £9/$14) – and still show a profit. All thanks to the hard work of Håkan Eriksson.

## The Kan-allt-shelf

During my first range week as Ingvar's assistant (which I wrote about earlier) he organized a meeting with a dozen trusted co-workers at Blåsippan, the council-like office of the range group in Älmhult. We were sitting around a table with plastic coffee cups and *snus* behind our lips. Present were the manager for kitchens Hans-Åke Persson, the now dead guru on kitchens Per Karlsson who Ingvar affectionately called Pelle Kartong (Cardboard) because of his background as a packaging technician, the political Jörgen Svensson, storage manager Per Hahn and a handful of others I no longer remember.

Ingvar held forth with his vision of the Multipurpose (MPS) system and carried on in his usual style for well over an hour. Anecdotes were mixed with thoughts and memories and Ingvar-type sarcasm. I was too new and full of admiration to really understand the jokes, but most people were smiling whilst others laughed uncontrollably. The Multipurpose system was anyway something Ingvar had dreamt about since the seventies, clearly. The idea was, as so often with Ingvar, as simple as it was brilliant. If all chest of drawers, bookshelves, storage shelves, kitchens and wardrobes at IKEA had the same basic measurements, the same basic drawers, the same basic doors, the same material, the same fittings and the same thinking in all other aspects, enormous amounts of money could be saved in all the stages. Involving both product development, construction, production, purchase of raw material and not least of all, the customers who would be able to easier understand the constructions since it all was based on the same principle. 'The perfect crime', as Ingvar put it.

After this not much happened with the Multipurpose system for a few years. That is rather typical of Ingvar's style of leadership, at least when it comes to questions about range, as we saw. He has dreams that he now and then discusses over a cup of coffee in some corner at Blåsippan. Then he lets the dream drift away in order to see what happens when a colleague takes it on board and into reality. Technicians from both the business areas beds and sitting rooms tried to develop a uniform drawer, but they could not agree about which measurements should be applied and any progress came to a halt there and then.

Next time I came across the Multipurpose system was five years later. I was then regional manager for the store division for storage units in living rooms and dining rooms and a few of my colleagues, a product manager, a buyer, a product developer and a technician, introduced the so called MPS-concept to me. They had taken Ingvar on his words and produced a Multi Purpose System for storage.

The very first version had a strange look (it was as ugly as sin), but it was functional and all the right ideas were there. One of the ugliest prototypes in history, I thought to myself. But the optimal measurements that suited both the customer and production needs had been integrated. The holy grail for home storage had finally been found. With simple means, there was the possibility to adjust MPS for the bathroom, the bedroom or the kitchen. For customers the starting point is always their storage needs: how many cupboards and of which size. After that these cupboards were given fronts as well as doors and drawers, which give the piece of furniture its expression of style. And the goal, to position the system at a price well below the veneered BILLY-shelves, would without a doubt be achieved.

We were convinced that the surface should be Japanese foil, a material which at the time was not used in IKEA. Japanese foil, a thin printed film, has the properties of a thin leaf, is cheap and is easily confused for real wood veneer. The reasoning was simple. If an expert could not distinguish between the real thing (veneer) from the copy (the foil) how would a customer be able to do it? And if the price difference was to be 40–50 per cent on the ready-made product compared to BILLY, the decision should be easy for IKEA's customers who, as IKEA has always assumed, have 'slim' wallets.

Swedwood, eagerly cheered on by Ingvar Kamprad, fought for us to use the wood veneer since they had already made a large investment in capacity for wood veneer and deciduous forest. They argued that the difference in price compared with competitors who used veneer would relatively speaking be greater than if they chose the foil. But if the customer could not differentiate between veneer and foil the price difference ought to be able to increase we argued. We even organized a so-called focus-group where customers, without knowing that we watched them from another room, discussed storage in general and surface finishing in particular. I will never forget how an officious guy born in the forties in a blazer got up from the table and exclaimed: 'Well, I will always choose the real natural thing!' at the same time as he was stroking the shelf with Japanese foil.

Five years and three regional store managers later MPS was a fact at IKEA. With Japanese foil. The name BESTÅ has become the new flagship for the group. Under the range manager Tina Pettersson-Lind's firm leadership the MPS storage system had matured into a beauty that sells like hotcakes.

'Straight into the woodshed', as one would have expressed it in IKEA-language.

The choice of material for the BESTÅ range was not to be, as one perhaps would have expected, normal chipboard or even a lightweight chipboard. Instead the business-area together with the BOF-people in Poland had come up with the idea of BOS, board-on-strips. In reality this is exactly the same thing as BOF, but thin like a chipboard and at a fraction of the weight as well as considerably lower production cost. So far it had all been very well worked out.

At this point Swedwood, whose board did not appreciate the potential of BESTÅ, entered the fray. They argued they did not know whether they would hold on to the many factories in Poland in the future in view of wage increases and other uncertainties. To build new factories to the required extent was out of the question. Bruno Winborg, chairman of the board, and the rest of Swedwood's management were reluctant. The range and purchasing groups were at a loss. Ingvar chose not to speak up, as did the chief executive Anders Dahlvig. Torbjörn Lööf who was ultimately responsible for the new BESTÅ product, wavered in front of the solid opposition.

The odd thing about this argument is that a furniture factory is really easy to move. It is a concrete floor, four walls and a roof plus machinery. The workers are perhaps less easy to move, but that usually does not count for much in the eyes of the factory owners. My point is simple. Even if they had constructed 3–4 proper BOS-production lines the same lines could if need be have been moved to the East a few years later. They had a great product – BESTÅ, 250 stores, 500 million visitors, 300 million catalogues – and they hesitated. They prevaricated.

The result was a disaster of rare proportions. The production capacity for BOF in the IKEA-world during the prevailing boom was not high enough. Not enough for LACK and not enough for BESTÅ. Despite the fact that the launch of BESTÅ was done cautiously in chosen markets the shelf was constantly sold out. For two years, up until the board of Swedwood (who lived in a world of their own) and the IKEA management had realized their mistake and put things right by constructing new production units. 'IKEA should never own its suppliers.' The prophetic words of Gydell resonated deeply in IKEA land. Instead of discussing purchasing, opportunities and alternative supply chains, time at Strategic Purchasing was wasted on talk – excuses – on behalf of Swedwood. Sub-optimization cannot be made more concrete.

Could this have happened ten years earlier? Hardly, since the attitude was different then. Its go-go spirit had since been curbed and been replaced by a careful bureaucratic rule as if IKEA was terrified of its own success. Twenty years ago the IKEA management made efforts to prevent problems. Ten years ago the focus shifted to solving them. Nowadays they seem to prefer to be ruled by the problems.

Of all the more or less costly board decisions and managerial mistakes that I have seen and witnessed during my twenty years with IKEA this one is without a doubt in a class of its own. Losses must have run into several billion kroner. Had the sensitivities of the Swedwood management been overruled, losses would have been much lower. Once again the loss is swallowed up by the enormous mass that is IKEA. Mistakes are concealed and repressed. And nothing is being learnt along the way.

## Death of the suppliers

The group of IKEA suppliers has in only a few years been reduced from several thousand to 1,400. The exact number of suppliers became a measuring device with its own importance within IKEA. If the only criterion for what you need to do well if you are a buyer, a purchasing strategist or a manager is to finish off suppliers, then you will eventually become really good at just that: finishing off suppliers.

It had begun as a brilliant idea by Sven-Olof Kulldorff, purchasing manager at IKEA until 2006. Like a commander in chief he led his men (as the women in purchasing could then as now be counted on the fingers of one hand) in a crusade across the world. The problem was just that nobody in the IKEA management had made a proper analysis of the influence on prices and supply of goods if you cut the number of your suppliers by 80 per cent. Apart from of course Ingvar, who kept out of the way until the damage had already been done.

The plan, which was carried to its conclusion by Kulldorff's successor Göran Stark, was lacking in most things. Nobody had proved why exactly 1,400 suppliers was an optimal number. Was it because it suited the manpower at the purchasing offices around the world? The mantra was that with fewer suppliers, purchasing volumes could be divided among fewer people. Larger volumes would mean lower prices. Today everybody knows how mistaken this was. In many parts of the home furnishing industry the ideal production volume is far below the massive orders now placed by Göran Stark. So the chosen suppliers were hardly able to offer lower prices without facing bankruptcy. In reality, IKEA risked becoming the only customer of the supplier, something that they had learnt to avoid after earlier experiences. Never take more than 70 per cent of a supplier's production used to be the internal IKEA rule-of-thumb.

A consequence analysis had still not been made, even as the goal of 1,400 suppliers was nearly reached. The consequences were not far behind however. A serious shortage arose time and time again. In all the business divisions. Shelves for textiles were empty in 250 stores. The same thing happened with wooden furniture, sofas, lamps, well in fact with the entire range. Sofas are usually sold in two parts. The frame by itself and the cover by itself. The frames are bulky and are therefore produced relatively close to the retail outlets, meaning that each product needs several suppliers. The cover on the other hand is often produced far away where the cost of raw materials and production are considerably lower. So each furniture cover had only one manufacturer somewhere in China or Pakistan. Naturally not all materials sell the in the same quantity. Twenty per cent of covers account for eighty per cent of the sales volume (the famous 80/20 rule). This means that you need to know with detailed precision what the best-sellers will be in order not to create shortages. It is a task that most people have difficulty in doing without a crystal ball.

So what happened? The best-sellers ran out as soon as the catalogue was published in August. Covers for all best-sellers were not there while an enormous surplus stock of frames were made. The relevant store area manager was threatened with dismissal. Colleagues were shouting at managerial group meetings. It took us ten months of hard work to restore order. What we did was simply to provide each important cover with a so-called supply chain management system, that is two or three suppliers. Exactly as things had been prior to the implementation of purchase manager Kulldorff's grandiose plan.

But after what I have heard and experienced, I strongly doubt that the purchasing management or strategic purchase realized the seriousness of their mistakes and why they were made. True to form the whole thing was swept under the carpet. The reduction in suppliers had extremely important side-effects, which must again have cost billions of kroner in falling revenue, but the worst thing was having to deal with disappointed customers. Customers who never seem to feature with the decision-makers in the growing empire of bureaucrats at IKEA. Ultimately it is all about a question of attitude. Arrogance we usually call it.

# 5

## 'The product range – our identity'

Blåsippan is situated in the centre of Älmhult and is as pleasing on its outside as any Swedish town hall. Three stories in whitish plaster with red fixtures. The sign on the front states IKEA of Sweden AB. In this building 750 men and women from all over the whole world, but mostly Swedes, work with the IKEA range. In the middle of the most dismal industrial community in the world, the majority of the IKEA-group's power is gathered and the by far most interesting task in the IKEA-world. Älmhult was not even the main town in the region before IKEA established itself there. Today it has 8,500 inhabitants. 2,500 of whom work for IKEA. For someone who is interested in more than pole walking and clear-felled areas of forest Älmhult has little to offer. Possibly the staff parties at IOS which could make anybody blush.

Älmhult is the central point in the IKEA-world and has always been so – by explicit decree from Ingvar Kamprad in order for the IKEA-culture never to become extinct. What exactly in this culture might risk becoming extinct, has never really been made clear, but it is bound to be some foreign influence. We will come back to the 'threats' against the IKEA-culture further on in the book.

The path to power

The fact is that the only powerful group that has ever left Älmhult since IKEA was established there 1953, is the group- and retail-management. And still a large part of the commercial power of the retailers has been returned to Älmhult during the last ten years: how presentations of the range should look in detail and in general in the stores is decided there. The difference in price between products in each range, the so called price-ladders, also. The absolute price for the main products. The number to be sold of each product and the number to be bought in. How to transport them. How to store them. All this is decided in Älmhult. At IKEA of Sweden AB (IOS) at Blåsippan. For 250 stores in forty countries with 500 million visitors. Year in and year out.

But above all, each individual product for each individual store around the world is determined in Älmhult. IKEA of Sweden AB is divided into eleven business-areas from sofas to seasonal furniture etc. In fact one of the worst battles ever between Ingvar and a group manager happened at the beginning of the nineties, when Anders Moberg introduced a new regional organization. Perhaps it sounds harmless enough. But the newly appointed manager Bengt Larsson for the northern European region suddenly considered the central IOS team and Älmhult to be 'just another wholesaler amongst others' as he expressed it in his broadest Skåne dialect. The power of Älmhult on the one hand was pitched against the dismissal of Moberg on the other: to navigate past the owner's vetoes had started to become an impossible task for Anders Moberg. Ingvar chose his chief executive over Älmhult. At least, for the moment.

I was too young and fresh at IKEA then to be able to now give a correct account of the effects of the regional division. Clearly the spreading of rumours and the power struggle amongst the top managers had repercussions which spread right the way through the organization. Göran Carstedt, Volvo's previous manager in France, was employed as manager of North America. An important manager from the pharmaceutical industry whose name I cannot remember (however I remember that Ingvar always referred to him as 'that fucking pill pusher' with barely concealed disgust) took on key responsibilities in Southern Europe. But what the indirect effects on the group were I do not know. Apart from one.

In the Moberg model the store organization at the time had been divided into three new regions: Market Unit Southern Europe, Market Unit Northern Europe, Market Unit North America, and a smaller organization for the up and coming Eastern European markets. Furthermore, and perhaps most important of all, the importance of IOS had been drastically curtailed and it had actually only become one wholesaler amongst many. The implications for IOS were many. The retail regions generated high overhead costs for administration, their own IT-solutions and management. The rivalry between the regions was costly as far as strength and focus went. To manage the logistics in an optimal way across continents became more difficult when each region had its own central stock. But worst of all was that the heart, the price and volume loop in the IKEA-machinery, was threatening to wither away when each retailer put great effort into making local purchases. With diminishing volumes the cost prices went sky high and the profit for the group was undermined. A confused IOS that still had not managed to get to firm ground within the new IKEA responded by extending its range with full force. There ought to be a product for each taste and the company was not even afraid to bring out heavy mahogany coloured bookshelves in English style, something which radically broke the business policy which dictates a selection in Scandinavian design. In the largest stores the number of articles soon grew from 10,000 to 42,000 articles. Its inefficiency soon threatened to block the whole IKEA logistical system.

At this point Ingvar Kamprad again put himself in the driver's seat and pushed through a comprehensive reorganization with great hullabaloo, 'the new organization'. The main reasons were most probably twofold. Partly the problems had accumulated so seriously in the wake of a weaker IOS and the rivalry between the Market Unit regions that IKEA's growth had started to seriously suffer. Partly enormous possibilities opened up when the Berlin wall came down in 1989 – possibilities that presupposed a strong, almost autocratic IOS that could control a strong price and volume spiral.

In 1995 the new organization was launched on a wide front. And now with the cream of the IKEA managers in key positions. The business-area managers were given ultimate power in the value chain. Factories were bought in large numbers in eastern Europe, mainly in Poland. Large volumes were transferred to these new in-house suppliers who all ended up within the recently bought Swedish industrial company Swedwood. IKEA – the world's largest production orientated retailer, became Ingvar's catchphrase of the day. Order had been reinstalled and both IKEA's and IOS's organizations have actually remained unchanged since then – a sign that both the organization and Ingvar's original ideas work.

Ingvar had had the last word and he had been confirmed right. The external managers were soon shoved aside, despite the fact that none of them in any way had achieved bad results. On the contrary, they were both popular leaders among their co-workers who achieved imposing results during the few years they worked for the company. Carstedt for example managed to stop the North American IKEA from haemorrhaging to death and even achieved results in the black during his time. (Interestingly, the financial collapse of the USA-company had been caused by no less than Björn Bayley, a cousin of Ingvar's. The nepotism within IKEA is something we will also come back to.)

The pharmaceutical manager, after a short sojourn as regional manager in southern Europe, took over the business section IKEA-at-work which he built up in Tibro around a newly purchased factory for the production of office furniture. During his years the business section grew at an unbelievable pace in a period when other sections were contracting. When he was let go of the whole lot was moved back to Älmhult. Since then IKEA office-furniture has been in strong decline. Today I would guess that the section only has around half the turnover it reached under the able leadership of the pharmaceutical manager. Yet again a loss of several billion lost kroner that has been absorbed by the great mass of IKEA.

## A product sees the light of day

Each year IKEA renews its range of around 10,000 products. In other words around 3,000 new products are developed every year. How do they do it?

Each and every one of the eleven business sections work in three-year cycles: the present year, the next and the one after that. At the time of writing this means 2008/2009 (IKEA uses a broken financial year), 2009/2010 and 2010/2011. In other words they work with three parallel focuses. For the present year the focus will mainly be on the supply of the existing range. Obviously especially on the catalogue range, since that is the only promise made by IKEA to the customer. At the same time a lot of time is dedicated to securing the launch of new products for the new range and catalogue. But the long-term plan and range for the following year must always be present.

To develop a product takes on average two years. That may seem a long time for something as commonplace as a candle-holder, a simple kitchen chair or a rug, but not even IKEA is free from the inertia that bureaucracy can cause. Obviously the energy and creativity that a younger organization perhaps can offer, is lacking. With this I mean the age of the organization not that of the co-workers. I mean that the IKEA range development, which has existed in Älmhult ever since the sixties, with time has become rigid in its structures, developed too many traditions, and has perhaps even become nostalgic with the years.

Products that take your breath away and knock you our

Throughout the years there are few areas on which IOS has placed particular emphasis in the process of developing products. Looking back at my years within the company show that it today has a model which I believe will last for some considerable time in the future.

It all begins with a so called range matrix which is a way of dividing the products into trends in tastes. Each part of the range is divided in four different groups of style and expression: Country, which is called peasant furniture by Ingvar, Scandinavian, typically light and Nordic home furnishing, Modern, which is perceived as attractive on the continent and Young Swede, which is all kinds of things in an extremely strange modern form with gaudy colours. The basic idea is that the customer should be able to mix and match from the whole range group in a particular style and achieve a homogenous Country inspired home or Young Swede home or whatever you prefer.

The four style groups are then divided into four price levels: high, medium, low and BTI (breath-taking item) – or products that take away your breath as it is called in IKEA language – and in this way forms a matrix. When the team from the business area gathers around the new range matrix they look for gaps. A square in the matrix which is empty or almost empty. If for example a coffee table in the Country style and low price is a gap in the range this must be filled as soon as possible. The reason is simply that the competitors are probably already active in this gap – and one wishes to at any cost nip the competition in the bud.

Let me just for a short while stay with the so-called 'breath-taking-items' and its cousin 'punch-on-the-jaw-items'. There is namely a further dimension in the range matrix. They are products with a very particular role in the range. 'Breath-taking' items are the most common and are the products within each product group – coffee tables, flower pots, piece-goods – which are so cheap that you as a customer will gasp. You could call them low price markers, since they reinforce the message about the low price in your consciousness with the help of their distinctive yellow price tags with a red border. But normally only one breath-taking-item is allowed in each group, otherwise it is thought that the message will suffer from inflation.

'Punch-on-the-jaw' is probably the most colourful role an article can have at IKEA. These articles are on the whole rare in the range, but in case the competitors become too troublesome IKEA does not hold back. The eighties was the period for mirrors. Everybody wanted square mirrors in sections which you could join with black or chrome coloured mounts. IKEA had ALG, but ALG towards the end was always beaten on price by the mirrors sold at every petrol-station in Sweden. The little brother of ALG was launched although it was not called ALG but JÖNS or something similar. A cheap alternative must never be able to be connected by name with the main product so that the trademark of the main product risks being depleted. This mirror was smaller, much simpler and dirt cheap. The mirror market in the country was soon crushed and ALG remained in splendid isolation after its little brother was soon retired from the range.

Another 'punch-on-the-jaw' example is the low-energy light bulb from the nineties. The formation of cartels, that mainly concentrated on patents, had fixed the world price for these at 200–250 (£18/$28–£21/$35) kroner each. A normal light bulb costs 2–5 kronor as a comparison. When you consider that a normal household has 30–35 light points you soon realize that the cost of being environmentally friendly was incredibly high. Ingvar urged the lighting team to find a Chinese supplier who could get round the patent in a watertight way. Soon enough the buyers found exactly such a supplier. Ingvar's idea was not to make a profit from the light bulbs, as they were sold at cost price, in order for IKEA to appear environmentally friendly. On the other hand it has to be said that IKEA of course made a lot of money at both the buying as well as the logistical stage. IKEA on the whole bought the entire volume from the supplier and were in exchange given a precipitously low price. IKEA sold their low energy light bulbs for twenty kronor. The market crashed and soon enough all larger retailers followed suit. It was not long until Biltema followed IKEA hard on their heels.

At this point it would be obvious to make a comparison with the LED lamps of today: their price point of 200–250 kronor and a market structure with complicated patents and cartels that are near enough identical. However in my opinion there is one fact which is different. Ingvar is today too old to inspire new great exploits, something that is totally understandable. But what is worse is that nobody else, neither Anders Dahlvig as chief executive nor Torbjörn Lööf as managing director for IOS nor the Kamprad brothers, manage to look the troops in the eye and inspire them in Ingvar's typically playful way. The same coup could be done today as well, I am convinced of that. Yes, the driving force ought to be even greater today, since our common light bulbs according to a EU directive are being phased out. But to find adequate alternatives has so far been difficult. Price levels have become too high since the patents behind the LED lamps, which today are the most credible alternative to light bulbs, create global monopolies. Furthermore the LED lamps give off a glare which is rather unpleasant to the human eye. Despite this, traditional light bulbs will disappear soon, which obviously ought to create opportunities for IKEA.

IKEA has today a handful of iconic items in their range that have been there for 30–45 years. POÄNG armchair, BILLY bookcase and IVAR storage are examples of such big selling products which have museum status. You cannot get rid of an icon from the range unpunished even if its replacement would be both cheaper and better, I am well aware of that as I tried it several times as business regional manager.

We can be fairly confident that IKEA originally copied each one of them from the outset. At its best the model was 'generic'. This is the reason that these and other icons exist at IKEA's biggest competitors as well. Not seldom at a lower price. In order to avoid a downward spiral of the cutting down of measurements, materials and price against the competitors Ingvar's solution in the eighties was a little brother to each icon. The little brothers who got the byname 'watch-your-back' are smaller, weaker, uglier and less flexible – but extremely cheap. WYB products have come and gone during the years. It is doubtful that they fill their purpose as well today as they did 20 years ago. I am saying this as IKEA often, too often nowadays, are beaten on price by their competitors.

The nostalgic element of IKEA culture has, with Ingvar's increasing age, become more obvious. During the recent years he has breathed life into a number of extinct IKEA products under the motto 'the treasure chest'. Of course the ghosts have almost immediately died out by themselves, as even the customers have realized that their glory days are gone.

Obviously it may seem a bit strange that a home furnishing giant like IKEA does not manage to keep its adversaries at bay when they time and time again maintain they have the lowest price in the market. The phenomenon was extremely rare fifteen years ago, but has now become common. To stand still for too long in a sector like home furnishing is fatal. It would never have happened before, but nobody seems to nowadays be able to fill in Ingvar's tactical genius when it comes to product range. As in so many other areas he has left a vacuum behind. The basic problem is that IKEA must make a profit from each stage of the value chain: purchase, distribution, product development and in the store. Despite this massive cost increment on every product, the stores are expected to sell the product at least at ten per cent below the market price for a comparable item (this was the decision of the group management already in the Moberg days). No competitor has equivalent cost increments. It is obvious that it is becoming harder and harder, not to say impossible, for IKEA to maintain this increment model at the same time as the competitors move their positions forward in the market. But this focus on profit – or greediness – is at the core of Ingvar's value chain. Ingvar preaches in his nine theses, which he formulated in the seventies and which form the basis for the whole IKEA-culture, that profit is a good thing and provides the company with means to become stronger in the future. A sharper competitive situation would probably force IKEA to adopt a different behaviour and lower the excess profits that the company generates year in and year out. By excess profits I mean that today's profit margins can hardly be sustainable since they depend on a sophisticated business model, the value chain with profits at each stage, which in turn is based on a situation with unusually weak competitors. The home furnishing market is still today too fragmented and regional for anybody to be able to really take on the battle against IKEA. The existing giants like Target Corporation and Home Depot, both considerably larger than IKEA, are very regionally orientated to North America and the competitive overlap between them is limited.

Developing a coffee table

The product development team always begins by coming up with an idea for, let's say, a coffee table. Obviously there are already general strategies about tables being media equipment friendly, having good storage for remote controls, being child-friendly – for example have a good finish and rounded corners, underneath as well as on top. Since the table has to be a low price item that puts demands on choice of materials and use. Pine and spruce are typical materials in a range box like this. They are relatively cheap and have exterior characteristics that are associated with country furniture from the past. The trick is to save on material where it is not visible anyway, as weedy-looking coffee tables are a sad sight however cheap they may be. The team lists their ideas about the coffee table that has now got a working title, lets say BOSSE (fictitious).

The project-leader for the team, a product developer, then meets with a designer. It can be one of IOS's own designers or one of the freelance people on the IKEA list. A discussion takes place and the BOSSE brief is delivered. If the brief is poor or the input to the designer inferior, the whole project risks being delayed by months. A good input in the IKEA-world should contain a thorough description of what the product should be and do. Meaning properties and usages rather than drawings. There are product developers who bring their own little pen-and-ink-drawing to the meeting, but they as a rule soon learn. Or they disappear through the back-door.

The designer then returns to the next meeting with a number of sketches of BOSSE. An agreement is reached on a couple of them and the designer goes off in order to make a regular design of the coffee table. Ideally a large part of these discussions take place on the factory floor at Swedwood or another supplier where model workshops and other things are available. This is done in order to avoid any mistake that might raise the price of production of the product. If measurements and phases are incorrect the whole cost-estimate might be ruined because of increased costs. In reality this happens rather seldom even if factory managers might complain for hours about silly constructions.

But as luck would have it for the less travel-prone production teams there is also a model workshop at home in Älmhult. Soon there is a sturdy prototype of BOSSE to gather around in the business area. Three-dimensional plans of Bosse are produced by the designers from the business area where exact measurements are decided, fittings, knock-down-functions (the functions that allows the customer to assemble the item) and the characteristics of the packaging like for example handling, logistic efficiency and capability to protect the content.

This entire process follows a carefully prepared schedule with particular obstacles that the product as well as the team must overcome. There are so-called washing instructions for the first run-throughs where the go-ahead is given to products which show enough potential. A hopeful product developer talks for the article and a jury of business and design managers will make the final decision. If BOSSE survives the scrutiny the product will end up with the range board where it will be given its seal of approval. Well, in theory perhaps, but not in reality. All range records are checked by Ingvar. With his signature he finally gives any item the green light. Or the business area gets the files back with Ingvar's sour comments in the margin. One needs to take those comments on board as Ingvar has the formal veto on range ever since Anders Moberg became chief executive in 1986. The wrong choice of material, ugly design, senseless functionality or too high a price are the things he will react to. 'Extremely stupid! Only costs 63 kroner (£6/$9) at a local store in Älmhult', Ingvar hisses in his sprawling capital letters in the margin of the product record. To be fair, a 'Well done!' also appears now and then.

At this point you probably wonder how the items get their, at times, ingenious names. That christening happens in a purely administrative way at the same time as the business section applies for the article number. Depending on which category it ends up in it will be given a specific type of name. Bookcases have for example usually male names or titles such as BILLY and KOMMENDÖR, tables and storage get place-names such as LEKSVIK, ÅBO or such like. Sofas always have place-names like KARLSTAD, EKTORP and BROMÖLLA. They are all taken out centrally in admin from a large file where all available names are listed. The name, the product term and the item number are then put into the computer system which gives the product its identity.

I myself among other things launched a storage system by the name of AMIRAL for the 2000 catalogue together with enthusiastic co-workers. We thought that the oak veneered, slightly futuristic system would be right for the time. It was to become the top-of-the-line for the living room. Already six months before the publication of the catalogue we showed Ingvar the prototypes. First he smiled. Then he laughed in his throaty way.

'This is the ugliest thing I have ever seen. It looks like an East German train carriage from the seventies', he merrily exclaimed.

He took my assurances that AMIRAL would strike the world with amazement calmly. Of course he was right. AMIRAL only stayed in the range for one year. This example says a lot about Ingvar's style of management. Few people have such an insight and calm as he. Or can be so tolerant. Because he realized that if he had stopped it, we would have become unmotivated without having learnt anything. Because none of us had forgotten his statement when we in the end withdrew the AMIRAL-series from the range. Believe you me, never has an uglier series of shelves seen the light of day in living room storage after that, despite the fact that I left the unit eight years ago.

Competitive advantages

I maintain that the range matrix definitely is IKEA's foremost competitive advantage in producing range. As IKEA's product management decided some ten years ago on the four style-groups and each group's expression, three obvious advantages followed.

First of all, as we have seen, it is relatively easy for a business area to find the gaps in its own range and to explain the desired expression to the designer. In other words: Country has many different stylistic expressions on the market. Previously IKEA sold models from suppliers (products that the suppliers develop themselves and store in a show-room) within the Country segment. People with good memories will perhaps remember ÅBO – the range that existed as bed, chest of drawers, bookcase and so on. Mediocre design and skimpy measurements of materials in order to keep the price down obviously meant failure. Each competitor of any value brought out an ÅBY-copy, which soon led to a negative price spiral in a battle for customers that IKEA could never win. The ÅBO concept simply meant that each furniture dealer gradually economized on wood, paint and fittings in order to get the price down in the battle to be the cheapest. Since the product quickly became generic it was only the price that distinguished one product from the next. Fairly soon the level of market credibility was crossed where the products became an ever thinner and rickety travesty of proper peasant furniture. Stick furniture which Ingvar somewhat contemptuously called them. It has to be pointed out, though, that the peasant furniture segment has been one of the biggest sellers by turnover for more than 15 years.

In order to avoid the dead-end scenario of ÅBO we got round the situation during my time in storage by launching two unique IKEA Country ranges (LEKSVIK and MARKÖR) in record time. MARKÖR, which was developed directly on Swedwood's factory floor, only took five months from idea to product in the stores. In other words in around one sixth of the normal time. The reason for this, apart from good teamwork, was that the factory in question had little work on and an enormous supply of spruce. Spruce was at this time considerably cheaper than pine. The disadvantage was that the spruce wood was full of twig holes and other blemishes, so it was difficult to produce IKEA's typical clear finish from the raw material. This problem was solved amongst other things by brushing the glued joints so that the surface was given an antique feel and was then given a dark stain. Each small part of the piece of furniture was analysed by designers, product developers and production technicians in order to maximise the usage of material and thereby minimising the price for the customer. The walls were made thin, but all corners and tops were made from solid pieces of wood so the impression was substantial and solid and so the quality was good. The price to the customer finally ended up being 895 kronor (£81/$121), perhaps a third of what competitors would ask for a similar product.

LEKSVIK was inspired by the range from the Gustavian period (Swedish Neoclassical style, 1772–1785) which at that time was being phased out. The bookcase in the range had an attractive soft image that the designer Carina Bengs made use of. At the first 'washing instructions' meeting where a prototype from the workshop was shown, we all realized that we were looking at the next best-seller. I will never forget when the purchase strategist proudly told us that we would be able to manage a sales price of 995 kroner (£91/$134). Completely spontaneously I asked why we could not produce it for a sales price of 695 kroner (£62/$94) – with a small profit margin. The colleague blushed with annoyance and said that was impossible, which was a completely understandable reaction. Because of the producers we had discussed production with, the lower price was impossible. A few months later we managed, nonetheless, by involving more producers in low cost countries, but also and perhaps most important-ly, by doubling or trebling the volume, to reach a sales price of 695 kronor – with a neat profit margin of 10–20 per cent in the store. Nothing in the quality, design or perfor-mance of the product changed in order to reach the lower price level, which for the competitors was completely impossible to beat. It is precisely this which is so ingenious when the IKEA-machinery keeps ticking over as it should. Extremely good and attrac-tive products that the competitors can only dream about selling themselves at the same price level.

So what is the difference between ÅBO and products like LEKSVIK and MARKÖR? ÅBO is a generic product, and so very generic in its stylistic expression, whilst the other two are unique or at least almost unique in their design. The only way to compete with a product like ÅBO is to save on dimensions and fittings. The product is simply not designed for anything else. With LEKSVIK and MARKÖR a low price was already decided on in the brief to the designer, and this low price was then realized in cooperation between able professional women and men on the factory floor from the best suppliers with the lowest prices we could find at the time.

Even if this sounds rather basic, you actually cannot plagiarize this process in the short or medium-long term. Nowadays IKEA has put the prices up over the years so that they are dangerously close to the competitors, in order to reach the profit levels required by the group. This means that the 'advantage' that once existed has largely been swallowed up. Today a LEKSVIK bookcase costs 995 kronor compared to the 695 kronor it cost when it was launched in 2001. An increase of 43 per cent. Certainly a lot of things can happen in seven years, but inflation has remained at 1-2 per cent. Obviously the market price of wood has followed oil and reached high levels. But during the last years the price of wood has gone back down, without IKEA adjusting their prices.

During recent years IKEA has seen this happen with kitchens and mattresses as well as wardrobes, to mention a few examples. The IKEA kitchens which are so much cheaper than those of their competitors have one of the highest gross profits at IKEA with more than 40 per cent!

Secondly the range-matrix clearly makes it easier for the customer in the store to mix and match from a coordinated selection when planning a home, than from a selection that has grown at random. Add to this that all colours are coordinated across the product areas in order to match in all of the four style groups.

It is also much easier for the product developer and his/her team to produce a beautiful and functional piece of furniture if the parameters are clear. It is after all IKEA's best home furnishing gurus who have determined its requirements. And the product developer, well, he/she neither has to begin at the beginning nor be entirely updated on the colour-scheme for the next years. It is already on file.

In concrete terms this means that IOS has the capacity to produce attractive and functional home furnishings at very competitive prices. Purchasing strategists are part of the production team from the outset of the process and safeguard the low price. Together the team can thus produce home furnishings at a low cost. And as we know that is IKEA's business concept.

A third competitive advantage that has given IKEA a good lead over the competitors is the year-cycle of IOS AB. The cycle describes somewhat simplified the decision forum for the commercial year, i.e. what meetings are to be held, when they should be held, who should be present in the room and which decisions are to be taken. In the year-cycle all parts of the product development processes from design to construction, production, sales prognosis and commercial treatment in both catalogue as well as stores are regulated. It is all kept together in the year-cycle model.

Two things are achieved with this planning model. First of all deadlines are kept. To slip, or even worse, completely miss the time of launch is considered a serious mistake which without fail will have an effect on the career possibilities of the offender. Secondly that it is possible to in time halt or start different product development processes. To promise something in the catalogue and not be able to deliver is also something which reflects badly on the offenders who in the future will have to contend with a serious credibility gap on part of management.

## IKEA taking other people's designs

There are some persistent rumours around IKEA that the company cannot shake off.

One of them is IKEA's bad habit of stealing other people's design by simply copying the original apart from a few details. Get hold of the original, let yourself be 'inspired' and voilà, a new IKEA product has seen the light of day. At half the price compared to the posh high-street product but just as nice-looking. Is this really how things are done?

Yes, in the seventies and the eighties the company stole the design for many of their best-sellers without shame. It is not exaggerated to claim that these 'stolen goods' to some extent helped build the IKEA we see today. That is how considerable the turnover from best-sellers must have been. Many storage ranges, armchairs and lamps were unambiguous copies with a light IKEA-touch.

The fact that IKEA, since the end of the eighties, hold forth about their designers whose photographs are shown all over the catalogue and stores is obviously proof of the ruffled conscience of the company – and obviously a way to attempt to improve its tarnished image.

Ingvar Kamprad, the master of apologies and excuses which are made to divert attention from the real issues, maintains that there is very little of new design that sees the light of day and that everyone is inspired by everyone else. Indeed. Try copying one of IKEA's unique products. Before you know it you have a pack of lawyers from Inter IKEA in Brussels on your back. Rest assured that they will fleece you to the very skin before they have done with you. So much for 'inspiring each other'.

In other words there is certainly unique design today as well and IKEA still steals it, only on a far smaller scale. In the product development process the designer has a central role, not that that is a guarantee against plagiarism. When I became business area manager for living room storage, I found myself in the middle of a case of plagiarism during one of my first weeks. An elderly product developer had been to a meeting with a designer in the prototype room. After the meeting he showed me his input to the designer. Instead of an analysis and complete description of the planned product's characteristics and purpose he showed me a cutting from the catalogue of a competitor. The picture showed a rectangular coffee table in beech wood with storage function in the top board which was entirely of glass with small compartments in the lower board. I was too new to know how to react and the wretched thing became reality despite the fact that it did not feel right. To top it all it became a best-seller and remained in the range for several years. That was the first and the last copy during my time in the business area. The decision to stop plagiarism was not taken because I have higher moral standards than the colleagues or feel compassion for the designers in the trade or the competitors. Not at all. On the contrary, I saw it as my duty to act with the best for IKEA in mind in each situation. To copy other people's work, I was and am still convinced of, is never a practicable route since you always end up one step behind. In other words, had I thought plagiarism was a good idea I would definitely have advanced it to become our key strategy on the storage front.

However I do not think that such obvious plagiarism any longer happens in the furniture range. The superior competence amongst product developers, range managers and others has put a stop to it. Regarding the areas of lighting and storage boxes I am more doubtful.

The last example I have of design theft is from a lighting project in 2005. The whole project team was in Shenzhen in China visiting a key supplier. The enterprising – and shrewd – Chinese entrepreneur showed us round and we ended up in his showroom. This was nothing but a hall packed with lamp models that were all stolen design with a touch of the unusual. Slowly it became clear to me that a large part of IKEA's lighting range, not least the best-sellers, came from this showroom and this factory.

IKEA's backbone

Obviously Ingvar has a large influence on the direction of the range as well as on purchases. But I would like to maintain that real enthusiasts at IOS also play a decisive role. There is a handful that I know of. People who are far down in the hierarchy, but who still manage to get their voice heard and gain sympathy for their ideas with the business area and with Ingvar – and their capacity to carry them to fruition.

Åke Smedberg, who unfortunately left IKEA's ranks far too early in 2008, was a product developer and a real enthusiast who I will always remember. He was certainly unusual, perhaps even a bit odd, but his creative brain was always revving fast. Always reflecting on things. Always cheerful. He and the technician Lennart Eriksson managed to produce MAGIKER and DOCENT, two big selling storage combinations, in less than 18 months. They, together with a subcontractor, even managed to breathe fresh life into the traditional print board technique. Print board existed already in the sixties, but it was then neither sophisticated nor efficient. Instead of veneer or foil the wooden pattern was now printed with rollers in the same way that you print newspapers or posters. It worked perfectly – and was in full production long before deadline. And, surprise, surprise, the supplier of the storage combination was Swedwood AB. Obviously it was the legendary Håkan Eriksson in Poland who was responsible for production.

A more recent example is the purchasing strategist Dan Persson (the name is fictitious). Perhaps no longer a young man, but equipped with as much driving force and ingenuity as a whole business area. Dan was also involved as purchasing strategist for MAGIKER and DOCENT. He has continued in this superior manner. The lightweight chipboard, for example, carries his initials. He was also one of the enthusiasts behind the flagship BESTÅ.

But his latest ideas led him even further. Ingvar got wind of them and he was asked to come to strategic purchase in order to present his thoughts. When Dan had finished talking Ingvar sternly looked around the room at his directors and managers. Dan had asked for 50 million kroner (£4.5/$7 million) in order to get started.

'Nobody leaves the room until we have decided about Dan's investment. My rough estimate is that he will need 200 million kroner (£18/$28 million) immediately to get going.'

Dan Persson got his 200 million kroner and is today working on developing the next generation of materials at IKEA. IKEA will never be better than this proximity between co-workers and highest management, between innovators and entrepreneurs who refuse to give in. What is Dan doing? That is an IKEA secret that I will not disclose – as I care for this old colleague and admire him very much. Keep your eyes open for the next catalogue and you may perhaps find it.

# 6

# Logistics – the journey of the product

During my time as furniture manager at the store in Wallau in Germany I initially trusted the advice from the logistics manager completely about how I should place my orders. Later I learnt the hard way that I alone was responsible for my department, around 45 per cent of the store turnover, volume of stock and space. My store manager's goal was that we this year should overtake the Munich store turnover, meaning that we, calculated in money, would become the largest division of the IKEA world. (Kungens Kurva in Stockholm was and is the largest store as far as space goes.) So I was to suffer for my trust in the logistics manager's talk of efficient flow of goods and how the system would manage everything. That nearly cost me both my job as well as my health.

The following year I did the opposite when I put my orders in and used both braces and belts when it came to the best-sellers. A few weeks later I was able to see my creation when the new catalogue was launched in August. Sales took off, we overtook Munich at throttling speed and everyone was content and happy except from the warehouse and logistics managers. For weeks on end I cluttered up the entire back of the store as well as surrounding areas with up to fifty loading platforms. A loading platform is the large wagon covered with a tarpaulin that goes behind an articulated lorry. I had to avoid the warehouse area and the warehouse manager on my daily rounds in the store, as he became angry each time he saw me and shouted abuse in his incomprehensible Hessian dialect. I can't blame him, as his job must have been near enough impossible because of me.

There is one cog in the IKEA machinery that Ingvar has very little knowledge of: logistics. This is slightly strange, since he is completely in command of all other areas. The forest, the industry, product development and the stores, all these areas Ingvar knows from the smallest atom to the strategic level – and backwards. But not logistics. At the same time some of the company's most important competitive advantages are generated precisely in logistics. My guess is that Ingvar's relationship with the subject depends on that he deep down sees the central warehouses and the logistics systems as large, costly and in reality totally unnecessary parts of the value chain. His and thereby IKEA's policy has been to constantly under-invest in the warehouse structure in order to force through as efficient logistics as possible. At the same time we need to remember that everything is relative. IKEA has a large number of central warehouses around the world. Each unit is enormous with room for tens of thousands of pallets with goods.

Historically it has always been the company's flow of goods that has been its

Achilles' heel. One of the first anecdotes I heard whilst I was doing my eight introductory weeks at the Uppsala store in 1989 was when IKEA had been on the verge of bankruptcy a few years earlier. It seems that they had grossly overestimated the sales prospect of the sofas on offer by the company. Or to put it more precisely, they were five years behind regarding stylistic expressions of the sofas. The sofas were in the wrong colours, wrong materials (mainly brown corduroy), wrong models at the wrong price – in short, they were totally worthless. And that was not all, they had estimated the volumes even more incorrectly, so there they were with thousands of unsellable sofas in Swedish stores, which at the time was the IKEA world's biggest country for sales. There were another tens of thousands in carriage trains across the whole railway network waiting. The liquidity of IKEA was being ploughed into sofas that were impossible to sell. The company was threatened by bankruptcy.

IKEA was salvaged from catastrophe by the managing director for Sweden at the time, Bengt Larsson. What Bengt and his Swedish team did was to put all their efforts, their whole focus into selling these sofas. No sales trick was forbidden in the exhibition of furniture and no exaggeration too gross. Just to lower the price on products that are hard to sell is usually not enough. You have got to work with every millimetre of the sales area, each platform, each hot wall in the whole store in order to manage it.

*A meeting room in the central warehouse, Älmhult, February 2000*
'Call business area Two and Johan Stenebo.'

The room was large like a normal lecture theatre in the seventies. Despite efforts to renovate, the gloomy beige shone through both the whitewashed walls and the worn floors. Now it was not a council facility, but the building was from the sixties if not before, and the company's restoration budget could not keep up with the rate of decay.

At the end of the room hidden in safety behind a rectangular table about ten stern colleagues were sitting. Highest in rank was Sören Hansen, the new financial director at IKEA. There was also Thomas Byström, who at the time was responsible for logistics in the group, and a number of other specialists in warehouse and distribution. All were middle-aged grey men apart from Sören who seemed as suave and alert as always. Thomas, an otherwise jovial man from Gothenburg, was acting chairman and led this inquisition session with a severe expression. It was not each business area that was granted the highly dubious honour of being present and to be shamed in front of the tribunal. No, it was only us who had put that bit extra in our orders. To be honest 'that bit extra' is an understatement. I too often followed my modus operandi from my years in Wallau and ordered too much. I was driven by enthusiasm, and far too early in the process did I shut my ears to warnings by my colleagues about surplus-storage problems.

'Let's go! This will be smashing', I arrogantly exclaimed and by that dismissed any opposition. That was leadership in my worst moments.

Each business area was responsible for purchasing, distribution and sales of its range on a global scale. My area of living room storage, coffee tables, TV benches and dining room furniture was already in those days a concern of well over ten billion kroner (£90/$140 million) yearly. Best-sellers like BILLY, STEN and IVAR were part of it.

Thomas turned on the big overhead-projector with a light push on the switch. The projector reacted with a sigh which changed into the loud hiss of the cooling fan.

'The situation is serious and we wonder what you from business area Two are going to do about it?'

Thomas was peering sternly behind his pilot frames with glass that changed colour with the light. Our business area on a daily basis made up 10–15 per cent of the group's turnover. Our part in surplus stock of the company made up twice that figure. Apart from the fact that space was lacking in warehouses and stores to house my enthusiasm, the entire logistical system was being put at risk before the imminent catalogue launch in August. It was namely at that time that all novelties were to come out in large volumes, the most critical period in the IKEA-season.

I was accompanied by Bengt, responsible for logistics and purchase in the business area, and Kjell-Åke, who knew how to count. The night before we had put together our plans for solving the surplus storage problem. They were not particularly sophisticated. But the urgent meeting held in order to solve the storage problems was not one which particularly impressed us to achieve great things. On the contrary, we all thought that the whole thing showed an arrogance and a self-importance that we did not recognize in IKEA.

During 1999–2004 the business areas were repeatedly told that if we were not careful with our forecasts the distribution system of the company would collapse. Almost as with a person suffering from serious heart disease who in the end collapses after years of debauchery with almost completely blocked veins where the blood can hardly be transported round. Parallel with these discussions a development of distribution centres of historic proportion was being implemented throughout the whole IKEA-world. But the warehouses were simply not sufficient since the increase in volume was extensive at the same time. On a couple of occasions, I have heard from the group's logistics managers, that a heart attack of the IKEA logistical system was not far off. Meaning that the point of collapse of stocks, transports and IT-systems had almost been reached and where the enormous flow of goods and the entire operation could break down.

The importance of the Autumn

It is really only during one period each year when it is of the utmost importance for all stocks to be complete, namely in the Autumn. During August as is well-known the catalogue is launched with all the novelties that IKEA promises the customer they will have in stock. And it used to be during that period that the warehouses were always empty of the products most in demand, both new items in the catalogue and best-sellers. IKEA sells just under 40 per cent of the whole year's volume during the period September – December. A bad beginning for the catalogue year, which begins in September, will usually never be recovered later on.

The root of the evil – when you arrive at your IKEA-store and everything you had planned on buying is sold out – is more often than not poor forecasting by IKEA. Around one hundred specially trained co-workers work at IOS making prognoses, meaning guessing the sales volumes of the thousands of items in the range. All these items are divided into service levels 1, 2 or 3.

Service level 1 are the key items, for example cross braces for IVAR or the legs for SULTAN sprung mattress base. But also the absolute best-sellers from each business area are here: such as nightlights, BILLY bookcase, BUMERANG clothes hanger and EKTORP sofa.

Service level 1 corresponds to a considerable part of the sales volume, but concerns less than 10 per cent of the items in the range. Service level 2 corresponds to the same number of items and to a reasonable part of the sales volume. Service level 3 is con-sequently the dregs or the tail, therefore the 'padding' in the range. We are talking about perhaps 5,000–6,000 items that put together do not correspond to more than a fifth of the entire sales volume.

So what raison d'être have the items from service level 3 have? Well, in order to be able to sell the best-sellers in your range you also have to offer a context, a framework. *Angebotskompetänz,* the Germans call it, which means the range on offer. I think the expression rather well captures what it is about. Just imagine you go to a boutique that only sells pleated pink skirts. You would have turned around and left even if you liked what you saw. Naturally you also want to see the red frilled skirt and the tight skirt in red-pink before finally deciding on the pleated one. Obviously you knew all along that it was the pleated one you wanted, but for your own peace of mind you also wanted to consider the alternatives. It works like that with curtains and garage storage as well.

Each service level is linked to certain performance requirements. Service level 1 signifies for example that these items are always prioritized throughout the whole value chain, from production to transportation and storage the whole way to the store. All this sounds obvious, but unfortunately reality is another thing. The prognosis-makers may often guess incorrectly, they as little as anybody else are capable of seeing the future and perhaps attach a service level 3 to a best-seller and vice versa. The result of this is, since the number of places in the first and second groups are limited, that important items end up in group 3 with constant and serious shortages as a result.

A reasonable question is why they do not start out from previous year's sales and so perhaps end up with a more accurate prognosis? The answer is that that would work in an IKEA that never changes in a world that does not move. The company changes a third of its range every year and new items have as we know no sales history. Furthermore items are given different weight through the positioning in the catalogue and other marketing activities each year. For good reasons certain items are given price rises, whilst others are reduced in price. To complicate things even further the trade outlook of the market keeps changing year after year. So there is no relevant sales statistics to build prognoses on, other than possibly the total level for a business area.

Instead when making a prognosis for range, catalogue and price, similar already existing items are used. For example in business area one, sofas and armchairs, we started from how well the predecessor KARLANDA had sold of each unit. Now this was certainly a somewhat less attractive sofa, even if it was rather similar and with a higher price. We also looked at the best-seller EKTORP, since we expected the new sofa KARLSTAD to become a best-seller immediately. But we could not only compare sofa with sofa, as EKTORP had a lower price and the price resilience on attractive sofas has been proven high. This means that if you lower the price on a best-selling sofa with for example 20 per cent the leverage effect, how many will be sold at the new price, will be considerably higher than 20 per cent. Expressed in real terms, if the normal price on an EKTORP is 4,990 kroner (£450/$700) and you lower the price by 20 per cent, you will not sell 20 per cent more sofas, but perhaps 50 per cent. The effect depends on how the customer sees the price. With the new price you have positioned yourself below the threshold for the customer resistance that depends on the fact that 4,990 kronor is perceived as a major investment whilst 3,990 is not.

In order to create a valid picture we instead looked at changes in volume of EKTORP at different price levels over the years. After that we added an extra buffer of perhaps around 20 per cent over and above the volume we had guessed. Sofas are a challenge that I have already talked about. If you guess incorrectly you can normally manage to produce more frames relatively quickly, whilst covers may have a six month delivery period from order to warehouse. This in turn may mean that you loose billions of kroner in lost sales. It is hardly possible to sell a frame without a cover and as always the 80/20-rule applies here too – in practice that one to two covers stand for 80 per cent of sales.

In the case of the KARLSTAD sofa in the 2007 financial year we guessed correctly. With that a new best-seller was born.

A reluctance to extend storage

The main reason for the problems with logistics and prognoses is a reluctance on part of the IKEA board, read Ingvar Kamprad, to extend storage and other areas in order to be able to handle the increased volume in the product flow. Consequently constant streamlining must be done so that the products get through at all. By making as few articles as possible at service level 1 or 2 you save on volume, i.e. space. A best-seller needs enormous movements of cubic metres. A full pallet corresponds to one cubic metre and we are talking hundreds of thousands of cubic metres per best-seller and year. Visualize this by trying to conjure up an image of 500,000 Euro pallets with the same EKTORP sofa on all of them. If prognoses are wrong and the suppliers carry on sending in a deluge of sofas you will not only have problems with capital tied in sofas – the question is where you can store them. When you come to IKEA next time and the very item you want is missing from its place on the shelf, don't be surprised. Excuses like the supplier has not delivered the item or has not produced it are nothing but smoke screens to hide the simple fact that the most important IKEA products should and will run out rather frequently, ultimately because Ingvar Kamprad wants to save money on the accessibility of goods in the stores. The unofficial mantra is that IKEA is so cheap and the cost of having 100 per cent access to products would be far too high, so the customers must simply take the rough with the smooth.

Many will perhaps be surprised. Do you not make more money if you have the products in stock and sell them than if you keep the stock and product flow under-dimensioned? That is certainly true, but only when it comes to the best-sellers, meaning 20 per cent of the range. In all other cases the opposite applies. IKEA's problem is that they allow the best-sellers to be hit by a management phobia that the flow of goods will overflow, and a costly extension of warehouses become an apology for inefficient logistics. The most important reason that you leave IKEA empty-handed on your next visit is probably in the end due to Ingvar's lack of interest in problems that deal with the supply of goods. I can actually not remember if I have experienced or even heard about him taking an interest in whether best-sellers are in stock. Today in the company all prerequisites for all best-sellers to be in stock the whole time exist: capable co-workers, able suppliers and a functioning logistics system. What is lacking is the required warehouse space to manage the assignment. Each article needs a buffer stock in order to manage the lead-time for new assignments from the supplier and for a natural variation in sales to take place. If a product like for example BILLY sells in millions every year this buffer obviously needs to be large. In other words BILLY, EKTORP and other IKEA best-sellers will be absent all the time because the company has chosen not to invest in further warehouse capability. And that is, as we shall see, not because they cannot afford it, but it is simply a cold calculation on Ingvar's part that the customers will come back anyway.

An interesting new feature which has been introduced recently by the logistics and purchasing manager for the group, Göran Stark, is the low flow- and high flow-stock. An enormous warehouse in Germany with a sophisticated electronic selection technique stores all slow selling products for the whole of Europe. In that way the high flow-units do not have to clash with such products that the store often orders in very small quantities, perhaps just a cardboard box instead of the normal quantity of a pallet. From what I understand the trials have been successful and the flow of best-sellers has been further improved. The idea came originally from Göran and shows how good ideas can crop up when someone tackles a problem with fresh eyes. Göran has a background as buyer and purchasing manager in different parts of the world.

Ingvar has been nagging the logisticians for years that the direct deliveries from the main suppliers to the stores must increase. The idea is in itself a good one. Without intermediate storage, costs would be considerably lower. The drawback is that you as a store have to order 1–2 months supply of lets say LACK coffee table in order to fill one articulated lorry. Normally a store will turn over its stock in 2–3 weeks. If you keep this enormous buffer stock of LACK tables in a store, which too often is under-sized in proportion to its sales volume, you will have a problem with finding enough space for other products. The problem has been accentuated because the constant and high growth during the last 6–7 years has resulted in the majority of the stores not managing the range. If both the display sample and the stock of a product are to fit in, space is required. If thousands of products are to fit in and be replenished on a daily basis the lack of space becomes acute.

Ingvar has despite this encouraged direct deliveries. The response of the retail management has been to cut the range, first on their own initiative but soon together with a mildly protesting IOS. The stores were classified by size as A-, B- or C-houses and the range was being pre-packaged to suit the three house sizes.

The number of items in a store

Ultimately the discussion has been about how many items IKEA needs in its range in order to be competitive. The stores maintain that 5,000 items, meaning the best-sellers and a few more should be enough. Mathias Kamprad, the youngest of the sons, was for a few years retail manager in Denmark. His opinion was more around 3,000 items. An opinion he angrily shared at each meeting he came to. If you have the Kamprad surname there are many people who will listen within IKEA.

'If you reduce the range to 3,000 items, Mathias, our competitors will jump with joy. That is when there will be no more IKEA left', his father replied sternly.

Naturally it may seem strange that a retail manager, having had the very best IKEA-education as well, brings forward such an extreme opinion. Not least as Mathias and his brothers are the crown princes of the whole company. Whoever understands the IKEA value chain and competitive advantages, meaning the overall picture, will see how risky his views were.

Anyway, the range was cut down at a rapid pace (depleted a lot of us were saying). The largest stores around the world were to keep a specified limited range of thousands of items and the rest a decreasing scale. The result was that most of the stores avoided the largest category and cut down even more drastically. Since it was up to each retail country themselves to reclassify single stores as they saw fit. In reality you could choose considerably fewer packets of items, but you could not influence the content in each packet. Smaller business units like Children's IKEA nearly perished, as its from the outset narrow framework was depleted further. When the customers were confronted with even less products on offer (IKEA has since the launch of Children's IKEA gone from 800 to 250 items), when there was no longer a choice, the pleasure of buying also disappeared and with that purchases of IKEA goods. And so also the financial results.

### The curse of instant gratification

There is one circumstance which further aggravates the current situation with a too limited and basic range on offer: instant gratification. The mantra at IKEA is that the customer wants their goods now. Irrespective of what you buy, a complete kitchen or a nightlight holder, you want to take the things with you home on the same day. A sensible person, however, understands that it would be better to wait for the home delivery service for a week than to find, collect and count all 300–400 kitchen parts yourself and to stack 4–5 trolleys at an IKEA-store on a Saturday. Most of us understand that instant gratification certainly is important when it comes to a cushion you have seen in the catalogue, maybe even a kitchen chair, but hardly when it comes to a sofa. Then you ought to be able to cope with waiting for a few days for home delivery. For sofas and kitchens you almost always have to arrange transport through IKEA home delivery at the exit of the store anyway. Few people own a car that can cope with several cubic metres of IKEA-goods. However this does not really matter anyway. The IKEA group executive board has decided that instant gratification must apply to both the egg cup as well as the leather sofa.

When it comes to the flow of cubic metres of items and the under-dimensioned warehouses, instant gratification plays a totally decisive role. If you were to remove all kitchen parts and white goods from the stockroom at the shops, because you can assemble your own kitchen in almost all stores, and all stocks of leather and material covered sofas, because you can also bring home with you a considerable number of sofas, the IKEA stores would suddenly have space for a 30 per cent larger selection of items than they do today.

But if Ingvar has said that is how it should be, then that's that.

### Competitive advantages

Despite all its shortcomings IKEA remains a logistical marvel of world class. Very few retailers make use of global purchases as efficiently as IKEA, move such mountains of cubic metres from one part of the world to another with such precision at such a low cost. Consider that around a third of the end cost for a product are made up of the cost of logistics. This part becomes the outside frame for what transport and storage is allowed to cost from the loading platform of the supplier to that of the store. As so often at IKEA it is similar key numbers that keep the price picture under control.

When it comes to the range on offer in the stores and the customer's demand for instant gratification I am part of a small number of people who believe that the range on offer, its size, depth and width, is more important than most things. IKEA becomes stronger when it offers its customers a larger and thereby more attractive range and not the other way around. The predominant opinion by IKEA's management is that the limited cubic metres in the stores dictates the size of the range. This approach stems from a time when IKEA, because of lower cubic metre volumes in proportion to the capacity of the stores, could allow itself a larger range and at the same time store almost everything as cash-and-carry items. At the beginning of the nineties there were stores that carried 42,000 items.

Those days are long gone. Competition is today razor-sharp in most markets. Before the customer enjoyed collecting the bits for his/her own kitchen. Now almost all customers think that doing this is a form of self-torture. You still have to pay for the transport following IKEA's unique graduated transport scale. The more you want brought home, the higher the charge. The opposite is obviously customary in the trade – the more you buy the lower the transportation charge relatively speaking.

If IKEA's range is their identity (the first commandment in the IKEA-bible that Ingvar wrote in the seventies) there is every reason to reconsider. An average offer of around a thousand items per store (I cannot give the exact number, as this is considered a trade secret according to Swedish law) does seem worryingly weak and is a direct competitive disadvantage compared to the dominant companies in Germany, France and North America. In units like Children's IKEA, sofas, WORK IKEA, lighting and textile the restrictions are already beginning to hurt giving lower sales and revenues.

Perhaps IKEA is on its way to getting stuck in its ways like old-fashioned department stores. Such stores wanted to be a player in all ranges: hardware, food, fashion, books, CDs, perfume and so on. Logistics, special and profitability restrictions resulted in them becoming weak in most areas. By weak I mean that the offer becomes too thin, too narrow and too shallow to attract enough customers. If you are to succeed as a bookseller you cannot just offer the best-sellers and a handful of other books on sale, because the customers will soon see through your credibility, your *Angebotskompetänz*. The fact that the Swedish Amazon, *adlibris.se*, have in a few years managed to take a third of the Swedish book market is no coincidence. Their range on offer is unbeatable and the prices attractive. And weak is never good enough in the retail trade. What happened to old fashioned department stores was that they cut and compromised until not much remained of the range already at the time when I worked there in the eighties. That is where they still are since then and they are moving backwards regarding profitability really completely unnecessarily.

The solution is of course not to sell everything, but each area of your range has to offer something which can compare favourably with the range of the more specialized competitors. As a rule of thumb the only exception is if you manage to keep prices 30 – 50 per cent lower.

## The store – the stronghold of commercial forces

So far I have dedicated a lot of space to the flow of goods. The reason for this is obvious. The prerequisite for success of a retail business which tries to reach a broad public is always the efficiency in the flow of goods. It was also this answer I gave to Anders Moberg's question when he hired me: 'What ultimately makes a retail business successful?' In other words it does not matter how attractive and well produced the products are, if they do not arrive on time, are too expensive to produce or too expensive to transport to the place of sale in the store the encounter with the customer will be ruined. Because the customer – and this is the only prevalent truth within IKEA – always has a slim wallet.

No part of IKEA is more well-known among the public than the stores. Many seem to think that more or less everything that goes on within the giant group does so behind the blue and yellow front. In reality the work going on in the stores is nothing but a confirmation that things have worked smoothly upstream in the value chain, in the cotton plantation, in the factories, on the container ships and in the warehouses. Not to mention the hundreds of decisions that have to be made in Älmhult before production can even begin. The number of items on a pallet has to be decided. The appearance of the cardboard box to the customer has to be determined. As well as the number of boxes that have to be ordered as a minimum by the store at each order. In other words a multitude of production decisions are behind each item where it is waiting for the customer at its point of sale.

## Room Sets and compacts

In simple terms a store consists of four parts: furniture display, market place, cash desks and warehouse. A furniture exhibition has two main keys for the furniture manager to play in order to maximize turnover: room sets and compacts.

Room sets are the well furnished spaces you see everywhere in the furniture display and they are perhaps 50–60 in total. The first room set in a display that meets you should be as diverse as possible since the visitors have different tastes and each and every one should find their favourite design already at the beginning. The room sets follow the range-matrix exactly with Country, Scandinavian, Modern or Young Swede. Normally the furniture manager decides which main products should be part of the room sets, like the sofa with a particular material and the storage with a particular colour and expression. Within each area, for example living room or bedroom, there are a number of room sets.

The main items in the living room sets, sofas and storage, are matched according to style group. After that interior decorators from the KomIn (communication and room sets) department take over in order to create and bring to life each room set so that the customer feels that it is not just attractive, but also so realistic that he/she would want to have this fabulous room at home. 'The best way to sell a product is to show how it functions', is the IKEA motto. Even if the customer afterwards only buys the bookcase or the sofa he/she has, by being captured by the room set, already experienced that IKEA can help him/her exactly. For maximum sales the skill of the furniture manager is to make sure that the best-sellers among sofas and storage have a space in the most important room sets. And by the most important I mean those room sets which have the most exposure to the flow of customers and are in their field of vision. In those room sets that are not in the field of vision along the route the customer takes, but are situated in the so-called backwaters, the products which are not best-sellers are placed. Those that according to the 80/20 rule do not contribute on a considerable scale, but that however have a role to play when it comes to the living room offer's *Angebotskompetänz*: that IKEA has something for everybody.

Experience shows that a furniture display ought to contain 120–150 strategically placed 'bins', that is white rectangular filled hampers with price tags. The bins should contain products that in themselves are highly tempting because of their design, function or low price. In many room sets the bins should be placed and contain a product which is shown in the display as well, for example a nightlight holder for 10 kronor (£.9/$1.40). If you cannot afford the sofa in the room set you will without fail pick up the nightlight holder from there as consolation and perhaps as a reminder of how you would like your living room.

'Open wallet'

*Schnelsen, Hamburg, store opening, summer 1989*
As a newly employed trainee I had been given the rather basic task together with a temporary employee over the summer, he too from Sweden, of taking on responsibility for the bins in the furniture display during opening day. Well the whole responsibility was not ours, our task was to attach a two centimetre long metal hook on each bin and then hang a number of IKEA plastic bags on the hook. That sounds like a task that anybody would be able to cope with, does it not?

Wrong, we failed.

The shiny blue and yellow building opened its doors for the first time this morning to the inhabitants of Hamburg. The Final Countdown by the pride of Upplands Väsby, the rock group Europe, roared out of the loudspeakers in the store. And people poured in by their thousands. Each staircase, each metre of aisles, each compact and each room set was filled to the brim with customers. And in the middle of all this organized chaos in the stronghold of commerce there was one thing which suddenly dawned on me. The customers had something quiet and focused about them and their gaze was staring. Strange, I thought whilst I and my colleague attached another pair of hooks. Suddenly tens of hands reached out and literally tore the hooks and the bags out of our hands. They all disappeared with the torrential stream of customers down the aisles.

What happened that morning in Schnelsen is symptomatic of IKEA. By creating a hype with the customers before visiting the store (irrespective whether it is a new store opening, the launch of the new catalogue or a normal Friday ad in the press) the customer is given expectations of what to expect at IKEA. Once in store a sophisti-cated commercial system takes over which literally massages the customer's brain during the entire visit. One could describe it as if IKEA grabs you by the hand and consciously guides you through the store in order to make you buy as much as possible. Lively exclamations from the loudspeakers, signs, displays, customer aisles, compacts, room sets and boutiques interact in this process to create an almost fanatical desire to buy. The same hype that made the customers in Hamburg pay a lot of money for metal hooks that were largely worthless.

A bag of nightlights is probably the most typical bait in an IKEA store. You will find them amongst the 10–12 bins in a group, just as you come up the escalator to the furniture display, which internally is called 'open-up-the-wallet'. The reason is that they can only contain impulse products that the customer – you – almost as if by reflex grabs because they are so cheap that you willingly will open your wallet for them.

Nightlights, are always useful, a set of nice wooden frames for 19 kroner (£1.80/$2.80), are always useful, a toilet brush in three colours for 10 (£.90/$1.40), is always useful. If you fall for these tricks and you pick one of these products you are hooked. IKEA has opened your wallet. Since by getting you to pick up the first item, other items will follow once you get going during the rest of your visit to IKEA.

'Things I did not even know I needed', as IKEA's customers usually describe the seduction – after the event.

If you have ever wondered about the name of the very ugly yellow bag with blue handles that you and everybody else is carrying around in the store, it is simply called 'Ingvar's bag'. The bag has only got one purpose, to allow you to pick as much as possible amongst the myriad of offers at irresistible prices that are always at the correct height for picking up, which pursue you along the aisles. If you despite everything forget to pick up a bag at the entrance you will notice that at each given point in the store, with your nose towards the direction of the exit, you will be able to find a bin with Ingvar's bags. Check it out at your next IKEA visit. You should never go through the store empty-handed but have a well filled Ingvar's bag over your shoulder.

But the function of the bins is far more advanced than 'open-up-the-wallet', since bins are strategically placed both in the furniture display, the market, the checkout, the self-service warehouse and the hot-dog stand after the exit cash-desks. After years of behavioural scientific studies on the store floor a handful of rules have been produced about the content and the placing of the bins. Obviously these studies are not academic but carried out in best IKEA-fashion, namely by the co-workers themselves on the floor. The result is that the bins are always discreet, always have an appealing content at a fantastic price and are always ready to tempt you when you really feel like it.

*On an inspection trip in Mälardalen, summer 1998*

Ingvar, myself and the MD for Sweden at the time Göran Ydstrand were on a tour visiting the Swedish stores. These could be rather cosy excursions since Ingvar was usually brisk and happy and never lost his temper during a store inspection. When entering we were met by total chaos from the customer entrance and the whole way to the exit. The three of us looked bewildered at each other because this was the worst any of us had ever seen. Litter, crooked signs, worn display furniture, well, on the whole there was nothing OK according to the usual normal IKEA-standard. The store manager, we can call him Ronny, was just as pleasant and obliging as always, apparently totally unperturbed by the fact that he had the founder of the company in front of him and that his store must have been the most filthy in the entire IKEA-world. Ingvar did not in the slightest show what he thought but walked around the customer aisles arm-in-arm with the manager. Now and then he would stop by a room set or a bin and discreetly give his new-found friend smart suggestions and ideas about what he might possibly change. I only know of one thing that makes Ingvar lose his enthusiasm during a store visit. That is if a product has no price. If for example an armchair or a vase has no price-tag he immediately becomes irritated and starts lecturing about the importance of pricing all products. It is usually enough for him to show irritation, for people in his vicinity to feel that the situation is really unpleasant. That is how powerful Ingvar's authority is.

'A product without a price is always wrong', goes Ingvar's most important rule for the retailers. The logic is simple: if the customer does not know what an item costs he/she will not buy it either.

The room set is as I said earlier the name of all the rooms that border your route through the furniture display. Compacts are the wide, rather neutral areas which come after a series of room sets. Each compact shows the customer more or less IKEA's entire offer of sofas, storage, TV furniture or desks displayed in straight lines or in groups. Everything is displayed according to colour, wood, style group, function or size. Then the furniture manager simply puts his 'peasant sofas' like the best-selling

EKTORP in a group, since the customer consciously or subconsciously is looking for a particular style or colour. The exception are the British who do not choose sofas with their eyes, but with their behinds. They literally sit through the entire compact of sofas or until they are satisfied with the seating comfort. Germans and Swedes wander about until they have found what they are looking for – with their eyes. After that they might lightly touch the sofa with their buttocks before they nod approvingly to the rest of the company.

Mechanical selling

Now it is not just a matter of placing all the sofas in the range in a large empty space. IKEA has made mechanical selling into an important competitive advantage. Mechanical selling means everything that can be sold without a salesperson (i.e. personal selling) but with the help of only the catalogue, price-tags and other signs. The price-tag can, for example, show EKTORP Lillemor yellow, shelf G, space 67. Thereafter the idea is that you 'mechanically' will go there, grab a customer trolley on the way and yourself load the sofa and the cover onto it.

The room sets that attract and tempt and that look so individual – are not always that. Nowadays readymade drafts for sets at least for all important items arrive directly from Älmhult. In other words the room sets are often, but not always, in all main details alike, irrespective of store and country. The compact is the rational opposite of the emotive room set. Because the compact will capture your attention just as you have been seduced by the room set and says: 'Look how much we have to offer, you will bring home at least one of these beautiful sofas won't you?' In other words what the Germans call *Angebotskompetänz*.

As if by chance the compact opens up to you where you stand. Before you know it you have gone astray amongst the sofas. And you are caught up in the process of buying. You hardly realise that all the sofas placed in your field of vision are best-sellers from different price groups so that you quickly will find something that suits you. That the sofa at the end with the large yellow-red price tag and the remarkably low price is there to attract you to the compact. That when you finally are standing next to the cheap sofa discover that it only exists with one cover, which you don't like, that it is hard to sit on and that it hardly has room for more than a couple of people despite being called 3-seater. At this point you have, without realizing it, chosen and discarded sofas in a matter of minutes. You have, as you yourself feel, come to a well considered purchase decision, since you have discarded a cheaper sofa for one a bit more expensive. 'You have to have room to sit as well. And the more expensive one is nicer, but IKEA is still cheap', you are thinking on your way to the purchase point to place your order.

Obviously the bins as well have a special task and don't just open up your wallet but also 'happen' to be placed amongst the sofas with a massive mountain of cushions exactly where you are standing. You pick up a cushion and squeeze it into Ingvar's bag. Even if it won't be a sofa this time, perhaps you can't afford it, it will anyway be a cushion. And in a month's time when you can afford the new sofa you already know where to go. Yes, you already know exactly which sofa you want. You already have the matching cushion in Ingvar's bag hanging over your shoulder.

Hot, hot-hot and cold spaces

In order to heighten the degree of sophistication about the commercial work of IKEA we can take a look at the so-called hot, hot-hot and cold spaces in the store. Imagine a plan of the entire interior of the store. Your route all the way from the entrance to the checkout is being monitored in secret. Every step and every stop you make is being observed and marked on the plan. Now imagine the route of a thousand customers through the store. Each customer generates a winding line from a plotter along customer aisles, compacts and room sets. The total sum of these routes creates a teeming swarm in certain areas and sparse lines in others. The most intense swarms, the areas frequented by most customers, are the hot-hot areas of the store and so on, on a sliding scale to the coldest area with sparse lines.

Why is it important to know this? Well, the best points of sale in the sofa compact, in the kitchen room sets and the carpet division in the market place should all be matched with best-sellers from each product division. The fundamental principal is as simple as it sounds. The more important the best-seller, the hotter the area for exposure. This simply depends on the fact that important best-sellers appeal to the needs of many people (otherwise they would not be best-sellers). And in the hot-hot or hot areas the best-seller comes into contact with many visitors and thus potential customers. And as you have already understood this is a general principle, the same applies to your grocery store or any fashion boutique.

The paradox is that rather few retailers, local, national or global, structure their commercial operations following these basic rules. Some of the fundamental principals I have mentioned exist in many businesses, but very seldom in as coordinated and consistent way as at IKEA. Maybe that is because the retailing business, with the exception of the world's large everyday commodity retailers in the world, still are not as sophisticated in their processes as for example the manufacturing industry. IKEA has consistently followed the basic principles about hot and cold areas, about bins, compacts and room sets in their stores for many years. A trained eye can quickly recognize the hot and cool areas in a sales spot without any difficulty. If one were not to use this principle it would be chance or the subjective taste of the sales personnel to decide where best-sellers, the most important products in the range, are to be placed. Or, even worse, it will be the single co-worker's preferences and not the taste of the customer that decides how the range is to be displayed. The difference between letting chance or basic principles rule the commercial work is roughly calculated at 30–40 per cent in sales revenue.

Three Aces and a King

IKEA has actually gone one step further in order to achieve complete leverage of its range in the stores. Each IKEA country produces a small manual called 'Three Aces and a King'. The reason it is not produced centrally is that local taste varies rather a lot. Germans hate furniture made from oak since the material reminds them of musty home furnishing traditions and is popularly called 'Eichebrutal' (roughly 'oak in a brutal way') meaning furniture from thick carved oak stained with dreary varnish. The British often prefer flowery materials, the Dutch like loud orange and so on. Even if the stores around the world in principle carry the same range at 95 per cent, local needs and tastes decide which products and style will sell best.

In 'Three Aces and a King' the most important items from the normal range are listed. The classification is simple. The range is divided into a number of range areas which normally would follow the material and function dimensions. So living room storage is business area 2, for example divided in range areas such as coffee tables, storage and TV furniture. Each range area is in turn divided into product areas. Storage consists of single bookcases like BILLY and storage combination like BESTÅ and IVAR. In the small manual are listed three aces and one king for all product areas in the range and they are several. It is simply not possible for the departmental head to focus on a larger number of products in the daily commercial work. One of the basic rules at IKEA is focusing and it is in that context you should view the 'Three Aces and a King' manual. Without it, and the obsession with best-sellers that it represents, it is impossible to succeed in your mission as sales manager.

The aces are divided into three categories for each product area: best carrier of turnover (best-sellers), best carrier of gross profit (highest profit margin in per cent) and the 'take your breath away' offer in the product area. A king is a new product believed to become a best-seller or possibly a carrier of gross profit. When you as a business are responsible for an area in the store plan your display of green plants or chest of drawers, the product type is of secondary importance as the principles are largely the same, you consistently follow the manual which in its turn follow the 80/20 rule. Unimportant products in unimportant spaces and the best-sellers in hot and hot-hot spaces. Of course IKEA is not alone in using the classifications of the manual or the underlying principles, but few if any other retailers are as consistent.

When you are seduced

One of IKEA's absolute competitive advantages is the fantastic capability to in a subtle way, almost unnoticeably, manoeuvre your purchases, something usually called purchasing process. This is done in a very ingenious way and with the only purpose to make you buy as much as possible. It begins already as you come up the escalator to the furniture display. Here you are met by the open-your-wallet market and bins with Ingvar's bags so that you will have room for all the extremely cheap products you without fail will pick up.

Then your stroll along the main route begins, the grey path. You continually find new tasteful room sets and interesting products. Wherever you go it is all so interesting and varied. To get lost is almost impossible. Signs in the ceiling, pedagogic plans and arrows on the floor lead you on with a firm but gentle hand. Your visit is going smoothly. Perhaps you won't even notice that no part of the grey pathway has a straight stretch of more than 10–15 metres (longer than that is called 'Autobahn' and is considered a serious mistake) before it is interrupted by a bend, then a short straight stretch and then a bend in the other direction. As you turn your eyes you will without noticing see new hot areas with new hot products. You carry on like this throughout the entire store: straight stretch, bend, short straight, bend, straight stretch. You cannot really tire as your eyes are inexorably guided towards new destinations and Ingvar's bag will be exchanged for a trolley in order to have room for all you have picked up and in the end there you are at the checkout with a full trolley. Consider that this entire process, all your experiences, the firm control over you strolling through the home furnishing department store happens so subtly that you at no time manage to perceive how you are being influenced to purchase decisions other than possibly subconsciously.

When you come to a decision

As you are strolling along in this fairyland of adventures ('*ganz wie im Märchenwald*', the Germans jokingly call it) and check your list of things to buy where at the top is written chest of drawers in large letters. You carry on and soon after the bedroom and the wardrobe compact you come across the chest of drawers compact. You thought the bedroom sets were extremely inspiring. In several of them you had seen exactly the chest of drawers you had chosen from the catalogue. Now you are seeing a sea of chests of drawers, but the difference between the competitors is vast. First of all it is not a disorderly sea of chests of drawers. Secondly no detail, no matter how small and insignificant, has been left to chance.

Almost stealthily 2–3 welcoming passages between rows or clusters of chest of drawers open up. The open pathways reach all the way to the back wall. The chest of drawers are normally placed by colour or possibly range group. A handful of products are marked with white signs with sales information and price. These are the best-sellers. The chest of drawers you have chosen from the catalogue you will probably find immediately, since it is very likely a best-seller. A chest of drawer a bit further back has a yellow-red sign with an extra bold price in black. This the take-your-breath-away product. This has only one task – to reinforce the message about the low price. Because even if the chest of drawers you want to buy does not have such a low price, the continual nagging about low price is contagious so that you without realizing believe that everything in front of you is cheap.

If you think that you are making a rational purchase decision when you are standing there choosing among the chest of drawers you are probably wrong. The combination of the same best-seller in the catalogue, in the room set and in the compact has already seduced you. The signs down to the price-tag level facilitates the process to such a degree that you really never even have to think.

## Commercialism elevated to philosophy

In this chapter I have tried to describe at a fairly detailed level how IKEA has transformed a good old sales spirit into a philosophy. When planning the sales area each small detail is given meticulous attention. Every detail needs to be looked at, discussed, gone over again and again. I myself have several times during my career spent hours, days, discussing whether for example a sofa in the compact by the entrance should meet the flow of customers at an angle of 45 or 60 degrees. Around ten people make up a group: the furniture manager, interior decorators from KomIn, the person responsible for sofas and perhaps the store manager. Arguments are twisted and turned in a discussion which must seem rather bizarre to an outsider. The central point of these discussions is the teamwork between the very knowledgeable interior decorators and the KomIn communicators and the sales people. It is precisely in this coming together of people with different knowledge and goals, the eagerness to increase sales and to create something attractive, that the principal competitive advantage of IKEA is created.

When competitors use hard selling by salesmen or sell from premises that mostly resemble a chaotic garage clearance, IKEA manages to seduce its customers in the fairyland forest. Until now no competitor has actually managed to break through this lead. The lead comes from decades of wisdom that have come out of the get-together between highly qualified, furniture managers eager to sell and aesthetically talented interior decorators and communicators. The dynamics of a well-run department store are a living organism which can never be put into a universal manual.

## The core business of the store

An IKEA-store has two central tasks:
1. to get as many store visitors as possible to become customers
2. to get these customers to buy as much as possible during the visit

Inversely, if a visitor only walks through the store without buying anything it is a considerable loss since IKEA has invested lots of money into attracting them to the store. And if they are there already it's obvious that they have to buy, and if they buy they should obviously pick up as many things as possible. Each extra little article ending up in Ingvar's bag is pure profit. A catalogue today costs 30 kroner (£2.70/$4.20) to produce and distribute and IKEA hands out hundreds of millions catalogues each year. This money has to be recuperated from somewhere – and that place is the store.

The marketing manager in each IKEA-country is responsible for the local marketing which aims to attract visitors. A visitor is a person visiting IKEA. At the moment the visitor picks up a thing he/she becomes a customer. Besides publicity and PR-work aimed at potential IKEA-customers the marketing department also distributes the catalogue, today the most widespread printed item in the world. The catalogue is produced by an IKEA-company in Älmhult whose studio is supposed to be the biggest in northern Europe. The print run is at the moment 198 million copies in 27 languages and 52 editions. Converted into need for wood this enormous number of copies demands the total clearing of an acreage of forest. This need for wood increases with the yearly rate of growth of IKEA, that is by 15–20 per cent.

The job of the store manager has thus nothing to do with publicity. He or she must together with the co-workers convert as many as possible of the visitors, which the publicity and the catalogue have generated, into customers and get them to buy as much as possible. The commercial part of the store manager's job is a lot about orchestrating the collaboration between KomIn – people and their well-developed creative talent and the sales manager's clearly acute understanding of the needs of his customers and the saleability of the range – to seduce the visitors and, once they have opened their wallets, fill their Ingvar-bags and trolleys with more things than they thought possible. And this without them even for a second understanding how it all happened.

The second part of the store manager's job is to create the right conditions for the buying process to work smoothly also for the store. The customer should in other words be able to buy as much as possible, whilst the operation should be run using as few recourses as possible and as smoothly as possible. The most important reason for this is that the operational process does not generate any income, not even a penny. On the other hand it is, if it is not functioning, extremely costly. A checkout with overstaffing, an uncontrollable flow of goods that is doing nothing but cluttering the shelves in the warehouse or badly planned delivery of goods, sometimes too few things sometimes too many, cost large sums of money.

At the end of the day there are only two priorities on the agenda: fill up and tidy up. That is how the work in a store is day in and day out.

The way to create a good profit margin at the retail stage is, simply expressed, to maximize the revenue, meaning converting visitors into customers who fill their trolleys, at the same time as you keep a keen eye on the performance and cost of the running process.

My own experience comes from amongst other things as furniture manager at the Wallau-store in Germany which during those years became the largest in turnover in the world and from two years in Leeds, England, where I partly built up, partly ran the store during its successful first year. I have to point out that our success in large parts depended on the hype that the marketing and PR-divisions from the Service Office, Brent Park, London managed to conjure up in our catchment area. When we opened in Leeds 1995, with a catchment area of five million inhabitants within 1–2 hours drive from the store, we paralysed every motorway within several miles radius for weeks. We had a constant queue of visitors up to 100–150 metres long who were waiting to be able to get into the store. The queues by the checkout could make you cry. The store sold so much over the planned budget that bottlenecks were inevitably created. My 500 co-workers and I worked terribly hard literally all days of the week and managed to ride out the worst storms. For a while Leeds was the most noted IKEA-store in Europe as it was built cheaply and quickly in just eleven months with the latest commercial solutions everywhere. We surpassed our sales budget by 30–40 per cent and went below the operating budget considerably. Colleagues made pilgrimages from near and far in order to see the wonder. One can quite rightly say that I established my IKEA career at this successful store. When I later left Leeds to become Ingvar's assistant, the rugs in the sales hall had started curling up from wear and tear. A change of these, but also other items, soon became necessary. According to the real-estate unit at the group's office in Humlebæk I had given the expression 'stingy' a new meaning.

# 7

# IKEA's company culture

The myth about moss on a stone wall

In the official IKEA-version about the rise of the company, as it is being portrayed in their own media and the commissioned work by Torekull, IKEA started out as a small concern by dedicated co-workers who defied all opposition in order to make the company survive. They were ordinary people with only the interests of the company in mind. And Ingvar Kamprad sat amongst them performing the same tasks.

One of the favourite official IKEA's images shows an ancient granite wall overgrown with moss and lichen in a summery Småland landscape in Sweden. It suggests that the cultural roots of the company grow in the barren soil of Småland.

There is a news item in the Swedish broadcasting corporation's archive from 1965 with an interview made in connection with the opening of IKEA in Kungens Kurva. It shows Ingvar, not yet forty, in a sober and tailor-made suit, stiff but with a pipe sagely placed in his mouth and with horn-rimmed spectacles on the edge of his nose. Far from the popular Ingvar without tie and jacket we have got used to seeing today.

It was also around this time that he owned his own Porsche. About ten years ago, during my time as assistant, I was visiting Kungens Kurva on an errand. At lunch I met up with a couple old furniture colleagues whom I had not seen for a few years. They had been sellers at the furniture department ever since the opening of the store. When they heard about my new job as Ingvar's assistant they told me with emphasis about his transformation. At the time of the opening they had spent some time in Älmhult on in-house training and had bumped into Ingvar on a number of occasions. At the time the company only had a few hundred co-workers. He had not once condescended to a greeting. Not once had he as much as exchanged looks.

'He seemed very shy', one of them said, but his look said something else. None of them appeared to believe in the transformation to the nowadays so popular image.

And this is exactly my point. A few years later, at the beginning of the seventies, a new image of Ingvar Kamprad suddenly appears. The Ingvar we know so well today. The era of opening businesses abroad had started. Ingvar using *snus*, whiskers and shabby clothes. The co-workers around him looked the same, albeit considerably younger. A rather impressive transformation one must say. A man in his forties changes style in a few years from tailor-made classical tweed to ugly seventies clothes, from pipe to *snus*, from restrained and taciturn, to jovial and vocal.

You may well wonder what Kamprad's style has to do with the IKEA-culture. Everything. This 'extreme makeover' by Ingvar is actually the birth of the IKEA-culture, I would argue. We may never get to know what he felt and thought at the time, what was behind this transformation. But whatever it was, Kamprad shed his skin. He went from the serious manager type, with or without fascist leanings, to become a modern business executive, who is one of the lads with tobacco under his lips and ugly haircut – even if he was just as uncontroversial as executive then as he is today.

I still believe that the transformation was more extensive under the surface than on the outside. It was probably at this time that Ingvar started working on his dogma about thrift and simplicity and other things which a few years later were published as 'The nine theses' or 'A Furniture Dealer's Testament'. These dogma make up, together with the business idea and the vision the foundation, what is today called the IKEA-culture. The reasons for Ingvar's sudden change of course, from old-fashioned strict to popular at ease, are just as obvious. It was happening during a period when the whole society was in a state of radical change.

Ingvar Kamprad had ever since the creation of IKEA always been quick to pick up and exploit the reshaping of society to his own advantage. He went from mail-order of small items to flat-pack home furnishing. At an early stage he realized the significance of cars and the possibility of out-of-town-retailing with all that it entails as well as DIY and its enormous significance for IKEA's success. He has as we shall see been quick to re-mould the foundations of his company a few times over the years. I mean that it has been exactly this ear for new ideas and currents that has been one of the most significant things of the Kamprad genius and thus the success of IKEA.

A lot of what IKEA launched were completely new phenomena. The pick-yourself stock for example, was in fact invented as a solution when the enormous assault at the new store in Kungens Kurva making it totally unmanageable a few days after the opening. They simply opened parts of the doors to the stock-room to the customers and let them drag the boxes to the checkouts. One could put it this way that Kamprad has always moved with the times. Or even a bit ahead.

From IKEA's vision 'to create a better everyday life for the many people' it is being described as a different type of company, which goes its own way on the basis of nine fundamental doctrines:

The Product Range – Our Identity.
The IKEA Spirit. A strong and living reality.
Profit gives us resources.
To reach good results with small means.
Simplicity is a virtue.
The different way.
Concentration of energy – important for our success.
To behave responsibly – a privilege.
Most things still remain to be done. A glorious future!

These new ideas, the nine theses in 'A Furniture Dealer's Testament', are a wonderful mixture of old Chinese philosophy expressed in Småland dialect, simple common sense and unusual brilliant thoughts of a shrewd businessman. My favourite is 'the product range is our identity', the first thesis. For a retailer to gather his activity precisely around the development of the product range was and is pioneering. Still today very few retailers in home furnishing entirely develop their own range. Instead they buy ready made models off the shelf. IKEA went one step further and said: 'We are what we sell', meaning that the range is given a clear and systematic profile in both design, functionality and price. But the range is at the forefront even more visibly than that. Everything depends on the range. To hang on to the idea that IKEA always sells typically Scandinavian furniture at a low price has been invaluable for the company during all these years of expansion abroad, where it in bad times might have been an easy option to introduce new products from heavy German furniture to British frills. Where each deviation from the established identity could have brought about a weakening of the company profile. Without doubt an extremely dangerous route for a newcomer from the faraway mould of Småland to take in a foreign land.

## Kungens kurva

A telling anecdote about the product range as identity comes from the seventies when Sweden was the great IKEA-country and Hans Ax was managing director. I only met Hans after his retirement, but even then he gave the impression of being someone extremely unpleasant and harsh who more or less knew everything better than anybody else. At Kungens Kurva in those days Bengt Larsson was store manager – the same Bengt who later was to become Sweden manager and finally Europe manager. Anyway, the two gentlemen were walking through the store and Hans commented with authority on things that were wrong. But this time there was not much and Bengt felt his satisfaction increase step by step. After a while they had gone through the entire store and were at the checkout area which was filled to the brim with crates of LP records with groovy dance music. Hans looked quizzically at Bengt. Bengt grew a further few centimetres.

'Yes, I got hold of a consignment cheaply', Bengt boasted in his broad dialect from southern Skåne.

'Will you resign yourself or shall I do it?' the small humourless moustached man replied sternly.

Bengt got to keep his job and that was lucky, but the important thing is the spirit. Nowadays it is expressed like this:

'We could even sell milk at IKEA in enormous quantities if we wanted to' but...

'What is not home furnishing IKEA should treat with utter care.'

Television sets and toasters have throughout the years not succeeded at all despite several attempts. Only white goods, where IKEA today is an important player, are the exception that confirm the rule. *'Ne sutor ultra crepidam'* (The cobbler to his last).

The theses in 'A Furniture Dealer's Testament' obviously also stipulate the greed, to achieve much with small means, as a lodestar. Precisely around greed a thicket of symbols have emerged throughout the years. The different way, my personal favourite, states that IKEA must always find its own way. To place the IKEA at Kungens Kurva in 1964 in the middle of a potato-field, or at least on the outlying parts of Stockholm, was a manifestation of this thesis. To paint the store metal boxes blue and yellow during the eighties was another (before then all IKEA stores were red and white for some unknown reason). This was the first step in making a gimmick of the Swedish character where Schwedenshop became a natural sequel to aquavit, gingerbread biscuits and Kalle's caviar.

In this and similar ways, in little as in great things, the business idea, the vision and A Furniture Dealer's Testament have been used as a safe rulebook to keep to over the years. Because of natural reasons the strength of the message has always been stronger the nearer you are to the epicentre.

In Germany there was a lot of talk about the unique IKEA-culture, but what it meant in real terms nobody really knew. Or cared about. At the time when I worked there, there were still a handful of politically correct cultural Swedes, employed as alibis to represent the so called IKEA-culture. In the case of Germany it was a rather odd marketing manager and his wife. That the two of them were breathing IKEA-culture as it was understood in documents and in Älmhult was doubtful. The big interest of the marketing manager was, anyhow, his Harley Davidson collection. The cultural diversity was shown by all IKEA co-workers using the familiar address of 'du' in Germany where the majority used the typical formal address. Something considered strange by outsiders up until the end of the seventies. This cultural marker is otherwise principally the only difference between IKEA and a conventional German home furnishing company.

In England there was no old eccentric Swedish marketing manager to rely on. At times the number of Swedish managers had been considerable, and a man like Anders Dahlvig has certainly had an influence over the cultural image of the managerial cadre in Brent Park or in the stores. But that the manner in which people relate to each other, cooperate, communicate which is so typical for IKEA in Sweden, has spread abroad I have so far not seen any evidence of.

The important cliché

What is corporate culture? A number of definitions exist, but one which describes it fairly correctly is that the phrase describes the values that distinguish a company from its competitors and how members of staff live up to those values in an everyday situation. If the opinion in one company is that punctuality is important they will succeed in keeping time in a better way than a company that does not have these values. Swedish Rail is particularly interesting in this context, since its management almost seem hostile to its customers with their late and overcrowded trains with very expensive tickets and investment decisions that always manage to arrive years too late. But the staff on the trains are extremely good at delivering excellent service.

The reason a company ought to invest time and money in its culture is simply that it has an intrinsic value, as it generates competitive strength against the competitors. If all co-workers have the same basic values and speak the same language, conflict and friction will be avoided since everybody is working towards the same goal. People are simply fairly like-minded. Processes that involve different cultures within a company, normally a common source of galloping prices and shortfalls in quality, will function better and result in better products.

Do bad and good corporate cultures exist? Definitely yes, and we will touch on that further ahead in the book. I want to suggest that the definition of a good corporate culture is that it develops the company and the society in a long-term tenable manner. I also maintain that what characterizes the good company is honesty, transparency and that you recognize the basic values of society. Interesting in this context is that Kamprad often criticizes jungle capitalism and praises the fact that IKEA is privately owned and so is able to act much more long-term than companies quoted on the stock exchange, who live a life ruled by quarterly accounts. In the following chapter we will see how well IKEA meets the criteria of a good company.

Symbols of everyday life

'A culture that does not hurt a bit is not worth its name', is Ingvar's thesis when it comes to corporate culture. And he ought to know as he together with his co-workers during the last decades has created a culture within IKEA which is as talked-about as it is singular. How do you do it?

There are certainly many different ways to create common standards and ways of relating among people in a company, but Ingvar's way has been to pick out symbols both for the desired and the less desired approach. Thus economists and other academics are out whilst the long road of IKEA-training is in. Now the company could hardly manage without newcomers and they are also taken on in their thousands every year to fill varying levels in the company. Interesting in this context is that Kamprad's own sons have attended both public school and university.

So simplicity is a virtue and IT in all its forms is completely out. The result is that IT is a black hole in IKEA's budget which consumes more money than any other part.

Actually the enormous costs for development of programmes swallows billions of kroner, they never work, and consultants sit and tick away meaningless hours in the company's enormous IT-colossus in Helsingborg. Nobody today has a clue about what to do to rectify the problem. A very well-informed person, an external senior consultant, estimated that by just changing the management and taking on real IT-managers (today it has become more like a parking space for the old faithful), tidy up the qualifications in the organization and choose the simple solutions one could without a doubt save up to half a billion kroner (£45/$70 million) – per year.

In the same spirit IKEA recently knew best and decidet to develop its own ordering system. The old system was a patchwork of thousands of ancient programmes so outdated that programmers who still knew it had become a species under threat of extinction. Alternative order systems like the market leader SAP did not 'suit' IKEA's needs. Ten years later their own so-called P3-programme has not delivered a tenth of what was agreed at the outset but has cost billions of kroner above the original budget. It is all so irrational that you shake your head in despair, but every P3-budget and business plan have been set out before Kamprad and the others at INGKA Holding BV, meaning the IKEA board, and examined.

My point is twofold. One, simplicity is certainly a virtue at IKEA but only when it suits Ingvar. The areas he chooses to neglect remain underfinanced irrespective of what the consequences for the company might be. Two, the so-called corporate culture, in this case the simplicity, has had extremely real consequences.

Other than that it is the dress-code which mostly distinguishes IKEA. Nobody in the company wears a tie, something which earlier made the company unique in industry. That was in the eighties. Today there is a myriad of tie-less companies. And even more that apply casual Friday, meaning you can dress down on Fridays.

An interesting fact is that even in a company like IKEA, which strives for equality with no obligation to wear a tie, hierarchical subgroups appear. For example many of the career-women in IKEA used to call the small group of top executives and young Turks the Dockers Boys with reference to the casual American Dockers trousers which everyone from this group were wearing. With the trousers they would wear a shirt of the label Gant or Boomerang. On the feet well polished flat or riding shoes, and to top it all a cashmere or lambs-wool pullover. The expression Dockers Boys has a deeper meaning as the group also stand for the invisible, but unbreakable, glass ceiling which stops everybody who deviates from the norm. Actively or passively this men's club for a long time made sure that women were few and far between in important positions in the company and that there were in fact none at all close to the significant power. Today there is certainly a different fashion than Dockers, but the men at the top of IKEA are principally the same. And so are the views about women.

Travelling has for many years been a significant issue where one travels business class and with cruising tickets (double apex). This means buying two return tickets which both cover a Saturday. One in each direction. The price for these two return tickets, where one trip from each ticket is never used, becomes much lower than one return ticket for the route but that is not valid on a Saturday. And overnight stays are done at special IKEA-approved hotels all over the world which keep a good, but never exaggerated comfortable class. When this was introduced at IKEA in the eighties it was remarkable in that it was above the industry norm. We are talking about an era when co-workers were expected to for weeks on end sleep head to foot in the same bed in an east European shabby hotel. However apart from long distance flying in tourist class, the IKEA co-workers of today are not exposed to worse suffering than most of the other business travellers in the country. You are however allowed to fly as much as you like domestically instead of taking the train. On the whole the restrictions on travelling are few compared to earlier.

Few people make more effort than Peter Kamprad, Ingvar's oldest son and crown prince to the IKEA-power, to set an example. All forms of waste with the company's money makes him, literally speaking, explode. When it comes to the cultural symbolism in order to stress thrift to the co-workers Peter works hard, but with headwind. He can for example fly across continents, wait for endless hours at airports only to reach his end destination hours or a day later with a slightly cheaper ticket. Thirty years ago this kind of thing impressed people, but people from the seventies and the eighties have decided that they would rather spend time with their family instead of at the airport.

He who laughs last laughs longest

It is still worse when the IKEA-culture is used to attack other corporate cultures. Recently Peter Kamprad was invited with a colleague to have dinner with a very senior executive from a large American consultancy firm in Brussels. This is one of the world's most successful consultancy companies in a different line of business and the meeting was about environmental techniques and risk capital. The aim was to create confidence and to discuss what type of assistance IKEA could get in these areas. At the end of the day the difference between environmental techniques and home furnishing is vast.

Young Mr Kamprad was as sour as a lemon from the outset because his father had suddenly decided at an IKEA board-meeting that all consultancy firms were bad. A veritable witch hunt was started against all consultants. The IT-consultants were quickly exempted, since nobody anyway had any idea about the black money-devouring hole, and efforts were instead concentrated on the consultancy despite the fact that the projects of the company generated IKEA billions in profits – every year.

In the car Peter started abusing the senior consultant. At the table the insolence carried on. With great calm the consultant finally asks:

'But what is it really that annoys you so much about us?'

'Well look, you are staying at the best hotel in town!'

The consultant calmly asked where IKEA-employees were expected to stay and how much that hotel cost. Peter answered sourly.

'The difference Peter is that when you pay €130 for your hotel, we only pay €150 for ours. And that is also one of Brussels' best hotels. You see we have an enormous discount and you don't. So really it is us who are saving money.'

When it comes to everyday technology such as laptop computers and mobile phones, IKEA finds it difficult to decide which leg to stand on. Of course the question may seem trivial, but in a company which safeguards its culture and its corporate symbols in everyday situations, this is an important question. Otherwise one could think that such technical aids ought to fulfil all criteria of good cultural symbols. Today 'everyone' has a mobile phone and a laptop as falling prices have made them equally accessible. As important everyday tools it ought to be possible to use them in a proper way as a symbol to mark hierarchy. Instead IKEA has chosen a strange middle-way where different IKEA-countries seem to follow different procedures. Both products were treated the same. First condemnation, since they were considered unsuitable yuppie symbols, and there was a total ban. After that, too late to be practically motivated (mobiles and laptop also help business within IKEA), there was a confused loosening of the ban. First only for managers and then reluctantly further down in the hierarchy. When a higher or lower ranking manager gets a mobile in a company like IKEA this is remarkable. At IKEA, managers are not supposed to stand out but should lead by the power of the good example, which has always been Ingvar's foremost managerial motto. Today a lot of things have changed, but just ten years ago it would have been absolutely unthinkable that managers had the latest technical gadget.

You probably have to go back to the early seventies, when IKEA took its first stumbling steps on the continent, in order to understand the original values of the company. These core values were simply a set of values and norms which had come to permeate the organization during its early development. Such values were for example that we are 'thrifty people from the Swedish region of Småland' (at the time the IKEA management was still mainly made up of people from Småland) and we lead by 'the power of the good example' (the manager sets a good example in an exaggeratedly ascetic manner).

The development of IKEA's corporate culture thus happened 20–30 years ago. From the middle of the eighties up until today not much change has happened in its culture, markers or symbols. Torekull accurately calls Kamprad the high priest in his book *The Story of IKEA – Ingvar Kamprad talks to Bertil Torekull* which he wrote on commission by Ingvar. Because obviously the founder must have been the high priest in the development of the basic values, but he was not alone. To be sure he caught on to currents and recurring themes in the organization, with his keen and sensitive ear.

Certainly he himself would have found a basis for his own leadership when he increasingly emphasized and praised certain behaviour and more or less subtly showed his disapproval of other types of behaviours. The corporate culture was thus formed bit by bit.

A parenthesis, but nonetheless interesting in this context, is how the founder is addressed. Each time I write Kamprad instead of Ingvar I feel a twinge of anxiety. My instinct formed during 20 years in the group tells me: 'Blasphemy! You will end up in disgrace.'

Because nobody at IKEA ever calls Ingvar anything else but Ingvar if he is present. He is not called Kamprad in the third person either. To do so would be unthinkable. In his absence IK or 'the founder' is fine as a the last resort, but then we are talking about senior colleagues who do not work in Älmhult. Everyone who works in his vicinity as well as the majority of IKEA co-workers simply call him Ingvar no matter where in the hierarchy they are. And this in while, as within the Swedish army, usually only surnames are used. But not when it comes to Kamprad – there it is Ingvar that goes.

Apart from Ingvar it is the previous IOS-manager and current manager for southern Europe, Mikael Ohlsson (from 1 September 2009 new chief executive for IKEA), who is the only person I have met who could be compared to a cultural priest. Most IKEA-managers live according to the company culture, but usually in how they act, in the power of the good example, and not in words. Mikael did, and still I assume, does both. He often applied one of the nine theses in conversation and for example talked about the importance of simplicity or about finding an alternative route forward in actual questions. He had the ability, more than Ingvar, to translate bombastic policies to the store floor. To us, co-workers, his reflections were always invigorating. To be able to get going with theses and business ideas in a concrete question such as how to plan the purchase of a low price product made the corporate culture feel both energetic and encouraging. Like a never-ending source for wisdoms about simplicity, thrift or to be able to find ones own way.

One's own responsibility

The personnel concept in the company describes rather well how you are expected to act as an employee at IKEA. Naturally this concept is an exceptionally important part of the corporate culture. In short, it is you yourself as co-worker who is responsible for your own development. And this development must take place on the floor, not at expensive study-centres or lecture-theatres. In reality this means that you yourself is expected to keep an eye on what support you need in order to manage your tasks. Ideally you bring your own list which describes your expectations to the annual development discussion with your manager.

As far as I know and have experienced myself the system works rather well. As a co-worker you realize two things from the beginning. Partly that you expected to take more and greater responsibility as a direct consequence of the rule 'to behave responsibly is a privilege', which is one of the nine theses. Most people enjoy being given more things to do and making decisions, so both employer and employee stand to gain from this arrangement. Partly that you feel that this company is different – and makes it into an important feature to always choose your own route – as a direct consequence of 'the different way', another of the nine theses.

It is exactly in this context that Ingvar's shrewdness becomes really sophisticated. Since by encouraging the company towards finding new, own solutions in everything, everybody who works there also becomes different in the eyes of the world. And if you can only get the wheels to turn so that the company is more successful than others, this creates its own choice of style of dress, habits, attitudes, way of doing business and so pride. Because that is how it is. One is proud to work at IKEA. Maybe not each co-worker feels like that, but definitely everyone with some degree of responsibility, regardless of how little. And that is enough. When I privately or on business met people outside IKEA this fascination about the phenomenon IKEA became something of a fringe benefit. As co-worker I was often able to bask in the glory reflected by the successes of the company.

As a parenthesis I believe this open admiration from the surrounding can corrupt. It cannot be very good for you to continuously walk around feeling a bit better than the poor outsiders. To believe that you know and can do everything a bit better. Because that is how it is. Beginning with Ingvar, through his sons and Anders Dahlvig, to most of the co-workers in the organization, they are all convinced of their superiority in a not totally pleasant way. I know as I was like that myself.

This coin of responsibility and pride obviously has a reverse side. As co-worker you are expected to each year accept a salary which is a lot lower than what you ought to have, given your responsibility and the local market. The IKEA-machinery is founded on this. The strange thing is that most people accept the miserable pay just because the job is inspiring and the open admiration you get from your surrounding becomes the cream of the crop. From IKEA the message is over and over again that they follow agreements and averages in the trade when setting wages. The strange thing is that everyone who leaves the company, almost without exception, moves on to better paid jobs.

A couple of examples. When I worked as Ingvar's and Anders Moberg's assistant I was ultimately responsible for the group's PR and communication, the environmental work in the group, travel services as well as assistant as advisor and project leader for a number of wide-ranging projects and also a link between Ingvar and Anders Moberg. At the time IKEA was also hounded by investigative journalist from several countries precisely because they never had done any environmental work worth the name or cared about their social responsibility as a company. This as well as much more I was expected to manage for a monthly salary of just over thirty-five thousand kroner (£3000/$4000) converted into today's money value. With a family to support and constant overtime and on-call duties around the clock throughout the year when there was a crises.

When Peter Kamprad was to take me on as MD for IKEA GreenTech AB he first wanted to offer a salary 50 – 60 per cent below the trade average with the motivation that I was only to have a handful of co-workers. Notwithstanding that this risk capital company easily was to become market leader with a war chest of half a billion kroner (£45/$70 million).

## Ingvar's crowing cockerels

Ingvar Kamprad has throughout the years consistently carried on with his network of spies. Since he already during the seventies left Sweden because of tax reasons his fifth columnists became a valuable link to the native country and the power hub of IKEA. From what I have understood, and partly experienced, Ingvar has had dozens of spies whom he asks for information. The prospect of spending time with the founder as well as Ingvar's utterly confidence-inspiring and persuasive manner, must have made them all crow like cockerels about their own manager, the IOS manager or about other intricate confidences they had received. Integrity is in short supply amongst IKEA's managers and co-workers, since you are expected to compromise with most things, even your own conscience, in order to further your career.

Ingvar's fine-meshed network of confidants spans a large part of the company's domains across the world. Directly or indirectly. Obviously this web does not only consist of spies without integrity, but many are key people who during many years have had fairly frequent contact with him. As far as I know many of them are concentrated in Älmhult and are to be found mainly amongst the company's reserve of talent in the district.

The purpose of a network of this kind is as smart as it is obvious. In reality the purpose is the same as for the state authorities and the Swedish military intelligence agency or the state authorities in the USA and CIA. Through a well functioning intelligence service degenerate behaviour is discovered – and taken care of – already at an early stage, something which saves enormous resources. You can react a lot earlier on threats of different kinds and you can often completely prevent potential problems by reacting before they have grown.

Even Anders Moberg worked in this way during his time as chief executive. Anders Dahlvig has on the other hand chosen a completely different and rather more formal way. This is probably due to the fact that Dahlvig never has had the contacts needed further up in the value chain, since he has had his entire career in retail, and most things that happen in IKEA do so a good bit further up the value chain. It is indeed the stores and the retail-business which are visible, but since these units are pure selling organizations their bearing on IKEA's development is very limited.

The best contacts are established early on in a career and when you work closely to the subject you spy on. I would imagine that the present chief executive's real reasons to do without pure undercover activities originates from a more principled attitude against gathering information sideways. As far as I have been able to judge he is rather indifferent to gossip and such things.

I was to in a very tangible way learn how sensitive the network of spies is in the autumn of 2008. Peter Kamprad had employed me as managing director for IKEA GreenTech AB, a subsidiary to IKEA with the task of going through the environmental lines of business with a fine-tooth comb looking for interesting products. The finance director at IKEA AB, a central company in Älmhult, was also funding my company. Now and then I received criticism through my chairman of the board and manager Göran Lindahl that some units at the travel administration were not managed correctly. The criticism was unjustified, but naturally irritating. In the end I contacted the finance director and asked him what the hell he was up to. Since amongst managers at IKEA there is an unwritten rule – you always go straight to the one irritating you and never further up in the hierarchy. Always. Two weeks later I was given a serious warning by Ingvar and the board. The warning had carefully been dressed up in certain platitudes and strange expressions, but my treading on the toes of the crown prince Peter Kamprad's spy, the finance director Anders Lundh at IKEA AB, was the central theme. The lesson I learnt was never to tread on the toes of a Kamprad-spy – and that it was time for me to move on.

## The IKEA group language

It is at least twenty years ago, if not more, that IKEA decided to make English its group language. For a long time Swedish had been predominant within IKEA. Many are the Swiss, Germans and Frenchmen who have had to learn Swedish in order to at all be able to work at IKEA.

Knowledge of the English language was until ten years ago very limited. I remember a poor Indian man, highly educated, able and experienced, who was about to start work within the business sphere 1, sofas. We are here talking about the very place where all strategic decisions regarding the sofa range of the company are taken on a global level. The business area that has an annual turnover of more than twenty billion kroner (£1.8/$2.8 billion). The problem was just that the business area was manned almost entirely by people from Älmhult at the time. And amongst them certainly no English was spoken apart from the odd visit by a supplier or during the range week. So the Indian, who had been speaking English since childhood, simply had to learn Swedish in order to survive amongst these men from the depths of Småland (there were almost only men employed). This happened only ten years ago, in 1999.

It is interesting to note how poor knowledge of languages inexorably creates isolation. I can really sympathize with the Indian colleague, as I have experienced the same hell. In my case the place of work was the IKEA-store in Wallau. The fact that my German was poor nobody took into consideration.

'*Hier wirt Deutsch gesprochen!*' (Here we speak German!) the store manager Joachim Stickel roared.

He pointed out that everyone in the room should ignore me as I had no command of the language and was mostly in the way anyhow. A comment that caused some merriness amongst the colleagues. I was after all in the country which has made gloating (*Schadenfreude*) into its own particular form of humour.

The distance to everyone around you is increased proportionally with how badly you master the language of your surrounding. Colleagues talk above you and around you, but seldom or never to you. The dignity and competence you had to start with disappear in step with the evasive looks and backs you meet. Still worse is it when you totally unexpectedly get told off in front of colleagues in the office or hundreds of customers and you cannot reply with anything but spastic stuttering. The only consolation you have is the indifference of your surrounding. This is another but still interesting side of the IKEA-culture, where you have to at all costs be part of the 'in-crowd'.

As a rule of thumb English proficiency is nowhere as bad as amongst IKEA's highest managers. Well, apart from Ingvar's English obviously, as long as nobody can hear him. Bengt Larsson spoke English willingly and loudly, always with emphasis, but few people could understand his variety of the Skåne dialect or English with a Skåne accent. Anders Moberg was well-known for his speeches in poor English, often improvised and always with poor vocabulary beyond comprehension. Instead he replaced his Anglo-Saxon shortcomings with phrases from Småland. Thus expressions such as 'How in sö hell', 'Pick sö low hanging froots' (pick the low hanging fruits) became favourites amongst his co-workers.

The Småland dialect, as it is used within IKEA in Älmhult, is peculiar as it is noticeably more evasive and indirect than normal Swedish.

'Indeed...', 'Well...', 'You don't say...' are replies you are most likely to get when asking an IKEA-co-worker with their roots in Älmhult about something. If you ask for a straight answer, you get: 'Perhaps a bit', 'Possibly...', 'You can never be sure...' or some other evasive and uncommitted reply.

So it is a toned-down language that becomes very vague and unclear to everyone apart from possibly the person talking. During the decades this has become the IKEA-Swedish. Many in managerial position at IKEA, however not everyone, speak in this incomprehensible way. The highest managers never do it. I remember when I moved to the Swedish sales organization after my three years in Germany. After a while when I had learnt to master German I came to appreciate the directness of the language. Once back home again I had great difficulty in understanding my Swedish colleagues and their empty talk.

I believe there is a culturally linked reason for this muddled Swedish and that is the way in which Ingvar takes decisions. Ingvar does not often say a straight no or yes to a suggestion. It is more in his nature to take in arguments for and against from his surrounding, let them mature for a while, force the discussion to go ahead and only after that make a decision. In other words this attitude with dithering and ambivalent language helps the co-workers to keep up with all the twists and turns which can be pretty difficult to follow. There are few things Ingvar detests more than people who are dead certain without having their backs covered. With the IKEA-Swedish you can be both for and against and in the middle without anybody really knowing what you think. When Ingvar in the end makes his mind up you can without risk join his way of thinking.

The most remarkable thing is that this method really works. I would guess that it depends on a couple of things. Firstly, that you calmly and methodically examine all issues before deciding. You also have to involve rather a lot of people in each decision so that the expert knowledge is always at the centre. Last, and perhaps most important, when the decision has been taken it has been done so with consent and so the realization, normally the most difficult part in all organizations, will be carried through speedily and extremely efficiently.

With Anders Dahlvig's entry as president in 1999 at least the Småland dialect disappeared and English achieved a more distinct and obvious role in the group. The IOS-manager Josephine Rydberg-Dumont who Anders shortly afterwards recruited helped a lot to give diversity an important place and to give English a major role within IKEA. Certainly since she as a woman had been hitting her head against the glass ceiling during many years before, but just as important was that she had an international background and was also married to a Frenchman. The aspects of diversity had always been part of her everyday life. This generational change-over definitely became the deathblow for the Småland dialect as the IKEA group's language. Obviously Josephine produced a number of favourite concepts that were readily taken up by her surrounding – often without anybody understanding the meaning. 'Alignment' was one of these concepts. Somewhat unpleasant, as the implicit meaning is that one should shut up and toe the line. 'The product is the solution' was another. You can suck that one dry for any amount of time without ever getting it. The concept was the main theme for a whole internal trade fair in Älmhult. Every retail manager of rank from the whole world came, but nobody understood anything of this stunning communicative approach. On the other hand they took with them home a standing joke that kept them going for months afterwards. The point is that when a communiqué from management becomes too philosophically fluffy and pretentious the recoil runs the risk of becoming difficult to grasp. The year before the retail-weeks at IOS, with every retailer on site, had carried the motto 'Go cubic!' as a heading and topic. Up to 500 visitors left Älmhult that time with an empty gaze. What the message really means still nobody other than a handful initiated around Rydberg-Dumont can understand.

## The power of achievement

'The only thing that matters is achievements', Ingvar usually preaches. This is one of the most important components in the IKEA corporate culture and a key component in the secret behind the success. As we have already established the IKEA co-workers are not just able when discussing problems and making decisions, they get the decisions realized as well. My career and that of many other colleagues was literally based on our capability to make dreams come true. Of course our talent was noticed quickly by our superiors and we were given new, bigger challenges to get our teeth into. If there is one sole talent that can push people forward within IKEA it is possibly this. To the uninitiated the ability to achieve may perhaps sound trivial. I maintain the opposite and would even go as far as saying that the ill that is rife in many companies today is precisely that decisions are left on the drawing-table. They never become reality. Within IKEA it is the capability to realize dreams which separates the wheat from the chaff. There is no better way of making a career than to drive through complex plans regardless of them being stores, suppliers or products that are to be realized. Neither is there a more efficient way to put a break on an otherwise promising career than to fail in this. Colleagues who did not manage to deliver were by Ingvar and his co-workers branded as chatterboxes who did nothing but make empty promises.

The secret of the power of achievement is mainly in the recruitment. Both Ingvar and his novices have been unusually skilful in attracting and promoting energetic men into the company. People who get things done and who can think pretty independently. Furthermore there is a spirit, an obvious expectation that things will get done, and will get done on time. Complicated follow-up systems have never existed and the company survived for a long time without either checklists or manuals. No, the right people and the right expectation is all that is needed. Of course even IKEA may slip at times, but never when it comes to key products or new stores.

## Invisible hierarchy

The most difficult thing for a newcomer in IKEA is to learn, irrespective of how experienced and talented this person might be, who it is that really makes the decisions regarding various issues within IKEA. The IKEA annual cycle which lists all important decisions and decision-forum throughout the year many with a bit of a keen ear and through their own efforts will be able to understand. Also how competitive advantages are created. The very Swedish expression 'freedom and responsibility' does not usually cause any headaches. But how decisions are taken at IKEA and why, remain a mystery for many years for new colleagues. As the entire company is largely governed by informal networks of single people or groups which pursue their policies on grounds that more often than not are unclear. You do not know for certain either who is inside or who is outside a network. Who belongs depends more on factual issues than anything else, which means that the decision structure is as accidental as it is casual.

The occurrence of invisible decision hierarchies go back to IKEA's gradual and organic growth first in Älmhult and afterwards in Helsingborg. Potentates have taken root throughout the years and gathered their faithful around them. Even if people move around, geographically or organizationally, the loyalty remains. If you for example get the idea to change material on a product, networks at IKEA of Sweden AB start rumbling. Few will speak to you, many speak about you and efforts are being made everywhere to undermine your position in the actual issue. Colleagues will perhaps approach you and clearly tell you what Ingvar thinks – an implicit threat that you ought to watch out. Others will not fall short of lies or pure intrigues. For the sake of convenience or because they actually can see something which you cannot.

Naturally enough invisible in- and out-lists occur soon enough in such a fluid organization as this. The spreading of rumours is at times ripe about imminent changes, the whims of the founder, who is about to be sacked and who will be given what job. The rumours are spread by word of mouth or by the memo-screens. (Memo is the ancient e-mail system which IKEA bought second-hand from Volvo in the eighties and still sticks to. Rumour has it that Microsoft Outlook is on its way in.) The random guesses about who is about to get a top job are almost always wrong, whilst those about who will be getting a summons to resign most of the time are correct. I think the latter depends on the fact that IKEA normally lets less successful promoted people stay on rather a long time in order to give them a chance to correct their mistakes. Something which is not always successful. To an onlooker from the outside this prolonged swan song can become pretty unbearable.

The IKEA anecdotes

At IKEA older, more experienced co-workers will always have a moral anecdote or two in stock for their new colleagues. Many are about Ingvar Kamprad as standard-bearer of stinginess and IKEA as its last bastion. Other describe his puritanical and industrious traits. All pay tribute to him as an absolute hero.

The essence of the anecdotes is clear: at IKEA we are all tight-fisted, even Kamprad himself. The implicit meaning is of course that your salary will also be meagre enough, but what does it matter when even Ingvar who is as rich as Croesus himself puts up with this simple life.

Early nineties, IOS AB, Blåsippan, Älmhult

Ingvar comes in through the entrance to the range company's office after a long period of travelling. His arrival is expected. Despite the fact that it is only soon after six o'clock in the morning the office building is seething with activity from hundreds of opportunists who have dragged themselves there despite the early hour. To be in the office before the arrival of Ingvar when visiting was an obvious thing for hundreds of IKEA co-workers.

But the entrance hall looks different. Only metres from the reception desk there is a café which could embellish any designer-conscious office in a large city. Cosy seating areas and tables to stand by in black and clear varnished beech. A coffee corner and subdued lighting.

Ingvar explodes. With resolute steps he passes by the reception, turns immediately to the left and steps brightly red and furious with rage into the office of the managing director without knocking. He literally takes the MD Jan Kjellman by the scruff of his neck and drags him to the new café in the entrance. Once there he gets a proper telling-off in front of co-workers and visitors during several minutes from an enraged Ingvar which will go down in history.

Why? Jan's mistake was that he had replaced the earlier boring and worn coffee-area with IKEA-furniture of a newer sort. Ingvar on the other hand saw that he had made the holy IOS entrance extravagant and that the range company thus had stopped setting the good example for the rest of the IKEA-world.

That this debacle really happened I am certain, since it has been told by eyewitnesses who happen to be colleagues with very high credibility. On the other hand I am unsure that Jan had his MD-office on the ground floor to the left.

Frankfurt am Main airport, early nineties

The old man boards the plane together with hundreds of other passengers. The steady stream of people are coming through the front entrance of the plane and into business class. Suddenly the old man, Ingvar, sees a known face. It is one of his top managers who is having a great time in a flashy seat on the wrong side of the curtain. That is in business class. Ingvar greets him in a friendly manner and carries on towards the back. A promising career is at an end in a comfortable first class seat.

Perhaps the best way for IKEA to consolidate its culture far into the organization is by story-telling. Obviously all the tall stories about Ingvar's various exploits as a stingy but odd nice old man are the most common.

The Gävle store, 1988

At six o'clock in the morning Ingvar and his assistant arrive at the loading platform of the store and begin to plough through the problems that the stockroom workers bring up. Incoming goods are controlled for unnecessary air in the containers (they have to be packed full to the ceiling) and badly packed containers with rattan from Asia are being discussed.

A couple of hours later the store manager finally appears shamefaced with hair ruffled by sleep.

'How nice that you too wanted to come, Calle', Ingvar says with a reserved expression. The inspection of the store could begin. After a demanding day the company arrive at the IKEA Accenten-department, that is glass, china, kitchen utensils and so on, when Ingvar stops and starts to criticize the presentation of the range. At this point Kerstin, departmental head of Accenten has joined the group. She listens to Ingvar's criticism in silence, but cannot stop herself and starts to abruptly interrupt Ingvar's wordy speech. She then continues by answering him back by referring to her own experiences from everyday life. Everyone in the group begins to squirm. Here they have been bowing and scraping all day at Ingvar's lectures. Suddenly Kerstin cuts his statements short referring to her own experiences. Ingvar brightens up and appears to become more energetic. He and Kerstin carry on bickering for a long while. At the end Ingvar does not know how to praise Kerstin enough, who has taught him so much about how to organize range in Accenten and many other things.

The first time I heard this story was in 1992 from my colleague Calle Pettersson who died far too early. Calle was the store manager in this anecdote.

The basement at the inn, Älmhult, late eighties

The group of men looked exhausted, but carried on discussing as animatedly as they could. The only one with a wide awake look and total mental presence was Ingvar. No question seemed too unimportant to him, too irrelevant to discuss together with the Swedish store managers. Earlier in the evening the inn had offered smoked sausages and beer, but the late light supper was conspicuous by its absence notwithstanding that it was past midnight. It seemed that Ingvar neither cared about the time nor about normal human needs. He was sitting in the middle of the store managers talking over his opinions, his worries and his suggestions. Exactly at one thirty in the morning his assistant managed to get the meeting to end. The company got up and started to scatter when Calle, the store manager from Gävle, turns to the assistant and says:

'Now it will be nice to finally get to bed.'

'Yes, you can think yourselves lucky, me and Ingvar start work again in four hours.'

Ingvar gets competition

During Bengt Larsson's time at IKEA, up until 2001, an astounding number of stories about him existed in his own area which towards the end included stores in the whole of Europe except Russia. Larsson did without a doubt have a huge influence on people in his vicinity. But with the anecdotes about Bengt a culture within the culture was created. The stories about Bengt Larsson mostly amounted to showing how great he was by stressing different parts of the culture. Kamprad was in that respect rather more banal as most of the stories were about his stinginess. Obviously the Larsson luminosity must have annoyed Ingvar, who would rather have the attention himself.

The inn, Älmhult, late eighties

'It had happened at a party two months ago. One of the meeting-halls at the youth camp was adorned with long cloths in the yellow/blue colours of the State, sketches were performed, speeches were held, marching through the hall to drumming and eating together.'

The inn lobby in Älmhult was filled with people to the last seat. Everywhere there were people sitting on the floor and on chairs. Some were standing. Everyone was quiet and there was a reverential atmosphere over the whole congregation where they were sitting like well-groomed schoolchildren looking straight ahead. At the front, sitting on a chair, was Bengt Larsson with an open novel in his hands. In his long-winded south Skåne dialect and with sweeping waves of his hands he gave body and drama to the lines in the book 'Kallocain' by Karin Boye.

How I have understood it from people present the entire retail management and members of the executive body had literally been ordered to attend. Because Bengt was an IKEA manager whose decisions were not questioned. That most people were embarrassed for their pretentious boss's actions he did not consider for one moment. Bengt Larsson namely lacked self-criticism, something which made him pompous above the norm and sometimes unbearable.

The fact is that I have never met a more authoritarian manager at IKEA. His authority always bordered on the choleric with frequently recurring outbursts. Twice Bengt summoned me to a face-to-face talk. Both times about trivial details, for example that I had opinions about the temporary accommodation for my family when I moved to England from Sweden, a view which Bengt did not share. Both times I left the meetings shaken, on the verge of tears and crushed by his threats. The man demanded immediate and blind obedience. As store manager in Leeds the day after the opening I witnessed how Larsson gave Anders Dahlvig (who then was MD for IKEA UK) a proper dressing-down during a store inspection that went on for over half a day. The plump man was shouting incessantly and the poor gangly Anders said nothing. And this in a store which at its time was considered the best in Europe. Even by Bengt.

One of the highest managers for IKEA Germany told me about a store opening in Germany just after the turn of the millennium. Bengt was European manager and always made sure to be present at openings. The entire German management as well as Larsson were standing at the entrance doors in order to let the masses in. Many had waited long in the queue and some had even slept outside the store entrance.

The area manager Joachim Stickel, the same Stickel who thought my German was very poor, together with his German store manager handled everything with skill. The crowd rushed forth when something happened. The entry went too slowly in Larsson's eyes. The customers had to wait too long. Bengt literally exploded in blind rage, took the small Stickel with the large grey moustache to one side and told him off in his characteristic incomprehensible Skåne-dialect/English. Stickel did not manage to utter one word but just looked terror-stricken at the large man in the tight-fitting linen suit, something which made Larsson totally lose self-control. He grabbed hold of Joachim with both hands and pushed him up against the wall so that the small German helplessly dangled his legs, at the same time as Larsson was roaring recklessly. In front of co-workers and customers. This is also IKEA-culture, albeit unusual.

Why do I dedicate so much space in this book to this Bengt Larsson? Well, next to Ingvar Kamprad he has been someone who has set the tone and been important to IKEA as a company and to the culture in particular and without him the company would have been considerably weaker today. IKEA has never had a more able retailer than Larsson and there is today nobody who can match him. Since Bengt left really no development in the IKEA store-concept has taken place.

What Larsson succeeded in doing during his time with IKEA is in a small way exceptional. I described earlier how the IKEA showrooms up until the middle of the nineties were similar to the Roman catacombs. The feeling of disorientation and veritable claustrophobia must reasonably have effected the visitors in a negative way. But the defence for these dark labyrinths was that an independent customer who is not influenced by the architecture of the building would buy less if he did not see the entire range. The fact that I myself was part of this school of thought I have to today reluctantly admit.

Being the freethinker that he was Bengt broke with these conventions off his own bat. He asked Tore (assumed name), a son of Älmhult with a rare talent when it came to questions of layout, to create a new solution for the furniture showrooms as well as sales areas. The starting point was that the customer himself should be able to choose whether to go through the entire furniture exhibition or to be able to choose certain marked shortcuts through the store, something which earlier had been unthinkable. IKEA's ambition regarding the customer paths through the store had until now been 'a short possible route for the customer and a long natural one'. When it comes to layout such an ambition will unavoidably be in the formation of a tunnel. Bengt expressed his pioneering idea of new layout in the following way to Tore:

'Wherever the customer is he/she should in the distance be able to see what to expect in the next department and the number of shortcuts have to be increased and marked out.' The customer should thus be able to find their bearing and even find the shortcuts which earlier had not only been unmarked but were cunningly hidden behind walls or similar things.

The furniture exhibition and the market place became brighter, more airy and so more welcoming. The new layout was given the name the 'European layout' and was incorporated into the earlier mentioned Moberg's musts and is since a decade the standard in all IKEA-stores.

Obviously a customer who feels safe in a bright and welcoming furniture exhibition is a better customer than a frustrated and disorientated one in a display in a catacomb. As far as I know no analysis of increased sales generated through the new concept was made, but it must have meant several percentage points in increased sales. Just imagine if Bengt had not had the courage to dismantle the catacombs – times 250 stores which also is considerably more today than ten years ago and with half a billion visitors – every year. Even if the idea may sound banal to an outsider, in this context it is always the simple solution which is the hardest. To just think 'we need a new layout in the stores' in Ingvarian IKEA requires an integrity and courage that few people possess. Furthermore, one would need a brilliance in retail knowledge when it comes to describing what effect the new solution would have on the IKEA customers in his discussion with the designer, topped off by an ability of carrying plans through which is unbeatable. All these things Bengt 'The world's best Karlsson' Larsson had. Previously Kamprad had always had the monopoly on thoughts of this magnitude, but that Larsson was the one who broke the store-code shows that Kamprad is possibly more able as buyer and range-expert than as store manager.

The same day that Larsson was later to vent his spleen on Dahlvig during the visit to my store in Leeds, he and I went through the store that morning. The tour took a bit under an hour and Bengt kept calm and was surprisingly quiet. Once finished he summarized his impressions. The store was on the whole brilliant, he thought, so brilliant that he would encourage my European colleagues to visit Leeds in order to see an inspiring example. But three departments were not up to the mark Bengt thought, amongst them the one with the blinds. A few months later when one could begin to see the contours of normal sales I remembered Bengt's comments. Imagine my surprise when he turned out to be right on all points. This further shows what an unusually brilliant retailer Bengt Larsson is.

About the same time as the 'European layout' became a reality thanks to Bengt and Tore, the former initiated yet another transformation of the layout and function of the stores. The cost of the stores' pick-up points (where goods are delivered to the customer) and self-service areas (where you collect the goods yourself) had begun to increase considerably. Bengt's idea was simply to once again do what had been done at Kungens Kurva thirty years earlier, that is to let the customers into the pick-up points. The brick walls that earlier separated the pick-up points from the self-service areas disappeared in all newly built stores and instead low mobile walls were used. The majority of the goods which the store co-workers earlier had collected for the customers was now moved out to the self-service area for the customers to collect, and the work, meaning the work of collecting a BILLY or a PAX wardrobe, was transferred to the customer.

Despite the fact that the IKEA customers suddenly had to collect their kitchens with hundreds of flat packs on several trolleys or drag along wardrobe frames of 80 kg or more themselves, the change became a success. Customers were satisfied and the costs for IKEA were lowered. But in order to arrive at this point Larsson first had to slay a number of holy cows, all with their roots in a thirty year old mind set. The principal resistance was naturally about the expected reaction from the customers. That they perhaps might refuse to lift heavy items or load too many heavy flat-packs on to the trolleys. That they might injure themselves if enormous wardrobe parts fell on top of them. That they would pick the wrong bits and that complaints would be endless. And also - not least – the doubts of the owner. But all these objections were side-stepped, the change became successful once Ingvar finally gave his consent. I seem to remember that this happened at a meeting on the store floor in Helsingborg 1996.

Rather unsurprisingly Bengt Larsson's strong personality, in combination with his lack of self-criticism, also became the reason for his fall from grace at IKEA. He fell twice and more or less simultaneously. Larsson had during his years made sure that by virtue of being the European Director, he also became a local celebrity in he Helsingborg region. That in itself was not that difficult, as the company was and still is one of the largest private employers in the region. He made sure he was rubbing shoulders with the local authority bigwigs and built up relationships which would further the interests of the company. As it turned out Bengt's personal interests were also safeguarded. At the building-industry-fair H99, which was meant to be a follow-up to H55 (at its time in 1955 epoch-making), Bengt thought that IKEA should clearly be the main sponsor. Kamprad was at the beginning against the idea but gave in. Moberg was as doubtful as Larsson was persistent and as usual Bengt ended up winning the discussion. In the end IKEA put up a large sum of money in order to be in the local authority's good books, with the aim of protecting IKEA's future interests in the region. Shortly after this Bengt Larsson obtained a prime piece of land by the sea in Helsingborg for a song. That this is really what happened I know from some of Bengt's nearest men, who obviously were disappointed, as well as from a Social Democrat municipal councillor who had been present and pushed through both the decisions about the fair and the plot of land and who was furious when the truth was revealed. According to him Larsson had actually maintained that the land was to be used to construct a guest-house for visiting IKEA-managers.

The press obviously destroyed Bengt's character. I know of no other single incident which has damaged the IKEA-culture so badly amongst the co-workers as this. Bengt Larsson is the only senior manager at IKEA that I know of who has done something comparable. I have myself heard Bengt complain about top management being kept on the outside of 'the growth of fortunes' within IKEA by Ingvar. On that point I tend to agree with him even if his opinion does not in any way excuse his action. There have been a good deal of billions that Bengt's brilliance throughout the years have been putting directly into Ingvar's private pockets for which he received nothing but a high-powered title and a very modest salary. Maybe he thought the plot of land by the sea was no more than what he deserved?

At the same period that Bengt got himself a plot of land by the sea Anders Moberg, the chief executive, left to move on to a top position at the American competitor Home Depot. Ingvar dismissed Moberg's termination of contract after twelve years as chief executive by saying 'he is only horny for money' when I bumped into him a few months later. I wonder myself who is hornier, the son of a crofter Moberg or the son of landowner Kamprad?

The strange thing was that Larsson despite his obvious violation was allowed by Ingvar to keep his job. Graft like this must still be the worst crime an IKEA co-worker can commit according to the values of the company? Still Ingvar covers up the story. I was still his assistant at the time and despite passing him several newspaper cuttings and letters about the scandal, which Ingvar was sent from co-workers and the public, he made no comment at all. Something he would always do and especially if something irritated him. I think he simply gave Bengt a second chance, as he realized the enormous value the renegade had to the company. Or perhaps he thought, that by choosing mercy before justice, he would be able to control the unruly Larsson better.

But the calm around Bengt was not to last long. A short while later Larsson was contacted on Ingvar's orders to take on his youngest son Mathias Kamprad as country manager. Larsson flatly refused with the motivation that nobody should be given priority just because of their surname and that the son in question was not capable of doing the job. Everyone I know and respect at IKEA with insight into the situation, would agree with Bengt's analysis. Nobody would dare say the same words. A couple of weeks later Bengt Larsson was given involuntary retirement and was immediately and in perpetuity from all contact with IKEA. But he still has his plot of land by the sea.

Leadership according to IKEA

Shrouded in a mist of cigarette smoke twenty pale IKEA-workers dressed in red were sitting around an enormous grey SIGNATURE table. Near the door an overhead-projector which had served its time shone on the wall with rows and columns of hundreds of numbers.

'*Das mache ich nicht mit! Das geht doch nicht!*' (I will never approve of this! This will never do!)

The small man with a grey moustache was roaring across the room so that our ears became blocked up, whilst hammering on the table with his fists.

'*Das ist eine Sauerei ohne Ende!*' (This is a mess that will never end!)

'*Dieser verdamte Saftladen!*' (This damned lousy place!)

With each new roar his lungs seemed to find more air and the force of the outburst grew.

'*Ich bin hier Chef! Ich bin hier Chef!*' (I am the boss here!)

By this time we were all holding on to the tabletop hoping that the outburst would soon subside. Although we knew that we were not to be that lucky. Instead the small man would soon point out the whipping-boy, who in front of all his colleagues would be castigated verbally.

As it turned out it was me who was at the pillory. And it was to go on and on, I was made to stand there alone at each managerial group meeting for six months. Every week. It was when the catalogue was released in 1990, the most important point in the IKEA-year. I was furniture manager, beginner and had listened to the logistics manager and ordered far too few articles. The angry small man made sure I was never to forget it verbally.

These castigations every week were unbearable. 'What the hell, are you sitting in here being idle when the showroom looks like a complete pigsty, you idiot?' he could uncontrollably shout in the staff canteen.

'*Ich bin Altdeutsch!*' (I am old German!) was his motivation for his leadership.

You will probably think that lunatics like Stickel however must be an exception at IKEA. Of course they are not a majority, but they exist more often than you would think and across the organization. Bengt Larsson, who was part of the group manage-ment, was totally comparable to Stickel when it came to uninhibited and nasty outbursts and when it came to using repressive methods for no other reason than to feel superior to others. During the period I worked in Germany there were at least another four store managers who were the same. The worst one was called Rambo and worked at the Berlin store. It was not just the fact that he always sat on the short side of the conference table so that he 'could keep the useless people in order' during the managerial group meetings, on one occasion he punched an older interior decorator in the mouth when he opposed him.

One thing that is typical of managers like Stickel and his equals is that they lick upwards and kick downwards as their most important strategy to further their careers. And his career was brilliant. Wallau became as I have said the largest store in the world during this period. I turned my initial failure into a sales success, and since my department corresponded to almost half of the store turnover it is easy to see Stickel's motivation behind the tyranny. But the pure personal cost to me and many of my colleagues was of course enormous. After three years in Wallau I was considered a veteran in the managerial group. Almost all other departmental manager colleagues had been sacked or had resigned.

Stickel was soon promoted to regional manager in Germany and later MD for IKEA Australia. Even today as a pensioner he has different commissions for IKEA Germany. All this has happened with the approval of Ingvar, Anders Moberg and Anders Dahlvig. They knew perfectly well what Stickel & Co were up to, but still allowed it to happen. Where amongst the IKEA-culture's bombastic phrases about 'the good company', the IKEA-family and the idea of 'co-workers' this fits in I cannot still understand today. I suppose, that is what we mean by hypocrisy.

# 8

# The winds of change

IKEA is and will remain a great company, I hope. The problem with companies which put up a façade is just that they neither want their actions to be examined nor appreciate discussion about what lies hidden behind the front.

The IKEA that gave my my first job in 1988 was a company with around 30,000 employees and a limited operation outside of Sweden. By comparison, IKEA today has a turnover of 250 billion kroner (£22/$35 billion), almost 150,000 employees, stores from Tokyo in the east to Los Angeles in the west, from Haparanda in the north of Sweden to Perth in Australia and a purchasing network which is global in the proper sense of the word. IKEA has, thanks to its unparalleled success during the last 20 years, been a company in a state of substantial change.

In those days manuals and checklists were unknown concepts. Everything I know about running an IKEA-store, both commercially as well as operationally, how to create advantages at the purchasing stage and the development of range and so on and so forth I have learnt on the floor through practical experience. The power of the company was really in word and meaning where it belonged, that is to say on the shop floor. The retail countries and the single stores had an enormous influence compared to today. So did IOS AB in Älmhult since they set the agenda for the product range. Who purchased the volumes and who made the purchasing forecasts was more wrapped in obscurity. The result was that the co-workers blossomed in the freedom given them but the mistakes, in the shape of serious shortages of best-sellers or just as serious situations of surplus stock, sometimes put a damper on the joy and cost the company enormous sums.

Today IKEA is a far more professional company. But at a high price. In 2007, my last year at the range division IKEA of Sweden AB, a couple of curious and ill-boding things happened in the small village of Småland. IKEA AB had acquired a great deal of control in Älmhult by forming a service division. In other words everything that was not core business was hoovered up on the fringes: switchboard, inns, IT, caretakers and whatever else there was. MD was Tommy Karlman (assumed name), previously a business area manager at the range division and fiercely loyal to Ingvar, but hardly the most talented in the IKEA managerial cadre.

'Only at IKEA can such an unremarkable person as Tommy become business area manager', as a previous IOS-manager put it. By saying that he did not mean to say that the demands on the company's managers are outrageously low generally. Rather that for someone like Tommy Karlman who was born in Älmhult and furthermore, one of Ingvar's favourites, career paths were open even to jobs far above his capacity.

Tommy seized the opportunity in his new manager's job to reorganize the service for the entire IKEA Älmhult. All his co-workers were each given a black jacket with the text 'Service IKEA AB' in white on the back. But the reorganization did not end here. A work life-balance coach was taken on in order to make the co-workers feel better. 'What the hell is a life-balance coach', a colleague wondered?

At the time nobody could answer that question, but within a couple of weeks a couple of thousand colleagues had, thanks to this new recruit and Tommy Karlman, lost the only fringe benefit that the job offered: Wednesday cake. This cake was a simple one of chocolate, but it was always an appreciated break from the usual dry biscuits (biscuits are called Ingvar-cakes in Älmhult). The Wednesday chocolate cake was replaced by unripe apples or equally inedible pears. After this followed a multitude of other silly reforms that did little for the balance between work and leisure or the health of the co-workers at IKEA in Älmhult.

This small example of the life-balance coach and the chocolate cake are symptoms of two maladies which have infected IKEA during the last years and which are threatening to seriously harm the company in the future. One of the maladies is the domination of bureaucrats which bit by bit has emerged during the last 15–20 years. With increasing age Ingvar has naturally been forced to limit his time and effort to fewer areas. A 70-year old cannot run a company of IKEA's size like a 50-year old. Especially if the company keeps on growing at a rapid pace. With age we are all affected by fading memory, a body which cannot cope, a judgement which perhaps at times wavers exactly because the body cannot cope and, often even, by fear of death. Obviously even Ingvar, today 83 years old, is to an increasing extent showing signs of these symptoms and has done so during several years. First unnoticeably to his surrounding. Then at an accelerating rate.

Bureaucratic domination spreads

The IKEA GreenTech's office, Lund, Spring 2008

I had asked my colleague Anna to order computers and a few other items which I thought would be necessary to run the activity of IKEA's risk capital company.

'Call IT-support in Älmhult and check what technical requirements there are.'

And Anna called. Two months on she was still making calls. But we still did not have any computers or accessories. Important in the story is that Anna is a highly educated, extremely talented colleague with a driving force which beats most people. But not the IKEA bureaucrats.

'Everything regarding the computers is fine now, Johan', Anna said one morning. All I needed to do was to go to the home page of IMS (IKEA Indirect Materials & Services) and all would be resolved. Now that is not what happened, as my password for accessing the page did not work. It did not help that the same password was valid for all the other systems that I had access to in the group. After reminders for help I realized that it would take me an afternoon to get access to their portal so that we could order IT-equipment for somewhat under ten thousand kroner (£900/$1400). I did not have an afternoon available in my schedule so I asked my colleagues to order directly from Dell and forget about IMS. It had worked fine until then without the involvement of IMS.

When the Dell computers were being delivered my telephone rang. It was one of the top managers from IMS and he was angry.

'You cannot do this!' he began in furious Skåne dialect.

I tried to explain to him that as long as he was not on the board of GreenTech he really had no right to either give orders or dictate the terms for our activity. That made him even angrier. We actually had to follow his and IMS instructions and what we thought was irrelevant. If I carried on buying directly from Dell he and IMS would immediately block that route. If I continued to be cheeky he would immediately bring it up with Anders Dahlvig.

'You can of course do what feels best for you', I continued, still surprised over the enormous rage that a couple of laptops for a few thousand could provoke.

Then I asked him how much IKEA and thus GreenTech saves by letting the able buyers at IMS do the business. When it comes to juicy discounts I am never difficult to convince. The reply left me dumfounded.

'We do not get discounts. We do this for security reasons.'

'Hang on a minute. You are saying that we have to buy from you without discounts because you view me and my colleagues around IKEA as potential computer thieves?'

'Yes.'

IMS is an excellent example of the new IKEA, where cadres of bureaucrats are charging around producing very little added value for IKEA. Helsingborg IMS has only five hundred co-workers, but the organization stretches over the entire world. Naturally there are parts of IMS which are rather a good business proposition, but the majority are not. When one because of incompetence or lack of interest cannot strike good deals one dedicates ones energy to the foremost raison d'être for a bureaucratic rule: to control your surroundings. Thus IMS has put rigid and compulsory agreements like a wet blanket over the entire company. Furthermore they have taken on the role of police with great zeal, mainly through the home page. Everything from light bulbs to fork-lift trucks must be ordered there and the password is linked to each user's exact powers. But you seldom get a good deal or save money for IKEA. The control becomes an end in itself and not the conclusion with the supplier. Control of what? Even if I through-out the years have seen some colleagues being sacked for irregularities they have all been more sophisticated than that. This is the upside-down world compared to the purchase organization which with great skill and great energy under the leadership of

Sven-Olof Kulldorff conquered entire continents 1995–2005 and created the conditions for today's IKEA. In those days low cost price was the focus not control.

When I started at IKEA Ingvar was 62 years old, had several more years before normal retiring age and was in extremely good shape. During the twenty years that have passed he has naturally enough aged rather a lot. Sure, compared to anybody normal Ingvar is very alert and mentally omnipresent. But his strength is diminishing and his memory is not cooperating as willingly, he says. In the wake of Ingvar's gradual phasing out as the ultimate person formally in charge at IKEA there will inevitably be a power vacuum in the company. Since he is so active as owner and leader of his lifework this vacuum will be enormous. Further on I will show that Ingvar's power within the company so far is still in principle absolute. Within IKEA the slow but certain diminishing commitment from Ingvar has so far been filled by an army of bureaucrats. In many cases such a development may be good for the organization. New blood means new ideas and new perspectives. That is also how it up to a certain point has been within IKEA. But the disadvantages that come with bureaucratic domination in the form of fear, incapacity to take responsibility and uncertainties about who thinks what, spreads with paralysing force throughout the organization. Exactly as everywhere else in nature and life, fear is one of the most devastating things that can befall an individual – or an organization.

'Our objectives require us to constantly practise making decisions and taking responsibility, to constantly overcome our fear of making mistakes. The fear of making mistakes is the root of bureaucracy and the enemy of development. No decision can claim to be the only right one.'

The words are Ingvar's, taken from the cultural bible of IKEA, 'The Testament of a Furniture Dealer'. An example of such fears is the recruitment policy which has been prevalent since the middle of the nineties. Many of those who have been given important jobs within the company since have been rather anonymous people with a dubious capability to deliver great deeds but with a brilliant talent to avoid conflict and questions. In other words a type of person unusually free of friction. A company may possibly be preserved under such a regime, but it will not develop. The capability to think strategically, to see whole pictures and to understand cause and effect is something which is totally lacking in a true bureaucrat. That which has always been the family crest of an IKEA-manager, to be aware of the questions, big as well as small, in every detail is today something very unusual in the company. Few country managers have been store managers and even fewer successful ones. Few store managers have started out as department managers. This is how it is right through the entire company which is why the qualifications, the solid knowledge about the core activities is delegated to completely different people than those that lead IKEA.

That is the reason why everything becomes humdrum and predictable. Unfortunately it is not just co-workers and boards of directors who love the well-known and the simple things. Competitors will sooner or later notice that their rival appears to be stagnant. Another thing which seems to happen when the bureaucrats take over is a transformation of how words are used in the organization. It appears that any trace of 'Let's do it'- and 'nothing ventured, nothing gained'-mentality has been replaced by a careful 'let's wait and see until we know more' or 'if this does not work it could cost a lot'.

The fear of making mistakes is however the most serious. This fear stems partly from the accountant-like character of the bureaucrats, partly from the incapacity to be able to see and understand the company as a whole. Bureaucrats love a comfortable life and to remain within their own competency. Life outside one's own comfort zone is unimaginable, since their world-view is that each and everyone should know their own responsibilities only and to disregard others.

The civil-service-disease is infectious even for able entrepreneurs. I know of brilliant people who used to sail against the wind at IKEA who within a couple of years in all respects have been transformed into grey bureaucrats. Reluctantly I have to point out that it actually has been under Anders Dahlvig, IKEA's present chief executive, that the bureaucracy has evolved. Reluctantly because I have the highest regard for Anders and the knowledge he has. The new era's suffocating bureaucracy is not Anders's idea or mistake, but I must say that he has done far too little in order to restrain the invasion of the bureaucrats.

Anders is by the way without a doubt the best manager I have worked under. There is something about him and his person, his concern, his courage which is completely unique. I was store manager in Leeds when he was MD for Great Britain and I know of nobody amongst the managers within IKEA UK at the time who did not feel deep admiration for him. My first day in the London office he handed me a flimsy hand-written A4-copy of the project plan from the four year old store in Newcastle. After this he made his expectations clear that the store should open eleven months later (a record speed with wide margin), that the budget was extremely tight and that he expected a glittering example of commercial strength. After this it was up to me and my KomIn-colleague Bosse Ahlsén to get to work.

He pointed out a new route to us, gave us confidence that amazed us all and then allowed us to take the limelight when we finally succeeded. My colleague David Hood, today MD for IKEA Australia, one day asked me in a suspicious way in his wonderful Scottish accent after having been told by Anders to construct the enormous Thurrock-store in London.

'What's up with Anders? Why is he so out of the loop regarding Thurrock? Do you think he has an issue with me?'

To a Scot Dahlvig the complete confidence shown him seemed inexplicable, almost offensive. For someone who has never worked operationally in a dynamic retail business it is naturally difficult to understand what kind of enormous leadership talent is required to do this. Expressed plainly, there are millions of things which may go wrong in a large retail-organization – all the time. Naturally leaders in such a situation are forced to do one of two things. Either ignore the problems and withdraw behind the desk or distrust the co-workers and rule directly. Anders chose a third way. He both had confidence in us and made us confidant. He was never far away from the facts and was always open for discussions about people or things, but always at our initiative.

Today Anders is understandably a completely different type of manager. To lead the IKEA-colossus of today demands a different kind of leadership. Without a doubt Anders has tried by opening up and restructuring the recruitment policy. For a period at the beginning of 2000 the company was breathing in fresh air. But Anders's boss Ingvar and his three sons literally take turns in bombarding him with the family view of IKEA's development. A chief executive is in most questions forced to give in to the demands of the owner-family. Of course he could object, but not regarding every issue and not the whole time. Kamprad would just reply by a veto from the INGKA-board. And Anders would lose his job within a few weeks. In this way the diversity within IKEA has collapsed, a developed and competitive e-commerce was stopped and IKEA will soon have lost every courageous entrepreneur leaving the grey bureaucrats to advance.

Ingvar would always maintain that 'an organization without people rowing against the current is doomed'. Sadly enough I cannot think of anybody rowing against the current in IKEA any more. The ones who did exist have either left or conformed.

Only he who sleeps does not sin

It may seem strange that a company which actually has 'the right to make mistakes' written in its rules as number eight of the nine paragraphs in 'The Testament of a Furniture Dealer', consciously chooses to go in the opposite direction. In real life it is nowadays definitely true that he who makes mistakes will be sacked. Earlier we saw how Ingvar, Anders Dahlvig, Torbjörn Lööf and others caused the biggest and most damaging situation of shortage ever in IKEA by being over-careful with the expansion of the production capacity for board-on-frame in Poland in general and for the BESTÅ-range in particular: only because they could not make up their mind about where the factories should be situated.

A mistake that cost IKEA billions in revenue and caused the co-workers in the stores to go through veritable hell trying to explain to irate customers who had received the catalogue where the products were promised. One can of course maintain that IKEA would never be able to maintain the low prices with all the products in stock. This is Ingvar's general rationalization every time a product is not there. Certain shortfalls will always exist. On the other hand it is clearly cheaper for IKEA to explain priorities and their consequences. If that had happened BESTÅ would never have appeared in millions of catalogues. Then no customer would have been wanting BESTÅ since it had not yet been launched.

Perhaps the most telling example of the power of fear is the investment in textiles 4–5 years ago. An able store area manager, Marika Ramping (assumed name), was entrusted with taking over textiles after her maternity leave. Marika had earlier worked wonders in the business area bedrooms, not least with the wardrobe range (her new PAX-series still sells for billions each year), so expectations were high. Marika is also a woman of action. Soon a new textile range was created, orders sent to manufacturers, distributors given contracts and the stores informed. Everybody believed in the new products from Ingvar, to Anders Dahlvig, the IOS-manager Josephine Rydberg-Dumont and not least Hans-Göran Stennert. The last person is not only Ingvar's brother-in-law and Margaretha's brother, he was also chairman at INGKA Holding BV and so technically IKEA's highest manager. He was also admittedly able and a heavyweight in range and purchase questions. Obviously people from the retail countries were moaning a bit about the inconvenience of having to hold sales of masses of existing textiles in order to take in the new stock, but on the whole the IKEA-world rejoiced. Next thing it all went completely wrong.

After the event it is not easy to understand what happened, but I understand the whole thing more or less like this. 'Everybody' believed in the new range and in their overoptimistic zeal they placed orders without considering how much 100,000 Euro-pallets with material in fact is. It is the same in cubic metres, in other words a very large amount. And that was not enough, the unprecedented large orders were also in the main to be flown in to the stores in order to be ready for the publication of the catalogue in August at an insanely high cost. Soon enough unimaginable volumes of materials were flooding IKEA-world by air, train, lorry and ship.

The whole venture crash-landed. Just as the goods wagons with the brown corduroy sofas that I mentioned above and IKEA was again shaken to its core. The problem was that the business area had turned a blind eye when they submitted the orders for the textiles. It was thought that the materials, the cushions and the curtains would at least sell twice, three times more than normal best-selling textiles. Naturally, this extravagant forecast had been signed off by Kamprad, Stennert and Rydberg-Dumont apart from the standard control-procedures existing amongst the matrix departments in purchase and distribution. A gigantic error had been committed and the costs would be monumental. Hundreds of thousands of pallets with textiles were sent out across the IKEA-world, but only a fraction could be sold at normal price. The products were too expensive for what they were. Furthermore the majority of the customers did not like the design.

Now something strange happened. As soon as the trouble hit the fan, every IKEA-manager of any rank disassociated themselves from the debacle, apart from

Marika of course. And furthest away stood Ingvar. I suppose that Marika at this point not even in her wildest dreams could imagine the duplicity that she would soon be exposed to.

Ingvar was the first to demand Ramping's resignation. Much time at the INGKA-meetings was dedicated to Kamprad's ugly and grossly disparaging attacks on her. He was even so aggressive that Josephine Rydberg (or 'the Rydberg bitch' as Ingvar preferred calling her) in the end could no longer resist and started to turn on Ramping. It was not long before Marika Ramping was sacked by Josephine Rydberg-Dumont in the most abject manner I have ever come across during my 20 years with the company. Without warning she was called to a meeting with the personnel manager in the Activity house which is situated just next to Blåsippan. 'You have been sacked', were the words from the personnel manager which ended Marika's 20-year long career.

So what mistake did Marika make? Well, she was reckless and had difficulties cooperating with the retail countries for a start. On the other hand her assignment, the new range, was entirely anchored with the IKEA top management. Furthermore, the initiative had been warmly applauded. I mean that her mistakes were two. Partly Marika is the wrong sex in Ingvar Kamprad's eyes. Of course there are other women in managerial positions at IKEA, but none so strong and courageous as Marika. Strong and courageous women or co-workers are something that Kamprad does not want. Her second error was that her initiative turned out to not to work. In the IKEA of today errors are extremely unwelcome.

The cowardice that characterized the entire management when Marika was on her way to being dismissed is symptomatic of today's IKEA. Ingvar is in many ways a far more risk-hating person today than ten years ago. The same wretchedness, the same cowardice, goes for all the others involved. Only one person, Hans-Göran Stennert, a man with plenty of integrity, publicly said that he also shared the blame, since he as member of the board in the business area textile and also chairman in INGKA shared in the decisions leading up the debacle. We will return to Hans-Göran further on in the book.

Female managers thin on the ground

At the end of the nineties Ingvar Kamprad and Anders Moberg had gathered all IKEA's most eminent managers: store managers, business area managers, finance managers and chief of staff in the group, for a tour amongst the stores and the factories in Poland. One peculiar afternoon we were taken by bus to one of the Stalin towers in Warsaw. The enormous Gotham-like building rose proudly next to its sister tower and formed the highest points in the silhouette of the town. The towers had been a gift to the Polish people from the Soviet dictator Joseph Stalin after the war. The

Poles actually had to pay for and build them themselves, but Stalin was hardly someone with whom you discussed such things.

However, three hundred IKEA-colleagues took the lifts up to an insufferably small and stuffy assembly hall in order to enjoy yet another painful speech in Swenglish by Anders. After a couple of agonizing hours we took the lifts down again and gathered on the steps to the entrance outside the building for a photograph.

The girls must stand at the front because then it looks as if we have plenty of female managers', Moberg instructed us half-jokingly.

That is exactly how bad things are regarding equality at IKEA to this day. With the exception of those 2–3 years when Dahlvig as new chief executive managed to break the trend, things are back to the same situation of male domination as before.

But those with a good memory will say, they often write about female managers in the press. Certainly IKEA Germany, IKEA Swedish Sales AB and, as we have seen earlier, the Canadian sales company are all run by managing directors who are women. There are also a handful of female business area managers. Nonetheless, that is it. Because Petra Hesser in Germany, Jeanette Söderberg in Sweden and Kerry Molinaro in Canada all stand at the front of the steps of IKEA, to use Moberg's joke. The jobs that these three have must absolutely not be underestimated, but they have on the whole no real influence over the IKEA corporation since these managers are in charge of pure retail companies. This means that they can really only decide over operational matters such as the running of the stores. They cannot make any decisions regarding the commercial areas or purchasing or range. When Dahlvig was MD for England he used to exploit the retail companies' limited influence as an argument to keep down the salaries of the store managers (as well as his own one assumes).

Looking at the group's leadership it has today only one woman, Pernille Lopez, and she is now the human resources director for IKEA, and no longer manager for North America as before. If the MD of a retail company has little influence over the corporation, then a resources director also has limited power apart from over certain administrative areas. Until recently the group leadership had two female managers, both with an enormous influence: that is to say Pernille when she was North American manager and Josephine Rydberg-Dumont who was director of IOS. But the stronger and more powerful the women around Kamprad are, the more stubborn his resistance seems to become.

A relevant question in this context is why neither Kerry, Petra or Jeanette are on the group's management team? The first two do definitely have the required qualifications after many years of various high positions, superior to the majority of the male colleagues on the team today.

From the outside it looks as if IKEA is a fantastic equal-opportunities company. You just can't judge a company, however, by the people it presents to the media.

The bureaucracy

The best way for a civil servant – someone who rules the world from behind his desk – to cope with fear is to create a future that is entirely predictable. At the time of the new frontiers (1975–1985) when IKEA built stores at a great pace in Germany, France, Holland and Belgium you needed a different type of leadership. The expansion required leaders who could act independently and had the courage to solve themselves each problem that came their way. Those were the days when procedures did not exist at IKEA. There were few rules, follow-ups, drafts or other steering tools. At its best there were reference guide-lines to steer with or against, but more often than not it was common sense that a store manager or country manager had to rely on. Göran Ydstrand, at present MD for Hemtex, Janne Kjellman, at present manager for IKEA's restaurants and Anders Moberg, previous chief executive for IKEA, nowadays amongst other things chairman of the board and a considerable stakeholder in Clas Ohlson, are the role models for this generation of managers.

Today's IKEA-leaders are recruited on different grounds. Because they have good values and are good leaders many would say. This is certainly true. The problem is just that for each marketing manager or human resources manager who is turned into the MD for an IKEA-country, thousands of retail experts in the stores get someone who has not got a clue about the retail business. And the newly appointed MD has hardly got the thousands of hours behind him which is required in order to understand what being a tradesman really means in practice. The feeling for how customers behave and their needs, for products and prices and the commercial interplay on the floor of a store which you can really only learn through daily work. Otherwise one will at best obtain knowledge without proper feeling for the job and you will always lack a deep understanding of your core activity.

At the same time, as the group's subsidiary managers are mainly civil servants without the experience of the core activity, top managers are also recruited in the same way. Anders Dahlvig is a controller, and as soon as he starts to feel uncertain about something he relies on the skill set of his original role. Sure Anders is a brilliant leader in many ways, but only within areas he knows. As we have seen it is in the development of products and the purchasing activity where the competitive edge of IKEA is created. Sadly these are also some of Dahlvig's blind spots, which he reluctantly concerns himself with and appears to have a lack of deeper knowledge.

Amongst the group's directors there is today really just one real retailer, Mikael Ohlsson. IOS-manager Torbjörn Lööf was to begin with a builder, a while later purchasing manager for Italy, then a business area manager with doubtful successes. His predecessor, Josephine Rydberg-Dumont, had if possible even more limited experience of the core activity in IKEA's most important company, since she was in communication and PR from the start.

There is in this context another, even worse example. Hans Göran Stennert, Ingvar's brother-in-law but also an acclaimed product developer and business area manager as well as the originator of the bathroom-range PERISKOP, was substituted by Göran Grosskopf, professor of law, as chairman at IKEA's highest board INGKA Holding BV.

In an IKEA where chairman of the board, group management as well as managers of subsidiaries consist of fairly unremarkable civil servants it is obvious that insecurity, fear of the unknown is spreading. At the same time the founder of the company is being marginalized bit by bit due to the realities of aging. The remedy against fear in a company led by civil servants is usually bureaucracy. The company is gradually formalized, made complicated and controlled. The standardization, that everything must happen in a certain way in each single question, will quickly replace the wide variety of ways of thinking of the co-workers. Of course this is not called standardization but best practice, quantification, measurableness, target control or perhaps even benchmarking. The result is irrespective of term always the same: stop thinking, stop being creative and do as you are told.

In the case of IKEA it is possibly the total lack of new development that is most striking over the past years. Earlier it was Ingvar who pressed on with the progress of the company. The move of large purchasing capacity to the east. The creation of IKEA's industrial division Swedwood which today produces around 10 per cent of IKEA's volumes. Despite all the doubts, the decision to make a massive investment to integrate in a production area which was not part of IKEA's core competence, was at the time a very courageous and far-reaching decision, as well as a decision Ingvar made against the objections from his close advisers. The entry into Russia – both on the retail as well as on the production side. The list is long. For 7–8 years, however, no new development of strategic importance in the company has happened. Just look at the curious decision to open a store in Tokyo instead of thirty in China. IKEA's most important place for purchasing is China! From having been the first in China IKEA has long since been overtaken by several competitors. With a large number of stores in China IKEA would have had the advantage of the local purchasing of volumes which were needed in order to nip the problems in the bud. Advantages which could have spread to the rest of the IKEA-world with more advantageous Chinese cost prices. That is not what happened. The decision about the Chinese expansion came far too late and was far too defensive.

This is also why IKEA's cost-prices are going up and there are no plans for how to lower them. Once the price increases have become commercially unsustainable, the frustration will start. Because if there is no solution coming from Ingvar there does not seem to be one from anywhere else either.

But it is not just the stifling of development that has damaged IKEA as the 'controllers' have been placed at the spear-point of the company. Another typical symptom of bureaucracy is mistrust. A mistrust of everything that deviates from the norm. Mistrust of people who are too colourful and independent and who have, the absolute biggest threat against the bureaucratic rule, integrity. All this is met with mistrust.

The most important advocate of this development has of course been Ingvar Kamprad himself. None of the above could have happened without his expressed approval. There are few people who are as acutely aware of themselves and their surrounding as Kamprad. I myself brought up the question of the growing rule of bureaucracy with him a few years ago when we met over a cup of coffee an early morning at his round table on the first floor at Blåsippan in Älmhult. His reaction was to without a word or expression make a comment but instead subtly change the subject. The most plausible explanation for the spreading of bureaucracy within IKEA, something Ingvar has always maintained to be a sworn enemy of, is that it has made the company easier to manage and predictable for him. In other words the earlier vigorous development of the company has been turned down to a zero position in order to suit the age of the founder. Perhaps this may seem understandable, apart from for two things. A slower development pace within IKEA will sooner or later work as an open invitation for more aggressive competitors. The IKEA we know today was developed during the eighties and the nineties. That is when massive forward strides were made. For sure IKEA opens a lot of stores every year now as well, but they are all down to the smallest nuts and bolts the same. That is not development in the right sense of the word but activity. And it is development and not activity which creates competitive advantages.

The other reason is that the company by this conduct is doomed to a life of bureaucratic passivity. Once Ingvar Kamprad exits the company, he will be replaced by his sons plus a handful of greying potentates. Not one in this group has the ability or the experience – nor the insight into the problem – to be able to remove the inertia from IKEA and to let it see creative light again.

Friends of order will perhaps object that IKEA despite the bureaucratic rule, despite Ingvar's aging and the new generation of managers is doing very well as a company. This objection is correct, but my point is that the entire foundation of the IKEA-machinery and culture which created these large profits was laid down 20–30 years ago. No company can in the long run remain successful if the mechanism and the culture behind the company is not being continuously developed.

Mistrust of the unknown

IKEA has always had a curiosity that was linked to suspiciousness of the unknown.

The entire store expansion in Western Europe during the seventies and eighties took a comparatively long time and Swedes were for a long time dominant in the running of these activities. In important IKEA-countries, like for example Great Britain and Italy, this is still the case. In the same way, Asians are only given below the line positions in IKEA's activities in Asia. Why?

The behaviour can only be described in one word. Mistrust. We are here talking about a suspiciousness which has its origins in the province of Småland and which has accompanied Kamprad from the beginning of IKEA. People who do not come from around Älmhult are all a bit suspect in his eyes. I am not exaggerating here. His first manager of the group was a crofter's son from Dihult outside Älmhult who was originally recruited because he was good at handball. His second manager of the group is I admit from the province of Skåne just like some of Ingvar's closest men.

My opinion about Ingvar's view of the world is that basically only blood-relationships can be trusted. Then, only real Swedes are OK and amongst them really only people from Småland and Älmhult and its hinterland. There are no able and dependable women in the world, you can only count on men. That is how I would interpret what I have seen and heard during my twenty years.

When a successor to me was to be appointed to the job of Ingvar's assistant, a woman was mentioned for the first time. She failed because 'Ingvar would never accept a woman', according to the men in the top positions at IKEA and closest to the founder. Exactly as it is when it comes to appointments for key positions in the group, Ingvar has always got the last word when it comes to choosing candidates, though the suggestions come from other people. A while ago his assistant was to be changed again. The name of an extremely able co-worker, Swedish but of Asian origin, came up. A stronger background and a more capable person at the right age did not exist anywhere within the group. Still the name quickly disappeared with the rider that Ingvar would function better together with a different candidate. This despite the fact that this person in no way could measure up to the first mentioned candidate when it came to qualifications, experience and talent. Of course I am not able to say exactly why he failed. But I know one thing: the final candidate is a tall, blond and blue-eyed Swedish protestant heterosexual man exactly like me. And just like all other assistants before us.

I wish to point out one thing. Anders Dahlvig is the first, and if the worst comes to the worst, the last chief executive in IKEA who has pursued questions of diversity. He recruited Josephine Rydberg-Dumont as IOS manager, de facto number two in the group and so had the approval of Ingvar to do so. Anders made Pernille Lopez North American manager. Thus IKEA had appointed two women in the group management. Josephine who is a dynamic and a driving force cast most of the prejudices away from Blåsippan, purchase and distribution. Key people from the entire IKEA were given training in diversity by an American-Israeli colleague Sari Brody, who was a doctor having graduated in the subject and captivated us with her enormous charisma. This was an IKEA where sex, ethnic origin, colour of skin, religion or sexual orientation no longer would be an obstacle for progress, but an asset. Where diversity, and not allocation of quotas, was a prerequisite when an executive body was being put together.

Somehow around that time this extremely welcome development came to a halt. When Anders was to write the policy documentation on diversity for the board Ingvar forced through considerably more restrictive wording. Exactly where Ingvar stands in this question I do not know, but I can guess. Because I can sense his mistrust of the unknown. And I know what his sons Jonas and Peter Kamprad think about the subject.

'I don't even mind employing a blackie', as Peter Kamprad in a rallying tone of voice says as soon as the question arises. Then he savours the phrase a couple of times more, sometimes jokingly, sometimes quite seriously. I have witnessed this on at least three occasions. I don't think I have ever been so shocked over a managerial statement. And then he adds:

'Just wait until we have got rid of Anders Dahlvig, then we will let such rubbish out. Maybe there is not that much wrong with blacks, but still.'

I am here talking about the man who is to take over IKEA after his father: the crown prince of IKEA and its future dictator. His brother Jonas laughs a bit hesitantly with his brother. Ironically Jonas's wife is from Iran. Thousands of IKEA co-workers have a different ethnic origin, skin colour and religion or sexual orientation from the Kamprad brothers. One may well wonder how they will find themselves in the IKEA of the brothers.

When I as MD for IKEA GreenTech AB was about to employ a deputy MD, the matter had to first be discussed in what was then the project group, later on the board. I argued that I wanted to employ a woman since the line of business was excessively dominated by men and that I saw diversity as an asset in the long run. The woman in question should be familiar with commerce and at least a technology graduate. I had not even finished my statement before I was attacked by all present in the room. The worst were Peter Kamprad and the future chairman of the board Göran Lindahl. (Strictly legally speaking this was not a board meeting nor was Lindahl the chairman since the company had not yet been formed.)

'No, you are to employ on the basis of qualifications', Lindahl shouted and shook his finger at me dark red in the face.

'So you are saying that there are no qualified female deputies?' I said.

This was the first time I felt the rug move under me and that my days at IKEA were numbered. To employ on the basis of qualifications only and to disregard diversity is, in my view, one of the worst arguments in the organization of Swedish industry since it means that the glass ceiling is not just going to become permanent, but will be reinforced. In any way, I appointed a woman and once she had started everyone was happy.

Another way of describing the winds of change is to look at the latest managerial appointments. When the former purchasing manager at IKEA, Sven-Olof 'Kulan'

Kulldorff from Skåne, left he was replaced by Göran Stark. Kulldorff's success as purchasing manager had been almost immeasurable. Kamprad and Moberg had handpicked the former country manager for Holland for this important post. An engineer, Kulldorff was wise enough to spend his first six months learning. He simply travelled to each purchasing office and learnt his new area of responsibility from the bottom up. It did not take long for him to become successful since his ear for the needs of the organization was excellent, as well as their loyalty to him. No purchasing manager, neither before or after him, has had such significance both for his co-workers as for the competitive edge of IKEA.

Göran Stark on the other hand was less talented and he lacked academic background. He was given the job because he wanted it and there seemed nobody else in the IKEA company of 100,000 employees. He was, in addition, from Älmhult. My point is not that Göran has failed in his job, which he has not. He has launched some important solutions in logistics which have increased the supply of the company's most important ranges in the stores. The problem is that he has not succeeded in it. Cost prices at IKEA have steadily gone up during Göran's time at the helm. Not one single idea of strategic importance regarding purchase has been hatched during these years. The interior parts of China remain inaccessible. To produce and export products from Russia has remained elusive, regardless of however many billions were invested. The result is thus that the internal price trend is steadily going in the wrong direction. For each krona IKEA loses in that area, the competitors move their positions forward.

The serious mistake I think is how he recruits. Supply Chain, which is what his area of responsibility is called within the company, is on the whole free from women on important posts. In the executive group for Supply Chain, that is the most important operative body for purchase and logistics in the entire IKEA, there are only men. Most of these men again come from tiny Älmhult. Three of them were in the same class at school, and any further formal education than that they have not, as far as I know.

Even if we move up one level in the IKEA hierarchy the picture is the same. Purchases and logistics functions fall under IKEA of Sweden AB and therefore the IOS-manager. At the time of Josephine Rydberg-Dumont, who was manager for the IOS executive group, an IKEA body which well reflected the multiplicity in the organization and society both regarding ethnic origin, sexual orientation, religion, sex etc. Therefore decisions could be made on the basis of a vast experience and from various points of views on life. For example 80 per cent of IKEA's customers are women. In Josephine's executive group half were at any rate women.

English was the language used in IOS during Josephine's time. Torbjörn Lööf, was her successor and a son of Älmhult with a college background with a 2-year long technical education. His English is a moderate to reasonable Swenglish. His executive group only has one woman, who comes from Älmhult, and one person who is not Swedish. In order to facilitate decision-making a special strategic group has been set up of which this non-Swede is excluded, so that all issues can be resolved in Småland dialect rather than Swedish. The person who differs the most in the strategic constellation does so through his origin – he comes from Tranås in northern Småland. The group we are talking about has to solve all big IKEA-decisions regarding purchasing, logistics and range, the world over. Questions about the size of the range, which products should be part of it, how much they can cost to buy in and how much they can cost when being sold in the store regardless of where. In other words also IKEA's profits are defined by this group. More than half a million co-workers at IKEA and the suppliers the world over are directly dependant on their competence for their survival.

Perhaps a colleague from another IKEA-country with a somewhat different angle of approach and background might be able to contribute – at least a little – to the decision process. It would seem that simplicity has been elevated to group strategy in what is IKEA's most powerful company, IKEA of Sweden AB. Decisions tend not to improve if everybody around the table is like-minded. On the contrary it is exactly as a result of this type of self-important and insider clubs that companies much larger than IKEA have foundered by discarding the idea of diversification – to enrich and improve decisions in the company. Somewhere it seems that a widening group of people within IKEA than Kamprad and his sons have elevated plainness to a group strategy.

When fear begins to rule

The fact that IKEA has gone backwards and not forwards in fundamental questions like diversification has only one explanation. Ingvar does not want it. At the turn of the millennium, when he allowed Anders Dahlvig to convince him to appoint Josephine Rydberg-Dumont, this probably happened because Dahlvig was new as chief executive. A long list of fundamental issues had already been looked into and discussed and Ingvar thought it unwise to put forward yet another veto.

Since then the founder has aged further. He worries about his own death, and about what will happen to his beloved IKEA. His sons have been allowed into the company in preparation for the inevitable. But apart from that it has been Ingvar's fears which have governed IKEA the last few years. Fears that make him look backwards rather than forwards. Towards old supply markets rather than new ones. Towards old faithful old servants rather than new employees. Towards long since discarded products instead of new ones.

When it was time for Ingvar to leave as chief executive of IKEA this viewpoint was already manifesting itself. When, twelve years ago, Anders Moberg was appointed Kamprad's successor as chief executive, at just at 35 years of age, it was considered a very courageous decision by the world around him. Many of the people among his old group felt ignored. Certainly Moberg was from Älmhult, but he had also made great strides as manager of IKEA France. Anders Dahlvig who succeeded Moberg was not at all as controversial. Dahlvig was well over forty and had made contributions within IKEA Great Britain. But above all he was a previous assistant to Ingvar and was considered someone the founder listened to like nobody else. The more logical choice, objectively speaking, would however have been Mikael Ohlsson who at this time was MD of IKEA of Sweden AB. The man who had taken the most important IKEA-company to heights nobody had imagined possible. Because of his background in retail, Mikael knew both retail and purchase, logistics and range better than Dahlvig, who was mainly a controller with a few years in retail companies. But the reason Ohlsson was not picked despite his more much more impressive CV was because he had his own views on things which he was happy to discuss and which he defended with brilliance whenever needed. As he has taken over from 1 September 2009 as chief executive can only be explained by the fact that for the last ten years he has done his penance. The question is how such a talented man full of integrity like Ohlsson will be able to keep on the straight and narrow and only run errands for the family Kamprad no matter how crazy.

Julie Desrosiers was without a doubt the logical successor to Josephine Rydberg-Dumont as MD for IOS AB, and was Josephine's as well as Dahlvig's clear choice put before Ingvar. With her brilliant flair Julie made IKEA-history when she developed IKEA bedroom both regarding design, functionality and low price. With the exception of IKEA kitchens, which was developed by Hans-Åke Persson and Pelle Karlsson, nobody has managed the feat of building up such a large business area in the way that she did and create a long-term sale and profit increase. Julie had it all: the qualifications, the force in her leadership, the respect from colleagues, the knowledge and that particular intuition for range development which is usually called brilliance. And she was keen. Still Ingvar discarded her in favour of a weaker and more insecure candidate, Torbjörn Lööf. Why? The answer you will now know. She is a woman and she is French-Canadian. He is a man and born in Älmhult. The fact that her Swedish is actually better than his does not mean much in this context.

# 9

# The world's richest man...

The importance of telling the truth

During the eighties, in the middle of the champagne-bubbling yuppie-frenzy, a man with the remarkable name Reefat el Sayed suddenly appeared as the new rising star and darling of Swedish industry. He was a bit of a strange bird among the other managerial swans in the pond since he not only dealt with unusual activities (raw material for the manufacture of penicillin) but was also an Egyptian. He soon became so important that he was even given an audience with the king of industry himself, P.G. Gyllenhammar. Soon, however, all came to a grinding halt.

There is no doubt that el Sayed was and is an able businessman. But he made one mistake. He lied. He invented a doctorate he did not have. And the fall from grace from the golden corridors among Gyllenhammar and Gyll (Sören Gyll was besides Gyllenhammar one of the foremost Swedish business executives in the eighties) to prison, since he was condemned in court, obviously was enormous.

The case of Reefat el Sayed was often referred to by my professors at Uppsala University where I studied. They maintained with certainty that it was the lie which caused the fall of el Sayed. Now, with hindsight, I think that the sentence of Reefat was deeply unfair. Certainly the man lied, but who believes for a moment that the rest of the Swedish executives are paragons of virtue when it comes to honesty and ethics? Unfortunately he was probably convicted by another ultra-Swedish virtue, envy, and without a doubt because he was Egyptian. Regardless of this, however, the example Reefat shows the importance of keeping to the truth.

How are things with Ingvar Kamprad in this respect? Why does he time and time again insist that he is not one of the world's richest men?

When the lie becomes truth

'It is a lie and pure fiction. IKEA has for a long time been owned by a foundation and neither me nor the family get a krona', Ingvar told *di.se* a little while back.

He has made the same announcement over and over again for as long as I can remember: to his 150,000 co-workers; to suppliers and to the Swedish public as well as elsewhere; to hundreds of millions of people.

When Kamprad and his lawyer Hans Skallin created the extremely complex weave of companies and foundations that became the Kamprad-sphere, that is the IKEA-group (consisting of the stores, all the warehouses, purchase and IKEA of Sweden AB) and Inter-IKEA (which is the proprietor of the IKEA brand), the aim was partly to achieve better control over the company and the flow of money and partly to control the division of his legacy after his death. But last and most important was to prevent public control of the company. The front which prevented any form of control from the outside was created mainly through an extremely complex company- and foundation-structure which is considered in a world league of its own. Behind this structure the balance of power between the different parts of the company could be controlled and ruled. No part was to become too powerful. Power struggles and tensions were incorporated in the structural design of the IKEA-stronghold, and Ingvar could completely without interference from the outside in peace and quiet rule over the division of his legacy. In other words which of the sons should have the ultimate power after his death. Who was to become dictator over the empire. Last but not least the high walls allowed for the flow of money to be entirely controlled by Ingvar. Furthermore he was in the position to without embarrassing questions avoid paying tax in all the countries where his empire operates by moving money between wholesale companies, trading and import companies, retail companies and sophisticated Dutch foundation structures.

Once more two of Kamprad's basic driving forces appear. The anxiety that someone will touch what is his and his alone or even understand it makes him create a company structure so complex that nobody from the outside will ever grasp it, and even less get insight into it. The mistrust of everyone around him which compels him to take on the role of dictator and to create a structure of command where he and only he decides.

That Ingvar Kamprad with great skill can rule over the range development without even getting involved in operational activity we have already seen. When it comes to questions of crucial importance for IKEA and the Kamprad-sphere Ingvar decides in the main everything, just as he decides everything on the IKEA-board INGKA Holding BV without even being a regular member, since his age forbids his membership under Dutch law. Therefore the people nearest to him are reduced to agents at best, and mere puppets at worst. Nobody can get the better of Ingvar and nobody would even consider opposing him, that is if you want to hold on to your job. Do so and you will be dismissed immediately, as in the case when IKEA heavyweight Bengt Larsson did not want Kamprad's son Mathias as a country manager. Ingvar interfered with the help of his chief executive Anders Dahlvig and Larsson disappeared. As an irony of fate Bengt had been the mentor of Anders for many years and the two of them were very close.

It works like this

The complex company structure can somewhat simplified and in short be described as follows[3]. The Kamprad-sphere consists in the main of two large groups which are independent of each other, Inter-IKEA (Inter) respectively the IKEA-group (IKEA). The reason I have not so far hardly mentioned Inter is that the view amongst many important barons in the IKEA-group is that Inter-IKEA is in reality a purely financial structure in order for Ingvar to make money and to avoid tax. The only big asset of Inter is the IKEA brand. In order to be able to use the brand in the stores IKEA must pay an annual fee of three per cent of turnover to Inter. It does not sound much, but corresponded to around 7,5 billion kroner (£.6/$1 billion) in the last financial year. The manuals and other items that Inter produces bring in, in comparison, very little in added value.

In the same way that INGKA Holding is the parent company of IKEA, Inter has a parent company in Inter-IKEA Holding. This company is registered in Luxembourg. This Luxembourg registered company is in turn owned by an identically named company in the Netherlands Antilles, which is owned and run by a trust company in Curacao. And in the Caribbean the law is such that the persons behind a trust (an Anglo-Saxon foundation structure) can remain anonymous. It is not only the profits from Inter that are being moved via the Caribbean to obscure accounts with shady owners. The foundations and other trust companies behind IKEA do exactly the same thing.

In 2004 the two groups had according to the accounts €11.9 billion (£10/$15 billion) in assets. IKEA paid Inter €800m during the year, most of it as franchise fees. In total the two groups together paid €19 million in tax (£15/$25 million), or 3.4 per cent, on a combined profit of €553 million (£460/$722 million).

Both foundations and trusts are based on a deed, a broadly written document about the aim and rules of the foundation, meaning general regulations and the type of activity. You may in the rules of this deed or foundation put anything you like as long as it does not break the law. And now we get to the beauty of it all. Ingvar and Hans Skallin must quickly have realized that as founder he could both eat his cake and have it. If Kamprad according to the deeds can appoint and dismiss each member of the board in these key foundations and trusts he maintains, in fact, the absolute power over his money. From the outside it obviously looks as if the foundations and the trusts are run by a handful of lawyers, but they are no more than puppets just like the members of the IKEA board because Ingvar and Skallin formulated the rules of the foundation in such a way that he has the absolute power in all respects. And since he controls the foundation and the foundation board he also controls every Euro which flows into the foundation. For Ingvar it is even better. He has indicated where the money is to end up after the stopover in Curacao. Is there anything that stops them from landing in a Kamprad controlled account in Switzerland within practical walking distance from his villa and the taxman?

In total Ingvar Kamprad should be in control of what corresponds to several hundred billion Swedish kroner through these foundations, if you add up the profits of IKEA over the past 10–20 years. Then add a modest yearly growth of at least 10 per cent over time and the sums become gigantic. As Kamprad has the ultimate power in this whole fine-meshed web, and he can decide and control what happens with each penny, then the money is his in every legal and moral meaning.

## A pattern

The foundation structure through which Ingvar filters the IKEA profits is a result of the same approach, an impenetrable front. Therefore Ingvar can safely lie to journalists and say that he and his family do not get anything. Both *realtid.se* and the *Economist* have made determined attempts to find out the truth, but stumble on the complexity and the sophisticated obfuscations that the foundations donate money to charities. Certainly, they give money to charity, but we are here talking about a very small percentage of the total capital.

I would argue that the reason for Ingvar not to admit to the real state of affairs is that his – and IKEA's – image would crack. If Kamprad suddenly were to confess to being one of the richest men in the world, that he himself has at his disposal all the money which IKEA's 150,000 co-workers and 1,400 suppliers toil night and day to create, he would become unacceptable to both the co-workers and the suppliers.

For each one-thousand-krona note (excluding vat: £90/$140) that you spend at IKEA the first 30 kroner (£28/$47) go into his pocket through Inter-IKEA. The gross profit, 10 per cent of the turnover, i.e. 100 kroner (£9/$14), also go to him. Part of it is reinvested in the group, which leaves more or less one hundred to Ingvar and his three sons for each one-thousand note. As an IKEA supplier you will of course ask yourself why you are forced to offer such low prices only in order to fatten up the wallets of the world's richest man and his sons, each one already good for several billion.

But is it not the basic idea of capitalism that an entrepreneur should be able to make plenty of money from an idea he has materialized? Absolutely. The problem arises when you deny making such money at all. When you maintain that IKEA does not fatten anybody else's wallet except those of the many people it serves. That Ingvar and his IKEA are opposed to limited companies and 'jungle capitalists' (the words of Ingvar) and that they are driven by a social mission 'which only wants to help the many people to have furniture at affordable prices' and nothing else. If you assume that role for three decades and press your co-workers with low wages and the suppliers with low prices, you yourself will have to play your self-assumed role of ascetic almost-pauper very well indeed. If you are exposed with your bank accounts full to the rim, as having lied about many things and bluffed about the rest regarding your company the boomerang is likely to come back even harder.

In other words there is a lot at stake for Kamprad around this issue. A totally justified question is why he is lying, another is what does he need this enormous amount of money for? The sums are so vast that they correspond or exceed the GDP of many countries.

The world's richest man

Four things convince me that Ingvar is the world's richest man (or among the richest).

First of all the money from IKEA's profits during all these years must have gone somewhere. Of course 20-25 stores plus land will cost a bit in investment funds each year but hardly hundreds of billions of kroner.

Secondly you erect walls around your company for a reason and not for entertainment. Ingvar has plenty of reasons: he wants to control the flow of money down to the last cent, he wants to pay as little tax as possible and he wants to keep his finances a secret. Otherwise it would be difficult to urge co-workers and suppliers to exercise extreme thrift. He also wants to control the approaching division of the estate he'll leave behind to the last detail.

Furthermore it would have been very easy for him to say to journalists who have persistently questioned him throughout the years: 'No I do not control IKEA or the company's money. That is done by a foundation led by N.N.' Ingvar has never responded like this but instead reacted with poorly disguised irritation.

The fourth reason is that the Ingvar I know, ridden by suspicion and worry about his IKEA, would not freely give away a penny of IKEA's money. His entire lifework is about him being in control. Ingvar is a dictator. Dictating over what? The assets of IKEA obviously, the money. The fruits of his lifework.

So what is he going to do with all this money? He looks as well as lives like a pauper. To most of us money is apart from the everyday security it gives us a way of marking our social position. We do so by choice of car and clothes and where we go on holiday. Neighbours and colleagues will maybe be impressed and we have achieved our goal, to stress that we are slightly more significant than the others. With Ingvar it is the complete opposite. The more money he has got the more he has instead moved down the social scale. In 1965 a tailor-made tweed suit was his choice. Today it is trousers and shirts so simple that they are normally found at Tesco's. He has no need whatsoever to mark his position with social markers. On the other hand he has a burning desire to increase and protect his growing fortune. But in secret.

When I worked at IKEA this was not something which either I or my colleagues worried about. To do so would almost have been considered a blasphemy. Once I was on the outside I started to reflect on my impressions from all those years. On how Ingvar actually functions. On his motives. Obviously I can not be absolutely certain that my arguments are 100 per cent correct. For that I would need certified copies of the deeds that govern each trust and foundation in the Kamprad-sphere and these are the most secret of secrets in this world. But there are some circumstances which anyway convince me that I am on the right track. When the Nazi flare-up happened Kamprad reacted within days and put all his cards on the table. Why does he not do that in this matter? If he has nothing to hide it should not be more complicated than publishing an outline to the foundation deeds and the flow of money? And also to name the people who in reality decide over the money, if it is not he who does so. But of course he could not do so if 'Ingvar Kamprad' is the name on every document.

Worse still

There is one further circumstance which has a bearing on the image of IKEA's founder. His philosophy throughout the years has been that IKEA should at all costs avoid paying taxes. Thus he and his company pay a minimum of taxes. Contrary to most of us, Ingvar does not for reasons unknown to anybody but himself, want to see that taxes go to the general wellbeing of people. Health service, schools and social care are, so to speak, not part of the Kamprad vocabulary.

The same basic principle applies very much when it comes to the structure of the group. The reason for having Dutch foundations as owners behind the companies is precisely to avoid the taxman. Dutch law is extremely favourable when it comes to consolidating enormous flow of money into not-for-profit foundations, so called 'stichtings', and then transfer it to a trust completely protected from openness in the Netherlands Antilles for further forwarding to an untraceable place. In principal, this entire activity thus becomes exempt from taxation. Since the sums are hidden from view Ingvar Kamprad does not pay much tax in Switzerland either, he claims that he has no income there to the authorities.

Naturally IKEA's subsidiary companies the world over pay local tax, but the entire value chain is constructed in such a way that even they pay minimal sums. Through a structure of trading and import companies (HanIm), wholesalers and others, goods are bought and sold internally in the company in order to minimize taxes. The same applies to the charitable foundations which, it is true, donate money to charities, but only symbolic sums. Of course you may call this normal harmless Småland greed. Then Ingvar will appear in a somewhat more favourable light. I would rather call it an incomprehensible cynicism from the world's richest man. An avarice so limitless that it is difficult to understand for any ordinary taxpayer.

Reefat and Ingvar

At the beginning of this chapter, I wrote that I thought that Reefat el Sayed had been unnecessarily harshly judged in Sweden. Who really cares about a doctorate? He had found a smart business model which you obviously did not need a doctor's hat to think of. With Ingvar it is the complete opposite. He lies because of pure and simple greed.

On a personal level it upsets me and I am deeply disappointed that the man who I have admired so has been telling me and my colleagues lies by the dozen time and time again. At IKEA you are given a lot of responsibility at an early stage, but you have to work extremely hard in order to get anywhere. As an employee of IKEA you feel that you are part of something bigger and better than any quoted company. IKEA is the company with a social mission. IKEA is the good company which is honest and which pays its way. If the founder of the company has deceived an entire world of co-workers and suppliers this is extremely serious. Business is about trust, and if the company is not honest the trust would tumble down like a house of cards were the truth ever to get out.

# 10

## An ethical company?

IKEA is today known across the world as a good company, as a multinational company with a business conscience wanting to do good. Maybe it fails at times, but IKEA always corrects its errors and mistakes. This is the media image of IKEA today. Completely in unison with the strategy that two co-workers and I drew up at the end of the nineties: everything that IKEA does must stand up to scrutiny. With this in sight, the boundaries were obvious to everyone who had to make decisions in concrete questions. You did not need to look further than yourself and your nearest and dearest in order to understand where the boundaries were.

The TV-team from SVT that produced 'The workshop of Father Christmas – IKEA's backyard' had travelled all over the world and caught IKEA literally speaking with their pants down. Children who were working in terrible conditions in order to produce IKEA-products. Workers who were subjected to life-threatening work situations. As always excuses and smoke screens were rolled out. They were not children, and if they were children they did not work, and if they were working it was the fault of the manufacturer and not IKEA's. Kamprad and his closest in INGKA Holding BV were saying, between you me and the gatepost it was better for the kids to work and toil than ending up in prostitution. Slowly we and Anders Moberg, who was the then chief executive, managed to change the attitude in the company. And the problems with attitude were mainly amongst the management of the company. The environmental manager I recruited to IKEA in 1996, besides being the first ever environmental manager ever, did a fantastic job regarding these issues. She travelled around and pleaded that 'everything IKEA does must stand up to scrutiny' amongst the purchasing managers in Asia. It was like talking to deaf ears. In the end, with the fieriness of a terrier, she managed to get these highly-paid cynics to leave IKEA. And with that a new era could begin.

The first order Anders Dahlvig as new chief executive gave, firmly reminded by the same environmental manager, was that IKEA should close its purchasing office in the military dictatorship of Burma. The reason that he had to order rather than ask for this was that IKEA of Sweden AB's then MD, Mikael Ohlsson, initially refused as did the purchasing manager Sven-Olof Kulldorff. None of the two saw a problem with doing business with an oppressive regime like the one in Burma. They were partly right. At least they followed the current IKEA policy, only to close down businesses in a country that the UN called upon to boycott.

Burma was not on that list. The example however shows what a generous conscience IKEA had and has in these matters.

After this several initiatives were taken. The environmental staff under Susanne Bergstrand was strengthened. A vast ethical sanitation programme was initiated with the motto 'the I-way' (the IKEA Way). All managers within purchasing were trained in social and environmental questions. Controllers were recruited who made notified and non notified visits in the factories around the world. A handful of foresters were employed in order to trace forest raw material and to make sure that no raw material came from the last intact natural forests of the world.

Marianne Barner, previously a business area manager, took over as information manager for IKEA responsible for social questions in the company. During the next 8–9 years she made an enormous contribution in the issue of child labour. She managed to get Ingvar to invest some hundred million kroner (£9/$14 million) into a cooperation with the UN-agency for children, UNICEF. The money made IKEA individually the largest donor in the organization and today IKEA is responsible for 40 per cent of UNICEF's investments in India. With this money and the aim UNICEF and Marianne developed together the funds that are used for rebuilding local villages providing schools and care. They found a realistic model where the economy of an individual family would become self-supporting at the same time as the children were being offered adequate schooling.

Did I not maintain earlier that philanthropy is not Ingvar's most favourite thing? Well, he can cope even less well with bad press. In 2007/2008 Kamprad was forced to speak up after media for a long time had branded him a miser. Then the media genius Ingvar releases the eye-catching news that IKEA is about to donate 420 million kroner (£38/$59 million) to children in India. A body of united journalists nods approval and Ingvar has gone from public miser to public benefactor of historic proportions. The rumble of media disapproval dies down.

The truth is that this UNICEF-project had been ongoing for many years, but had been set aside. hidden from the media, for an occasion such as this on. Furthermore the decision about the money had been taken long before the discussions about Ingvar's greed started. So no new money had been committed. Also the 420 million Swedish kroner were budgeted over a period of five years, meaning 84 million (£7/$10 million) each year. By adding up the allowance over the years it is obvious that the end sum becomes enormous in the eyes of a journalist and a newspaper reader. By comparison this corresponds to a Swede with an average income donating 77 kroner (£7/$11) a year to charity.

Naturally you may think that all this amounts to a lot of money, but if you add this sum to the annual profits of the group of 20 billion kroner (£1.8/$2.8 billion) or to Ingvar's wealth or the value of IKEA, the discrepancy is grotesque. One should remember that IKEA has been selling handmade rugs from India since the sixties and has made billions from them.

The Greenpeace partnership

It was a few years before these developments in the environmental field took off that Ingvar asked me to read his memo about how the devastation of forests in the world would accelerate in pace with the population explosion.

Twelve years later, I realize, as I am writing this book, that his oncerns have become reality. Ingvar is as always someone who looked ahead. But this memo was obviously not only written with a pang of philanthropy. The real aim was to secure the forest raw material for IKEA in the future and at the same time to do some good along the way, that is to say to liaise ourselves with Greenpeace. So far so good. However when I was about to announce the result of our many meetings and discussions with INGKA Holding BV, I suddenly encountered a surprising scepticism from the members of the board. Ingvar had shown doubts on a couple of occasions weeks before and had clearly shared his thoughts with the members of the board. Thus he had in a subtle way arranged what was to happen. At this time, people like H&M's Stefan Persson and the industrialist and director of Volvo Håkan Frisinger were members of the board. Especially the last-mentioned had together with Jan Ekman (previously Handelsbanken) difficulties in seeing the point of putting money into the conservation of forests. The decision was to reduce the agreed sum by 30 per cent, something which created both disappointment and problems for Greenpeace and their partners. This was in a year when the IKEA-group made a net profit of just under 10 billion kroner (£.9/$1.4 billion). We are here talking about a sum of around .3 per cent of the net profit for the year from something which in fact was the most important raw material for IKEA. Not to speak of the importance of forests for mankind as a whole.

Borneo

Parallel with the Greenpeace-initiative and the media crises which began hitting the group during these years Ingvar gave me another task. Inspired by his memo on world forests he thought that I should contact a man with a doctorate at the university of forestry in Umeå, Jan Falck. It appeared that Falck and Ingvar had exchanged letters about the forest and the idea was that Falck should introduce me to a commendable forest project somewhere in the world. A project which was worth supporting financially according to Ingvar.

Sabah, a province that is part of Malaysia, is situated on the northern tip of Borneo. At the beginning of the eighties, its forest was significantly cleared and today only slivers of the impenetrable jungle on Borneo remain. Jan Falck's idea was that he would lead a project together with scientists from a state-owned forestry company with the aim of restoring the cleared rain forest. This was the same forestry company that had cleared most of the Sabah forest. It was so to speak like getting into bed with the devil. That is at least how Greenpeace saw it when I told them about our plans. We met in yet another smoky beer café in Amsterdam, but this time Christoph Thies had gathered a dozen colleagues. I chose to relate the idea as matter-of-factly as I could. Tell it as it is, has always been my motto. Many of the 'tree huggers' were clawing the ceiling with anger before they were pacified by the group's pragmatists.

Falck's plan was not to cut down more rain forest, but to replant it. It may sound rather odd, because a rain forest is very different from a Swedish forest of spruce. The belt of pine-forest which spreads across the globe's northern parts, of which the Swedish spruce and pine forests are part, is compared to Borneo's forest jungles extremely poor in variety of species. Whilst a Swedish forest has may be a handful of species if left untouched by the forestry industry, these jungles have hundreds, perhaps thousands of species. Nobody knows exactly. And that is obviously also the case when it comes to the rest of the flora and fauna.

But there is yet another crucial difference. The forests in our part of the world are ruled by the so-called 'big fire' every 200 to 300 years. All vegetative and the animal life is prepared for this. Out of the ashes grows a budding vegetation which will soon be followed by the returning animals. In the rain forest on the other hand each fire is unnatural and really only happens as a result of man's action. This means that jungle flora and the fauna are extremely sensitive to human intervention. The most important species of trees drop their seeds within 70–80 metres from where they stand and the seeds remain there. Furthermore trees only flower at long intervals. Not even in a thousand years would a cleared area rejuvenate itself, though a brushwood forest called macaranga will immediately grow and will preclude the return of the original plant and animal life.

Because of these reasons IKEA decided to support Jan's initiative. As far as I can remember the agreement ran for ten years and IKEA was to pay a total sum which more or less corresponded to how much Global Forest Watch received. A certain and poorly accessible area chosen by Falck and the forestry company of 14,000 hectares was rented by IKEA for a long period, in order to protect the replanted forest from being cut during a few generations. A number of simple greenhouses were built to house the nurseries. Local workers were hired in part to collect seeds in the surrounding forests, and in part plant out the small plants they had managed to grow. Replanting is not as simple in the rain forest as on a logged Swedish forest where one spruce plant after the next is planted in rows. Part of the research was to find models for replanting, so that the fully grown forest should end up looking as natural as possible. Over a hundred different tree species were planted as well as many different fruit trees that were crucial for a large part of the animals.

With fifteen years hindsight this initiative, despite all, seems commendable. I am saying despite all, because the road has not been easy. To start with the idea was for funds to be collected from the customers at IKEA stores around the world. IKEA would double each krona collected. We tried it in Sweden under the motto 'Sow a seed', but failed since both store colleagues as well as customers appeared to be genuinely uninterested.

Furthermore, only a year after having signed the agreement with the forestry company on Sabah, the Malayan government made an agreement with the Chinese that enormous areas of reasonably well preserved rain forest in this part of Sabah should be cut down for the production of paper. They simply wanted the small IKEA plot to be swallowed up by the Chinese project and to move our licence (right of tenancy) to a different part of the island. Of course we in IKEA were deeply divided. Some wanted to shut down completely in order to avoid potential interest from the media, something typical of IKEA's fear of the media 'imagine if the papers get hold of this...' Others wanted to stay, 'hold on' in IKEA-language and to build an island of hope in the middle of the great devastation. Hans-Göran Stennert, chairman of the board at INGKA Holding, led these delicate discussions. The decision was to stay and simply deal with the media as and when the situation arose.

Today IKEA's 14,000 hectares plot is thanks to the work and the extensive research going on there a world leader when it comes to restoring cut-down rain forest. IKEA has extended its commitment and work is continuing in the forest with undiminished fervour. The project is today seen internally as a big success and also receives praise from the environmentalists.

Another part of IKEA's commitment was to protect an extinct volcano, Maliau Basin, whose enormous crater had a completely unique area of highland rain forest. My wife, Falck and I visited the crater in connection with the ceremony to sign the agreement at the end of the nineties. According to representatives of the forestry company we were among the first Europeans there. A helicopter dropped us off by a shed in the middle of the forest. The beauty and the diversity were completely overwhelming. The following day the same helicopter picked us up and we flew towards the west and Kota Kinabalu, the capital of Sabah. As soon as we had reached the edge of the dazzling greenery, it changed into an infernal grey devastation. During the two hour long flight we saw a landscape which had been scorched down to the soil. No sign of life, not a tree stump as far as the eye could see in any direction. Only greyish smoking ash. The proud rain forest with all its diversity which only a few years earlier had covered these enormous areas had been cut down. The macaranga brushwood forest had only needed a couple of weeks in order to take over the entire landscape. As opposed to rain forest, macaranga brushwood burns like tinder. I will never forget the ageing Swedish forester who cried in his sorrow when we flew over the lunar landscape.

## A Teflon strategy

*Newsweek* covered IKEA recently. Among other matters, its cooperation with Greenpeace was discussed. IKEA was being called Teflon IKEA, where a good company policy is synonymous with teflon. A company that socially as well as environmentally strives to do the right thing in every direction, and which actively does so, makes it difficult for the media to criticise it even if mistakes were to be revealed in their activities. Just as food does not stick to a teflon pan, so no criticism sticks to IKEA.

Implicitly this also means that the company can use its teflon shield in order to hide damaging activities which are considered necessary for business. Consequently that investment in environmental projects and relations with the environmental movement happens intentionally in order to hide other activities.

The question is, then, how is this done? The obvious policy would be to spread awareness about these matters throughout the organization and never put one's foot in it. IKEA does not do that. The group has instead liaised itself with a handful of so called NGOs (Nongovernmental Organizations), that is organizations which are independent of governments. Whether they are independent of commercial interests is however a different matter. IKEA gives contributions to organizations like UNICEF and the WWF. With Greenpeace the cooperation is more idealistic, but there is also the odd project sponsored as in the case of Global Forest Watch. In the case of WWF the contributions are made in such a way that some of the workers in the organization in theory can be described as being completely paid for by IKEA. Here then the practical and financial ties are so strong that the WWF can almost be considered to be linked to IKEA. What I mean is that the organization regarding these issues cannot afford to seriously criticise IKEA if there was to be case of serious exposure of environmental pollution.

The teflon strategy of IKEA is as well planned as it is cynical. What they do is to establish connections with some renowned NGO, begin a more or less intimate cooperation and constantly tempt them with money. The only thing IKEA demands in exchange is the support of the organization if they were to be exposed in some awkward situation. One example of this is when Assignment Scrutiny a while back described the felling of intact natural forest in Karelia by the Swedish paper manufacturer Stora Enso, one of the biggest environmental villains in our part of the world. IKEA on the other hand, despite having completely new and vast forest concessions in the same area were once again portrayed as the good guys. Why? Well, before IKEA, or rather the group's industrial division Swedwood, established factories and started to fell they had more or less walked through the area with Greenpeace. And then the industrialists together with the environmentalists found a solution which both satisfied the demands of commercial forestry as well as the environment.

All this sounds rather good, but there is a drawback. In the case of forest felling you establish a link to Greenpeace and the media with the good example in Karelia. You could say that they reinforce the teflon shield. At the same time IKEA behaves, which I will come to soon, completely unscrupulously in their felling on the other side of the world far away from the scrutiny of the media and the environmental organizations. You could express this in two ways. The strategy of IKEA is to link the organizations firmly to them with money and to win their loyalty. In other words, as in the case of WWF, the company simply takes the organizations financially hostage. Expressed in a different way the concept of teflon should be understood as an alibi. If anything unpleasant were to happen the organizations will come to IKEA's rescue. I have several times described IKEA's and Ingvar's partiality as fronts to hide behind. Teflon is a typical such front. And in order to further reinforce this front IKEA funds a number of unknown projects.

In the same way as with the earlier mentioned Indian project IKEA, together with the WWF, also sponsors a development project in India, but this one is about cotton cultivation. The cultivation of this crop is one of the most water intensive and dirtiest activities you can be engaged in. Cotton grows best in dry areas, but will with plenty of irrigation, fertilizers and pest control grow best. The result is devastating for the surrounding as people are deprived of their most important resource. In this project, simple but functioning water management methods have been found for these poor farmers which at the same time allows for good cotton harvests.

Obviously it is a good thing that IKEA has the resources and the inclination to carry out similar projects. But the company has from the start had its own agenda. Just like NGOs that are forced to act as alibi the day when IKEA is caught out, the company can point at all these commendable initiatives in order to show how righteous they are. It is precisely and always because of this reason that IKEA never boasts about or even mentions the funding of environmental or social projects. They keep that for a rainy day. In so many words, the internal strategy of the company regarding this is that 'IKEA never talks about its environmental work or its charitable donations to people on the outside'.

The reality behind IKEA's teflon

In connection with this I wish to point out that IKEA in my view seldom commits environmental crimes deliberately. Most often they simply put their head in the sand and keep their eyes shut to the effects of their actions. I am not saying that the giant group is acting in good faith, it is not as they have enormous resources in the form of all the experts of the world at their disposal. Instead they choose to carry on regardless while they ponder what to do about the eventual mess. They can probably think for a decade or more whilst the environmental crimes continue. At times they are perhaps not crimes in a legal sense but an ethical extremely doubtful treatment of the world around us. I would argue this is just as bad.

It was not until after I had left IKEA that these patterns began to appear. When you are in the middle of your work, you do not mistrust your colleagues. As an IKEA co-worker you are proud of the environmental work the company does. I know the range-, the purchasing- and logistics-departments at IKEA of Sweden AB inside and out, both from a commercial as well as an environmental point of view. During my years as business area manager my colleagues and I made deals far away in the most northern parts of China, in Eastern Europe and in Russia. The problems you encounter on location and how they can and should be solved are familiar to me. Furthermore, I have worked on other projects which, from an environmental viewpoint, are sensitive business areas such as sofas and textiles.

When it comes to the highly topical environmental scandal where living birds were stripped of feathers (in itself not illegal but nonetheless, an ethically indefensible activity) IKEA was in all probability not telling the whole truth. IKEA's textile people and buyers are misstating the facts if they say that they did not know where the down in the company's down pillows and down quilts came from. It is obvious that they knew that the down was picked from a living bird in a completely brutal way. Let me explain why. A down pillow consists of 1 per cent thin cover and 99 per cent down. The cover is not something which drives the price of the item since cotton is much cheaper than down. Thus it is the down which drives the price and it is exactly around this raw material that negotiations centre. In price-negotiations with the supplier and also certainly with his subcontractor, the price and the quality of the down is discussed. Like any other raw material down is divided into different quality categories. The cheapest category, when it comes to goose down, is down plucked from a living animal since these poor wretches can be harvested in this way several times before being slaughtered. This means that IKEA always buys (or has bought) down plucked from a living animal in order to safeguard the low price. Even if it were the case that IKEA did not know where exactly the down came from – they blame it on the Chinese supplier who has thousands of subcontractors – they cannot plead ignorance. All these excuses that they cannot control all the subcontractors were also used at the end of the nineties when SVT and other media again and again caught IKEA out using child labour. It was always the fault of the subcontractors, and since there were so many of them one could not reasonably expect that IKEA would be able to keep track of all of them. They did not suspect child labour was involved. The fact remains that a company with the enormous resources IKEA has, can choose any supplier they want, where they want them. For example, one who has only got a handful of subcontractors which are possible to control and where production is done in an ethical way. What makes IKEA choose suppliers like the Chinese down factory with thousands of subcontractors depends only on one thing, the low price. And the knowledge by IKEA's purchase management that it is always possible to blame someone else. However IKEA does not only know exactly what is being bought in, they will have made at least one visit to the supplier at the establishment for animal torture each year. Anything else would be breach of duty in a company honouring itself on having complete control over the entire value chain and all the price driving factors. IKEA has in this way had down pillows and down quilts manufactured for at least thirty years. Is there anybody who believes the empty excuses from the company that they did not know, that it was the fault of the subcontractors and that IKEA cannot control them since they are so many?

Marianne Barner, IKEA's information manager, who was given the delicate task of meeting the press after the investigation into the matter on Swedish TV certainly did not know the whole truth. Neither probably did the chief executive Anders Dahlvig: he knows too little of what is going on in the IOS-sphere to do so. But the business area did without a doubt know, as did purchasing. In total at least one hundred co-workers knew the full truth. All of them chose to lie. Or at least not to tell the truth, the whole truth.

Once this messy activity had been found out the company did not opt for the most obvious alternative, like for example another story, by recalling and returning the down products. No, they were instead as usual sold at full price.

Natural resources

IKEA is not a gangster company, but it does actually do plenty of good things regarding the environment and social issues. On the other hand a company does not have to be criminal in order to buy and sell a tremendous amount of wood from intact natural forests. Just deeply unethical. The primary villains are those who fell the forests and transport the timber. The secondary villains are those who process and sell it on. But blame must be distributed equally in this value chain, and IKEA is not acting in good faith when it comes to intact natural forest timber. On the contrary.

The forest that will never grow back

The image of illegal forest-felling that public has is that it is only shady companies that take part in this destructive activity. The facts are alarming enough. Within one generation the world will no longer have any intact natural forest left, that is areas that have never been affected by human activity or illegal felling. With the forest, its unique flora and fauna will also disappear forever. The same applies to the very important ability these forests have to transform carbon monoxide into oxygen. Our grandchildren will one day look us in the eye and say: 'Why did you do it when you actually did not have to?'

There is no need to fell forests on a large scale and without control. In the tropics many cultivable species of trees that can be used as timber and fuel will grow to full height in 10–20 years. In Sweden the growth of forests, for example, is a lot higher than the felling that takes place. It is not because of necessity that the devastation happens, but because of greed. Illegal timber is simply much cheaper than, for example, Swedish forest.

If we turn and look at the enormous bulk of mainland China, we'll see that, since the Cultural Revolution, the Chinese have ruined their forest resources and without consideration for the environment. Landslides and other natural disasters with enormous human and ecologic suffering have been the result as the forests no longer bind the masses of earth in the river valleys. Chinese forest-felling was in many ways delegated to the local government authorities or single companies or a combination of both. In the wake of these natural disasters caused by man, China has imposed strict legislation which partly aims at replanting forest in critical areas and on a large scale, partly stipulates that felling should be done at a rate which more or less corresponded to growth. Last but not least the forest raw material should first of all benefit the Chinese people themselves and not multi-nationals like IKEA with their unquenchable thirst for cheap timber.

In 2002, when I was business area manager, the situation was the reverse. We established cooperation with a number of companies and regional authorities in the area around Harbin in northern China. The idea was that we were only to buy the part of the twiggy top of a birch trunk that had never been used before, saw it into suitable bits which we then glued together. The result was very attractive table tops with the pale iridescent pearly shimmer and a twiggy pattern. The large NORDEN-table with room for up to ten people we were able to sell for 1,995 kroner (£190 / $300) at a profit thanks to this cheap Chinese birch.

We had foresters at IKEA who during the summer months rode into the felling areas to make sure that the right trees were felled. That was the only way of reaching the areas since the distances were long and there were no roads at all. During the winter months the amount we had ordered was felled and transported down to the sawmills on to the frozen river beds.

Today the situation is different. Given that there is a huge shortage of available and cheap forest timber in China, the logical decision by IKEA's purchasing team would be to abandon the country when it comes to this raw material. Ostensibly there is none left to buy. That this is not happening is because the purchasing team with Göran Stark at the helm are not anywhere near their quota of wood supplies from Russia. And Russia and its neighbouring countries have the only areas in the world that can supply IKEA with really cheap forest raw material outside China. But our Russian neighbour is a big source of uncertainty from IKEA's point of view. Billions of kroner have and are being pumped into the country but little comes back in return. Throughout the years such great efforts have been made in Russia which such little effect that the failure there has become accepted within IKEA nowadays – in Russia you cannot make any money, only lose it.

And so the decision to remain in China has had devastating consequences which IKEA won't talk about. At least not openly. Because there is still plenty of forest raw material to be had in China from a different source. While the Chinese are extremely enterprising businessmen, their business ethics have never been particularly strong. They cross the border with Siberia and fell illegally in one of the world's intact natural forests most in need of protection. One of the keenest buyers of wood from the China border with Siberia is IKEA. A highly placed forester in the group some time ago expressed his concern that the possibility to trace the origin of the forest raw material in China was only 10–20 per cent. Companies have a duty to trace their forest raw material back to where it originates from. Everything below 80–90 per cent origin-traced and controlled forest raw material is considered very poor. 80–90 per cent of the forest raw material that IKEA buys in China may thus either have been illegally logged from the last forest areas in the country or from the intact Siberian natural forests. That is also the explanation I had from the forester at IKEA.

It is perfectly possible to trace the origin of forest timber in China. It just costs a lot of money, which means that ethically and 100 per cent legal timber is much more expensive than what can be bought today without this expense. In order to source legal timber IKEA would need to employ a large number of foresters or to engage independent forestry consultants. Furthermore you then need to choose suppliers of forest raw material who are so close to the place of origin that controls can be done on the spot in the forest. In China timber is seldom bought directly. Everything is handled by a long chain of middlemen. Normally it is the supplier of furniture himself who gets the timber from his subcontractors, who in turn have bought it from a subcontractor, who in turn has bought it from a middleman and so on. If IKEA were to be caught out by an investigative team of journalists they would exclaim: 'Our supplier of furniture has so many subcontractors for timber so it is impossible for us to control the origin of every log.' In other words, they would use the same excuses as with the goose down scandal, and child labour in India ten years ago.

When one considers the efficiency of China's legal apparatus, the conclusion seems inescapable that Siberia is a far more attractive place to commit environmental crimes. So a reasonable assumption is that a large quantity, or may be ever nearly all, of the 'Chinese' timber comes in fact illegally from Russia's Taiga region. China accounts for about 25 per cent of IKEA's total purchases of 75 billion kroner (£8/$11 billion). And 60 per cent of these purchases consist of wood in a variety of forms. In other words IKEA is likely buying illegally logged timber from Siberia up to a value of 15 billion kroner (£1.4/$2.2 billion). Converted back into forest this means that IKEA buys up to 5 million trees from intact natural forests. Every year. That would easily make the company the 'World's Largest Retailer of Virgin Forests', a title which ten years ago was given to Home Depot by the environmental movement in USA. It forced the DIY-chain quickly to reverse and completely revise their environmental policy.

It is at this point that IKEA's Teflon strategy becomes apparent. As IKEA has such close ties the WWF, both regarding cooperation as well as financially, it is highly unlikely that the organization dares to be critical of the hand that feeds it. It is the same for Greenpeace, who certainly are more independent but who have for many years been part of the supporters of the group. In some ways perhaps Greenpeace has dug themselves into a deeper hole after all. It is now more than ten years ago that I started IKEA's cooperation with them, a cooperation which over time has deepened. Greenpeace has had deforestation and climate-change high on its agenda for years. It must have know or at least suspected that their large and important partner IKEA is involved with serious environmental crimes in China and Siberia. Yet their silence remains complete and, thus, China's environmental crimes have become an efficient strategy for survival for both parties. Greenpeace is perhaps blameless in financial terms, since they do not accept funds directly, but hardly morally. UNICEF and WWF on the other hand are without a doubt dependent on IKEA's money.

It is exactly this shield of bought and muzzled NGOs and a handful of others equally-bought charity projects that IKEA can wheel out if a media tornado is on the horizon. For the management of the company it is in reality always more important to look good to the outside world than what is in fact happening every day behind the blue-yellow façade. Up until a few years ago, it was even forbidden to reveal the number of IKEA catalogues produced to the outside the company. Ingvar was very worried that someone would convert the volume of the catalogue to number of felled trees and hectares of clear-felled forest. IKEA is in other words not much better than the 'jungle-capitalists' condemned by Ingvar. If anything they are worse, since very few multinationals or other companies have such vast needs for access to forest timber as big and steadily growing IKEA.

The climate – an interesting question of no importance

The earth's climate is the great challenge of our generation. Never before has an environmental question been so high on the agenda across the world. Even people who previously arrogantly dismissed any consideration for the environment, heads of governments and company managers, have bit by bit been forced to change tack. And time is short. The combined carbon monoxide emissions of humanity have to be drastically reduced for the climate not to change dramatically. Never before have such great expectations been placed on one area as now – environmental engineering. Those in power all over the world continue to think that we can go on driving cars, travel by plane and carry on polluting like before, and believe that everything can be fixed by new green technology. That any technical sector anywhere ever would be able to solve even a fraction of these major problems in twenty years must be the biggest self-deception of the century. The truth is probably that only a dramatic change in consumer patterns will solve our climate problem. Obviously environmental technology will help, but the basis is and remains, help to self-help. When you and I realize that driving to work every day or travelling by air to Thailand on holiday cannot continue we will at least be nearer a solution.

IKEA is unfortunately not a fortunate exception to environmental problems. On the contrary IKEA's carbon monoxide emission is enormous compared to other big groups of companies. An outsider might think that all the transports from far away to stores in Europe and North America are the villains in this drama, as well as all the customers who drive to IKEA-stores. In fact, more than half of the company's carbon monoxide emissions come from the manufacturing of products in materials such as plastic, metal, glass and other materials which vast amounts of energy. The solution would obviously be either to change materials or make the manufacturing process more energy efficient. Transports correspond to 6–7 per cent of the total emissions of the group, the pollution from stores even less.

IKEA have started a new project at group level in order to diminish emissions from the stores. They have tested solar panels and the idea is also that many stores will be issued with their very own wind turbines on the roof. The only problem is that today's wind turbines need an average wind speed of 9 m/s. I dare say that no roof on any IKEA-store experiences anywhere near such an average wind speed. But it will lead to positive publicity. At IKEA such manipulation is usually called a 'false nose'. Meaning that you take an ineffective decision, a non-decision, instead of solving the real problem: in this case, the enormous emissions of carbon monoxide from the group. And so new state-of-the-art energy-efficient spotlights are put in the stores instead of finding a substitute for plastic in IKEA products. They plan electric sockets for electrical cars in the store car parks instead of looking for new manufacturing processes for metal.

These non-decisions become a façade to hide behind. The truth is that the IKEA-board has not got an ideas how to tackle its massive emission problem. There is no agenda, no believable strategy. Only the publicity plan to put wind turbines on the roof of the stores. There have been attempts at tackling the enormous emissions, from within but IKEA's leading environmental manager (but not the most senior) left recently because of purchasing manager Göran Stark's and others' die-hard opposition to effective measures. An opposition which is not only sanctioned by Kamprad, but also has his finger-prints over it. Ingvar is really very mistrustful about environmental issues in general and the climate question in particular. His conviction is that every step taken which could really put a break on IKEA's emissions, for example to replace all plastic materials and to introduce new manufacturing techniques, will drive up the price on the end product. For him a lower price at IKEA is obviously far more important than the environmental question. On the INGKA-board he has therefore opposed every suggestion to take charge of IKEA's emissions.

Ingvar's line of reasoning must be that nobody should ever be able to penetrate what exactly is going on at IKEA with regards to the environment. So wind turbines and solar panels are used as diversions for the public while IKEA's pollution remains unchecked. IKEA is as opposed as other multinationals to measure and to make their emissions known: the public, and the media have no idea what is going on. And what others don't know can't damage you, seems to be the argument. It is not only an environmentally loathsome strategy, it is also a dangerous one as no improvement whatsoever is happening with regards to the harvesting of raw material which is the big villain of the piece. This means that the emissions of carbon monoxide caused by IKEA increase with the growth of the company, that is at least +20 per cent annually. Put in a different context, IKEA will within a maximum of four years double their emissions of greenhouse gases at a time when almost all companies are doing their utmost to reduce them.

IKEA has furthermore had a weak environmental manager for many years in Thomas Bergmark who rubs shoulders with the environmental movement and environmental journalists at conferences instead of using his position to make much needed changes internally. The image of IKEA as the good environmental company has, I admit, been created by Bergmark, but with Ingvar's approval. Once he let it slip that the company was about to cut emissions by 25 per cent, but then he was very nearly fired by an irate Peter Kamprad. A not enviable situation exactly.

If you compare IKEA's non-existent climate strategy with that of General Electric, GE, which for many years competed for the place of the world's largest company, the differences are striking. GE is quoted on the stock exchange and has subsidiaries in the most diverse of sectors, from the television network NBC to parts of nuclear power stations and airlines. Large groups of companies or conglomerates, which run a great variety of varying activities, are unusual. On top of that, it also has good profitability and an uninterrupted successful upward trend of success, which is still even more unusual. The company's group managers are not only considered to be the best of their class, they have, like the former manager Jack Welch, become legendary within the business world.

That is why it is not surprising that GE has a strong climate strategy which was introduced by Jack Welch's successor, CEO Jeff Immelt, a few years back. Immelt was subjected to a lot of criticism both from big shareholders but also internally, but was determined to follow the road he thought was the path to future success. He called his plan *Ecomagination* and it quickly became a veritable success, since the managerial structure and culture of the company created an imposing discipline. The first step was to produce efficient measurement methods and to put a diagnosis on the enormous emissions from GE's industrial activity. After this review, strategies to stop the carbon monoxide increase were developed. One of Jeff Immelt's closest co-workers was given the task of directing the challenge. Within 3–4 years GE managed to through focused and hard work reduce the carbon monoxide emissions by 30 per cent. And this while it preserved or even improved profitability. IKEA and Kamprad closing of their eyes to IKEA's enormous emissions of carbon monoxide because a reduction would drive the price and so diminish the profits of the company is not only deeply irresponsible, it is a complete moral failure of the company.

Scratches in the façade

The modus operandus of IKEA is to hide behind façades, go long on excuses or blame subcontractors. If a scratch appears in the façade, charitable ventures or the negligent subcontractors are promptly high-lighted or blamed. Look how good we are!' IKEA exclaims and so divert the attention from the down factory to the children in India or whatever it may be. As mentioned, the media was not aware of IKEA's projects on Borneo or in India earlier since those trump cards were literally speaking up IKEA's coat-sleeve. The surprise effect always works and a quick change in focus happens in the media to the good guy who 'happened' to make a mistake, but who still on the whole does so many good things.

Soon WWF or similar closely linked organizations will come to the rescue, terrified that the financial support from IKEA will run dry. They'll say: 'Of course it is unfortunate, but no company tries so hard as IKEA to do the right thing in a part of the world where mistakes often happen.'

The media, always looking for news and are not in any way familiar with these complex questions, quickly swallow the bait since they automatically want to think well of IKEA. Voilà, the environmental villain IKEA becomes the good guy of the media in an afternoon. How does this happen?

First and foremost the magic trick depends on IKEA's extremely strong brand which over the years through hard work has created the image of the good company. With the successes both Ingvar and his lifework have achieved a status of national treasure. And nobody can or wants to think badly of the good company and its founder. IKEA and Ingvar are and remain infallible in the eyes of the journalists, of the public and also amongst the group's co-workers, after all that is why they work for lower wages at IKEA.

Ingvar Kamprad has during the last years been accused of greed in the media. His standard reply is: 'Me and my family do not get a penny of the IKEA money' and that he therefore is not the world's richest man, sounds more and more hollow. Successful companies and rich people are expected to donate money to different charitable projects, unless they want to seem mean and stingy. Bill Gates and his wife donated a large part of his enormous fortune to charities in the third world. So did the legendary financier Warren Buffet. Giving away your fortune has complicated life for Kamprad. The difference between him and Buffet and Gates is that the latter two realize that money in itself has no intrinsic value. If the money can help others in difficulties then they should lend a helping hand where they can. To Kamprad the money he is hiding, at a rough estimate at least 250 bn SEK (GBP24/$40 billion), represents his own intrinsic value, his raison d'être.

It was exactly the same when I led the project with the Ingvar Kamprad School of Design at the Lund Technical University as with the UNICEF project in India, where the end sum was high but the annual payments less impressive. The yearly contributions were stingy, but over a period of 10-20 years the investment seemed enormous. Ingvar claimed it was the largest donation to the academic world in Swedish history. A statement I today strongly doubt, but my point is a different one. If a donor gives the total sum in one payment the recipient can profit from the growth. Even with modest growth of a few per cent the value of the capital will double every 5-7 year. Ingvar instead seems to prefer to dole out donations over time and so he can profit from the interest on the remaining capital himself.

For as long as I was around Ingvar has been swinging to and fro between unwillingness and loathing when it comes to charity. Up until the middle of the nineties he and his company donated only symbolic figures, an amount of a few million Kroner, to the cancer foundation of Berta Kamprad. The projects with Global Forest Watch and Greenpeace and the rehabilitation of rain forests were the first charitable investments that IKEA became part of. After that followed the designer training at the Lund Technical University, UNICEF and a few other things.

In all instances the amounts were very modest. Kamprad and his colleagues usually maintain that they do not want to donate larger sums since the charities cannot manage to look after the money. Is it possible to be more arrogant? Would it not be more honest to say that you do not want to help further simply because of greed or avarice? A large number of human beings in our world live a life of unimaginable poverty, with serious disease and in many cases not even food for the day. And as always it is the children who suffer the most. The world's last intact natural habitats on land as well as at sea are on the brink of collapse. Perhaps our grandchildren will never be able to experience what we today take for granted. The only ray of hope in this darkness are all the NGOs and UN agencies who actually are doing an enormous job against all odds because the funds are lacking. To say that Médecins Sans Frontières, Greenpeace or the Red Cross neither cannot handle more money from IKEA is twisted. Especially if these words come from a company that prides itself on being ethical.

# 11

# The Kamprad monarchy

*The Russian expansion, INGKA board meeting, a day in late summer towards the end of the nineties*
It all began when Moberg asked me to 'check if we should not establish ourselves in Russia'. Obviously Ingvar had already subtly raised the question with Anders and he thought the idea was brilliant. So I went to Russia a couple of times, I met IKEA's small mail-order company there and people from the Moscow embassy. After this I put together a memo about risks and possibilities in the country where IKEA only a few years earlier had been robbed of an entire sawmill by the mafia.

I need to point out that this was at an early stage of Glasnost so people, buildings and infrastructure were still tragically shabby in a kind of eastern European way. And in this realm the mafia and the newly rich oligarchs reigned freely. One of these oligarchs courted his beloved by putting her picture with the text 'I love you' on all the big billboards (and there were thousands) for two weeks – in the whole of greater Moscow. It was also because of security reasons impossible to move around freely in the chaos that was the capital of Russia at the time.

I presented my memo to the group managers. Everyone, apart from Moberg, was against setting up in Russia, since they thought that the risk of losing the entire investment was too high. Everyone gave in with the motivation that 'if you want this Anders, we will back you'.

Later in the summer I presented the same memo to INGKA Holding BV in a hut just outside Älmhult. The decision concerned several billion kroner. The basking sun made the air in the room stifling despite open windows. During the run-through two of the older members as well as Ingvar's three sons slept soundly. Despite the snoring I plodded through my analysis of advantages and disadvantages with an establishment in Russia. A few lame objections were heard from two members who were awake. Ingvar asked a couple of questions. When it came to a decision both the older and the younger members woke up. Everyone nodded mild approval. The decision involving many billions to expand IKEA in Russia had been taken and the autocrat Ingvar looked pleased with himself.

A business family will soon change generations for the first time. A patriarch, a company legend will sooner or later have to, whether he wants to or not, pass on the baton. Can anybody from the family step into his enormous shoes? Who are the three Kamprad sons urged forward to the throne by the elderly monarch? And how will the IKEA of the future look without Ingvar at the helm?

Questions pile up when one attempts to understand what will happen when the generations change at IKEA. Ingvar has on a number of occasions said that none of the sons will become chief executive, but that all three will be involved in the running of the company in different ways. This will not be a problem according to Ingvar. The truth is according to me a different one.

IKEA's hundred top managers who have experienced the trio during a few years, are deeply concerned about the future even if discussions about it take place in private. I myself have witnessed Peter, Jonas and Mathias Kamprad for 15 years. To begin with, at a distance. Then as direct managers and members of boards in a company where I was MD. Ingvar Kamprad is today 83 years old. A fractured thigh could happen at any time and forever remove him from power of his lifework IKEA. What will happen then remains to be seen.

How the division of the estate will look like is on the other hand not so difficult to predict. Certain issues have already been mentioned by the media, others are becoming more obvious within IKEA. Basically the inheritance will be divided equally between the sons when it comes to the assets, that is the entire IKEA group and Inter-IKEA. Where Ingvar's wife Margaretha comes into the division of the estate I do not know. The IKANO-group, an independent company wholly separate from IKEA has already been owned by the trio for many years. On top of this there are all the hidden assets which are controlled by foundations, that is the 250 billion salted away over the years. Everything but an equally divided partition would provoke unnecessary conflict between the sons. And it would run the risk of becoming really complicated since the structure is based on Inter-IKEA taking money out of the group at the same time as it balances the power. Inter-IKEA decides what the stores shall look like on the outside as well as the inside and through that creates an opposite pole to the in assets the much larger IKEA-group. An independent IKEA would otherwise become too strong. Ingvar's work together with the lawyer Hans Skallin when the giant IKEA was construed had as a goal to eliminate conflict between the children and to maintain the balance of power.

The sons' mentor

Göran Lindahl, the previous ABB-manager, is according to what he himself says the person Ingvar has chosen to guide the three sons towards the enormous responsibility they will soon shoulder. One may well consider how wise this choice is. Lindahl, who I have worked closely with during a long period when he was my chairman of the board, is someone who had a poor judgement during his years with ABB  as well as being rather self-centred. When it comes to conflicts between Peter, Jonas and Mathias Kamprad they have been many and bitter, even at INGKA meetings. Göran who is on the board of INGKA Holdiing BV praises himself with having reprimanded 'the boys' (all brothers are well over forty) strongly several times, and so finally settled the arguments. I urge the reader to take this statement with a pinch of salt as in IKEA GreenTech AB where both Jonas, me, Göran and Peter worked together it never happened that Göran dared tell them off harshly. This was irrespective of how serious the situation was. But he was and is rather a powerful force on the side of Peter.

The massive criticism that Peter Kamprad's initiative with the risk capital company GreenTech initially received from the IKEA-group board that he was using IKEA-money to speculate with, as if it were his own, was justified. he had more or less forced a quarter of a billion Kroner from Inter-IKEA and the IKEA-group respectively to fund GreenTech AB.

'I already consider that money lost', the chief executive Anders Dahlvig declared referring to the poor judgement he thought Peter and Göran had shown.

One example was when IKEA GreenTech was about to make its first investment. Contrary to established business practice and business ethics it was Peter Kamprad and Göran Lindahl who themselves chose the first investment object. Let's call it company Q. I am here talking about the fact that a board in a risk capital company both suggests and approves an investment object. They are so to speak keeping a foot in both camps and any assurance that the deal will be done correctly disappears.

This was not enough. Göran Lindahl also appointed himself as chief negotiator and by doing so disregarded me as MD. The fact that a chairman of the board in a company like this himself both negotiates as well as approves the same investment is extremely unusual. Definitely unethical. In practice it meant that Göran and Peter made all the decisions, whilst I as MD had to take responsibility for the deal. As negotiator he carried on in a grand way with very little interest for the views of the opposite party or the company. Lindahl has a reputation for being the world's best negotiator. Here however he did not show any such talents. On the contrary we suffered for almost a year with endless negotiations and increasing lawyer's fees. Neither the lawyers, the accountants nor the patent expert approved our investment after the analysis, the so called due diligence. Despite this Göran continued to push the deal to the end. Finally it all fell through as the experts found a small, but important, technicality which hid a potential claim for damages from the investment of several hundred million.

Earlier on, the crucial question of technical due diligence had emerged. This means that one or more experts in the technology in question analyse the technical portfolio of the company. In the case of Q this was extremely important as the whole deal stood and fell on their very advanced technology. Arguments started about who or whom should be granted access to make the analysis. The Q management were understandably afraid of industrial leakage. When they, despite pressure, refused to let any outsider in, Lindahl simply told GreenTech's board the story that someone he knew, a professor in USA in the same area, had done this due diligence. Obviously no professor from the American West Coast could have seen the company's technology, since it was according to them unique and furthermore locked up in a laboratory on the opposite side of the world.

Perhaps it is easier to understand Lindahl's behaviour if you know that Peter Kamprad paid him a bonus for each investment that was carried through. Something which, as it had happened at ABB a few years earlier, seemed to influence Lindahl's judgement. To anybody who had been watching Lindahl over a period of time, this became clear, but not so perhaps to IKEA's heir to the throne, Peter. Peter, the oldest in the trio, will have the last word once the sons take over.

Personally, I never felt that Göran contributed very much value to any situation I was part of. Well, he is an able chairman at meetings and tactician when he puts together the agenda and determines who speaks. My view, and certainly that of other colleagues, is that Göran Lindahl makes many promises, but he seldom delivers. The edge that the group managers of IKEA have, not to mention Ingvar himself, he certainly does not possess. This did not stop Göran from often brushing aside chief executive Dahlvig (when he was not present) by saying that he lacked the contacts on the ground and would soon be finished.

When it comes to the power between the brothers, the balance is different from the equal division of the assets. Ingvar has several times told the media that Peter has the casting vote precisely because he is the oldest. To anybody who has been part of the board of a company or an association it is obvious that he will become the boss of Mathias and Jonas. In reality this makes Peter Kamprad the IKEA crown prince and after Ingvar, the head of the entire group. In other words he will inherit his father's role as autocrat.

Acquire, inherit, destroy

Ingvar Kamprad has dedicated a large part of his life to finding a way of making IKEA immortal. 'As long as there are human beings on earth there will be a need for IKEA.' This Ingvarian motto covers up a fear that IKEA, his lifework might disappear.

The mistrust which has marked everything he has said and done over the last 70 years, is obviously also about how control over the company can stay with the Kamprad family. We have seen how his mistrust has led to a situation where a disproportionate number of positions of power are filled with people from Älmhult, a place with 8,500 inhabitants of which 2,500 work for IKEA. When it comes to the control over IKEA it is natural for Ingvar for the genes and nothing else to rule since he really does not trust any outsiders. He hardly trust his sons, but they are immediate blood relations and therefore as close as you can get.

'Acquire, inherit and destroy', a saying which suggests that it takes three generations to build a good company and then run it into the ground. Regardless whether it takes two, three or four generations to ruin a family business it is a big challenge every time a new generation is due to take over. How has the succession worked in other Swedish family run businesses? Jacob Wallenberg was appointed at the same time as his cousin Marcus and they have bit by bit built something which has their characteristics and which works in the present-day. Cristina Stenbeck entered both the company Kinnevik and the media scene when her father died unexpectedly and too early. From the beginning she surrounded herself with able bodied managers and put continuity first. At the same time the appointment of Mia Brunell Livfors as MD for the mighty Kinnevik company was perhaps a bit unexpected in such a typical male dominated world as the Stenbeck-sphere. But the sceptics have had to swallow their words as the enterprise has had a positive development over the last years. Finally Karl Johan Persson has taken the throne for H&M in 2009 at a mere 33 years of age. According to information from colleagues who are in a position to judge him he is mature enough to cope with the task. After all his father Stefan Persson did the same things at that age and his importance for the company has been immense throughout the years.

It seems obvious which qualities these persons have in common. First and foremost a sharp intellect which allows them to understand complex matters typical of companies of this magnitude. An intellect which allows them to think strategically, meaning to be able to see the complete picture and to understand the choices at an aggregated level. Furthermore they seem to have a judgement which goes beyond the ordinary and which is their inner compass when they are trying to navigate between the hidden rocks under the water. Last but perhaps not least they have a pronounced social ability which makes them win the trust of their co-workers, that is what we normally would call qualities of leadership.

Not surprisingly both the present chief executive Anders Dahlvig as well as the previous Anders Moberg had exactly these qualities but in a slightly different way from each other. Moberg fits into a group of people with his charisma and ability to lead in a natural way. You see and hear him. He also has a memory like an elephant and a rare capability to understand the most complex questions. 'Your judgement is in reality the only thing that counts' he often said.

Dahlvig is more reserved, but with his razor-sharp intellect and his captivating way he always becomes the central figure in a meeting. A mixture of rational reasoning power and simple common sense. He seems to always know when to speak and when to be quiet and just wait. The leadership of Anders was a shining example for us who worked under him in England.

Ingvar began introducing his sons 3-4 years ago by placing them on all the strategic boards. As fast as they have been working their way into the company and been seen in different places the unease amongst the top managers in IKEA has begun to spread. Many realize that not only will it be extremely difficult to work together with the trio of brothers, rather a few of them also understand that they will possibly lose their jobs within a few years. Most of these managers have worked at IKEA for many years and possess a deep and absolutely necessary competence within the company. Not least in a post-Ingvar IKEA they are extremely important for continuity.

The problem is that the brothers are only familiar with fragments of the activity. On top of that that they often do not recognize their ignorance and either indulge in pure opinions or disregard reality and run the company entirely on the basis of business ratios. This means that they only have a vague idea about what is to be done when larger or smaller problems affect the group. Both Mathias and Peter are despite this ready to have an opinion about most things. The IKEA leadership which will now have as its task to solve problems following Mathias and Peter's criteria, in the smallest detail, has two alternatives. To follow the directives to the letter and stay. Or to leave. I myself have worked with Peter and experienced these threatening situations many times. Senior co-workers like the IOS-manager Josephine Rydberg-Dumont and the chairman of the board on the INGKA-board Hans-Göran Stennert were both dismissed on the orders of Mathias and Peter respectively. Obviously not directly, but Josephine was given a silken brush by Anders Dahlvig and Hans-Göran from his brother-in-law Ingvar. With such a record before they have even formally taken over we get a hint of what is to come. If you can dismiss the most senior managers in the company without hesitation the situation for a manager with a smaller area of responsibility becomes even more serious.

## The Kamprad brothers

So who are then the three brothers? Before answering that question I wish to make the reader aware that this has been by far the most difficult chapter to write. Not because I lack material, despite everything I do know Jonas well as a colleague and Peter rather well on a personal level. Exactly like with everyone else appearing in the book it is the IKEA co-worker and not the private person I am describing. In the case of the sons I only use examples from their private lives in exceptional cases. I wish to point out that my intention has not been to make fun of the IKEA-heirs, but reality is unfortunately as bizarre as I am describing it.

Jonas, the middle brother, is 43 years old and lives in London with his Irish wife and children. He has a clear designer-focus in his education and his interest is in that field. Earlier he designed a handful of pieces of furniture for IKEA, however without any success as sales go. On the contrary, if one is to be honest. As a person Jonas is reserved. That may in part depend on his problems with stuttering, and he seldom answers with more than two to three sentences. From what I have heard he is more assertive at certain range discussions at IOS. Otherwise Jonas is a rather pleasant person in as much as he does not have the same marked need to assert himself as the other two. On the contrary he appears to be content with subordinating himself to the leadership of his brother Peter. I have never heard him bring anything of importance into a discussion. My impression is that he is forced by his father to sit on various forums where the future of IKEA is decided. He appears to be mostly interested in design and range.

If Jonas is a tall and fine-looking man, his younger brother Mathias is short and rather plain. He has a boyish look with staring eyes and a wry smile which indicates a weak self-esteem. Mathias is 40 years old and separated since 5-6 years from his partner with whom he also has children. Their relationship started when they were both working for the Children's IKEA in the nineties. It soon became a 'scandal' in the Småland village since she was a few years older than Mathias, and if I remember correctly she also had children. Not much to complain about one might think, but in the small industrial village of Älmhult this was a big thing. The parents of Mathias were not very enthusiastic.

But to defy conventions and parents is significant for Mathias in more ways than one. He is for example the only one in the family who has been twice exposed in the press for living like a rich man. He lived in a house in a rich area of London which he had trouble selling in 2001 as the market had turned. He asked 1.8 million pounds, which the British tabloid press hackled him for. Some years later the same thing happened again, this time in Sweden. When Mathias bought a house in Falsterbo through an IKEA-company for more than 20 million kronor, the media was bound to find out about it. (This is the house where he lives today.) He lives like a bachelor with alcohol, late nights and ladies are part of his everyday life. A while back, a colleague who knows and is also in a high position told me that, he by himself wrecked a whole restaurant in Copenhagen on one of his many nightly raids there. IKEA immediately paid for the repairs and a fair amount of hush-money. This episode hardly shows the judgement one needs to run a company with 150,000 employees in the future. Just imagine that another IKEA-manager irrespective of level, had done something similar – from what I know it has never happened – he would have been let go off just like that and with great speed.

In the end Mathias was given the job of MD for IKEA Denmark, when the at that time European manager Bengt Larsson paid by losing his job when he refused to comply with Ingvar's wishes. The official version is that Mathias managed to turn the company's negative growth around. The correct version of Mathias' actions is that all strategic decisions required for a turnaround had already been taken. All he needed to do was to sit back and wait for the success. On the other hand he managed to become intolerable amongst his co-workers during his two years there. As a character he becomes violent and autocratic as soon as something goes against him. I have amongst other things seen him during the range weeks in Älmhult when the entire IKEA-world's managers are present. As soon as he does not like something during the pre-sentations with maybe 30-40 people in the room he goes on the attack. He forces through his ideas, his truths. It is an embarrassment in a company which has discussion as one of its principal tools. Mathias was at the time (and probably still is) convinced that his range framework of 3,000 items was the only correct one. The fact that nobody else, neither in that room or anywhere else, agreed with him seemed in no way take relevant to him. I have not worked with Mathias enough in order to be able to have an opinion on his talent. But his lack of judgement is worrying, and he seems to have decided that because of his surname IKEA shall be ruled with a rod of iron in the future.

Peter is the oldest of the brothers with his 45 years and the Kamprad brother I know best. He lives with his Danish wife and their two children in Brussels. Peter has the equivalent of an economics degree, but with a pronounced technical interest. His favourite read is the magazine *Photon* that everyone in the solar energy sector reads. The magazine is dull and thick like a thin telephone directory. A subscription is extremely expensive but Peter made sure that IKEA GreenTech AB paid the bill. Somewhat strange it may seem since he himself is a multibillionaire.

The weight of taking over IKEA after his father unfortunately seems to have gone to his head. It has gone so far that people are laughing behind his back. In his eagerness he has done all he can to be like his father. Facial expressions, the walk, the laugh, the phrases, 'the dyslexia' where he also writes artickle like his father, the dialect, the look, well even the voice. At times he manages to do perfect imitations of how his father characteristically talks to people. The problem is just that it becomes strained. Furthermore he seems to have inherited a surplus of his father's worst sides. He has a fiery and unpredictable temper and from one minute to the next he can let off violent tirades. A temper that can be triggered when he does not get his own way 100 per cent. He has a fixation on detail and can force a board or a business advisory meeting to occupy themselves for hours with silly details while he is totally uninterested in strategic questions. He lacks his father's ability to move between the smallest level to a strategic level and to see things in context and as a whole. From what I have seen and heard all three sons lack exactly this vital capability to understand context, to see totality and to think strategically.

Peter also lacks leadership qualities. He will after all any day now become the boss over a giant empire and lead 150,000 people. His leadership works for as long as things are going his way, if not he becomes furious and issues his ultimatum, no matter how insignificant the issue. This is something that both myself as Göran Lindahl brought up on several occasions but he just carried on in the same way. However Peter has a social skill and he can be both charming and pleasant. Sadly that helps little when the charm quick as lightning and without warning can change into a fit of rage. The result of his unpredictability is that everyone around him walks on eggshells. Therefore the creativity his father so skilfully brings out in people never happens. Instead people near him are reduced to helpers who are there only to carry out his decisions. Peter is furthermore hardly more than of average intelligence, apart from one area, techniques such as solar power and LED-lamps. Here he has a Asperger-syndrome-like memory down to the tiniest detail. He is however convinced of his own excellence in most other questions, too. He does ask specialists for advice at times, but most of the time it is as if Peter has already made up his mind in advance and is only looking for confirmation for his ideas.

One thing I often thought about during my time with Peter and Jonas was why they were so frenetically protected from the media by the people around them. There may of course be pure security reasons, but the threat against their father must be far greater and he appears on TV and radio from time to time. My conclusion was that the brothers were being protected from themselves, from their own incapability becoming exposed in the headlines of the newspapers and on the television screens.

One thing is beyond doubt, nobody in the trio has inherited the business sense of their father. Ingvar is as we know capable of getting blood out of stones. A colleague told me how he had participated in meetings with Ingvar and his sons and how Ingvar had given all the brothers a good talking-to exactly because they had been such clots both in share dealings as in their private lives and lost enormous sums of money because of their incompetence.

If you want to find an explanation as to why one son stammers to a degree that he hardly says anything, another son is driven by a massive inferiority complex and drinks and parties like an immature 18-year old and one son who tries to become his father at 45 years of age you must possibly look towards Ingvar. Just as funny, charming and cuddly as their father can be, he can also be just as patronizing and domineering. No other human being I have ever met has Kamprad's ice-cold authority when he is in the right mood. He has an inimitable ability to instil fear in everyone he meets. I believe that the arrogance and autocratic ways that Peter and Mathias have as their distinctive characteristics and also Jonas's withdrawal is a direct mirror image of a partly brutal and always authoritarian upbringing. Ingvar has said on TV that his father Feodor raised him with the belt in one hand. When the reporter asked him if that was not awful he was first baffled as if child battering was the most natural thing in the world.

How it was at home with the family Kamprad in the sixties I obviously cannot know, but how else can you understand that none of the three brothers, who obviously all lack both interest and aptitude to become big company leaders, have rebelled and chosen another route than IKEA? Or have become so brutally dictatorial? Or that they still in their forties have such respect for or rather subservience to their father that they hardly dare open their mouths in his presence?

Fear of death

As he has grown older Ingvar has on occasions been affected by mounting fear of death. In his eagerness to put a damper on his fear that IKEA will collapse after his death he turns to his trusted old friends in the organization. They in the latter part of their middle age. A close colleague told me about Ingvar's worries in the summer of 2008. 'My three sons are hopeless. Promise me, dear Bosse, to make sure that IKEA survives despite them...'

After such talk to a number of old men at IKEA, the rumours about the founder's fears spread like wildfire. And obviously the message sooner or later reached the Kamprad sons. If, during your childhood you have been subjected to such an authoritarian upbringing as they were, your only mission in life becomes placating your father. Everything else is of secondary importance. Clearly rumours that your father thinks you are stupid is a harsh smack in the face which erases any self-esteem you may have managed to foster in the meantime.

I myself experienced this at the beginning of August 2008.

We launched IKEA GreenTech AB in the media and the result was a success. They wrote about us in 50 different countries, and newspapers from near and far away got in touch. We had not expected such attention in our wildest dreams. After the board-meeting Peter was reading through an article from *Svenska Dagbladet* and an interview with me as MD. Suddenly he jumps up from the chair and stares at me:

'Why did you say that there will be 8-10 employees?'

'Because we will probably need a few co-workers more in order to wisely invest the sum of half a billion. There is hardly any risk capital company in the world working with less collaborators to invest this much money in a sensible way.'

'I have no confidence in you any longer, Johan', he replied and went back to the article.

In IKEA-language that means that you will be dismissed. Immediately, there and then. I must say that I was rarely threatened with dismissal during the two decades at IKEA. Not just because I had been doing a good job but also because that type of threat was not used in the company. Obviously people did get dismissed at times just lasike in other companies, but they were not threatened first. For Peter Kamprad this was a normal reaction, however. From well-informed colleagues a while later I heard that it was precisely the fear of their father that made Peter and his brothers behave this way.

I was not dismissed, but it was the beginning of the end for Peter and me. As soon as he had calmed down he would apologize, but then the damage had already be done and the trust, my trust in him anyway, gone. For the first time in twenty years it occurred to me that it was time for me to separate myself from IKEA.

The mistake of his life

At a family meeting a few years back perhaps the biggest mistake Ingvar ever made regarding his succession at IKEA happened. At that time Hans-Göran Stennert

(Margaretha's brother and Ingvar's brother-in-law) was the chairman of the board at INGKA Holding BV. The career of Hans-Göran at IKEA has been long and successful. The bathroom series PERISKOP is one of his pet concerns and despite the fact that 20 years have gone past since he as product manager brought it out, it still lives on. It is a success that is only granted to a few products since 30 per cent of the range is changed every year. Hans-Göran is a very talented person with a judgement in tricky questions which goes beyond that of most people's. Both within production, purchase, range development as well as retail and logistics he has an imposing breadth and depth. Far more than anyone else within IKEA that I have met, apart from Ingvar himself of course. Furthermore he has an authority and a winning way in all relationships with colleagues at all levels in IKEA.

But Hans-Göran Stennert made a mistake. Frightened by all the weaknesses and poor judgement of Peter Kamprad he tried promoting Mathias as a suitable head of the family after the retirement of Ingvar. Peter's reaction was brutal. Shortly afterwards Stennert was dismissed as INGKA chairman. What happened was that the discussions were so heated that Stennert felt obliged to ask if he as chairman of INGKA he had the trust of the sons. Peter was clear that he no longer had any trust in his uncle, which meant the same thing as his dismissal. Stennert was replaced by Göran Grosskopf and was banished from the absolute top of IKEA to a few marginal appointments in IKEA's equivalent of Siberia (Japan and China). Peter remained as Ingvar's choice and as the strongest amongst the brothers.

To us on the fringes of the family, the decision came as a shock since Stennert was and is the only person connected with the Kamprad family with the ability to lead IKEA in the future. I personally think that he not only has the capacity to do this, I also believe that he would be able to develop the company in a number of areas. Many have for years tried to understand why Ingvar chooses his in most things useless sons over Stennert but that will remain a mystery. And Ingvar's choice of Peter as head will without a doubt dictate the future of IKEA. In which direction remains to be seen.

The result of Hans-Göran's brutal exit had some unfortunate consequences. A stream of key people, some of IKEA's absolute best co-workers, have left or were dismissed sacked by the brothers. Obviously not directly but on their orders.

Blood is always thicker than water in Ingvar's world. Obviously even if it might risk the survival of the entire IKEA.

That the Kamprad family owns and will carry on running IKEA is obvious to all of us. But it would have been wiser if Ingvar had allowed each of the sons to develop their skills where they would have preferred. Peter would without a doubt have become an able technician. Jonas has an artistic gift and seems to feel unfamiliar and uneasy in the board-room. At the same time he is the only one who has found his own platform within the company, the work with the range. I do not know Mathias well enough to dare say where he would have fitted in. If Ingvar allowed the brothers to leave all the

IKEA boards and work on limited platforms within the company like Jonas, the new Kamprad generation would have been able to take IKEA into the future in a totally different way. Then they would have been working with key processes within the group and not with the totality. For the totality you need a completely exceptional talent. If then their uncle Hans-Göran Stennert was to come back in favour and went on the most important boards of the company then IKEA could go stronger into the future even after Ingvar has left.

Ingvar's latest chief executive

In April 2009 Ingvar and his sons selected as was expected a successor to Anders Dahlvig. Completely unexpectedly it was Mikael Ohlsson who was appointed chief executive.

A more qualified candidate than Mikael does not exist anywhere within IKEA. During his thirty years with the company he has led and developed activities in the whole value chain in different parts of the world. As IOS-manager he showed his social side when he wandered around the open-plan offices in the business areas in order to ask people how they were and how things were going. It may sound banal, but no IOS-manager neither before nor after him has ventured out into real life in that way.

Now and then Mikael gathered all 700 employees at Blåsippan in the small lobby in order to give his view on the state of things. Always easy to understand. Always engaging. 'You often hear that you should consider local variations in price. Don't bother!' he would say in his typical Skåne dialect.

What has characterized Mikael during his career is probably his exceptional intellect. I have earlier talked about his enormous knowledge which at times can almost measure up to that of Ingvar. Like no other Mikael could sit quiet for hours in a meeting to suddenly get up and not just summarize the important bits in a few words on the whiteboard. He was also able to formulate a conclusion out of the hour-long discussions which lifted the entire room.

However perhaps the principal quality of Ohlsson which makes him suitable for the role of KIEA's chief executive is his leadership quality. The top managers I have experienced during my years with IKEA can be divided into two categories: the ones who are self-centred and take over and dominate each meeting they attend, and those who normally don't say very much even when they should. To the former group people like Bengt Larsson and Josephine Rydberg-Dumont belong. To the latter Anders Dahlvig who very rarely raised his voice. Mikael Ohlsson on the other hand was sensitively capable of altering between being quiet and observant, to more active and inquiring in order to bring the process forward to actually putting his foot down. In particular, I remember a meeting with a business area during a range week with Ingvar when Mikael seriously told off a couple of colleagues. It wasn't out of order, I thought, as they had expressly disregarded agreed outlines and were now giving a vague excuse instead of admitting their error in a straightforward way. But I particularly remember that afterwards Ingvar felt sorry for the culprits and complained about Mikael's temper to his brother-in-law Hans-Göran Stennert. The fact that the offenders were responsible for their part in a multibillion enterprise which was put at risk by their incompetence did not count.

This was as far as I remember the first time Ingvar criticized Mikael. During the following years his criticism became more serious. And Ohlsson was to become more and more worn-out by the enormous task he had been put in charge of. Because he was not only IOS-manager, responsible for all range, purchase and logistical questions at IKEA. He had also taken charge of a divided and rather amateurish department in the forests of Småland while being charged with transforming it into a world-class enterprise.

Since he managed this undertaking with honour it is not strange that Mikael pictured himself as the obvious successor after the chief executive Anders Moberg. Moberg had been doing the job for twelve years and was now looking around for other tasks outside IKEA (at the American Home Depot to be precise). But the chief executive job did not go to the favourite Mikael Ohlsson but to Anders Dahlvig. My guess is that there were two things that made Mikael unsuitable in the eyes of Ingvar. First of all Ohlsson has an integrity based on his self-esteem which is difficult to cope with even for Ingvar. I have myself witnessed this during discussions between Ingvar and Ohlsson, where the latter has pushed his ideas far beyond the acceptable. By the acceptable I mean that in a relationship with Ingvar you need to be able to read him in order to understand when you have gone too far. Who is right and who is wrong does not enter into the equation. Ingvar decides. This happened on a couple of occasions and it irritated Ingvar.

The second characteristic of Mikael Ohlsson which was hard to accept for Ingvar is Ohlsson's ability. Despite being the quiet type Mikael managed to completely dominate a meeting with his charisma when he presented his well-informed contributions. Not very unlike Bengt Larsson, with whom Ingvar also had problems, even if he was always brilliant. I believe that Mikael Ohlsson did not get the job of chief executive ten years ago simply because Ingvar could not stand having a bright star next to him.

As a result Mikael was sent into quarantine which was to last ten years. He accepted a job with responsibility for the retail business in southern Europe. Then two strange things happened. One of them happened to Ohlsson and the other to Dahlvig but both were closely connected as Mikael still wanted Anders's job.

The fact that Dahlvig was 'tired' was a recurring mantra for Peter Kamprad and Göran Lindahl. The expression should be viewed rather as condemnation of a chief executive with ten extremely successful years behind him. What it referred to was a reluctance to carry through the developments that the owners, the Kamprad family, are aiming for, rather than 'tired' in the exact meaning of the word. During my last months at IKEA I met Anders on a number of occasions, and since I had known him for two decades I can testify that he was not tired. On the other hand he was in the way of the development of the company that the family wanted.

'Once we have got rid of Dahlvig then...', as Peter often said. As if something would open the floodgates for a fantastic development within IKEA. INGKA Holding's present chairman, the greying taxation professor Göran Grosskopf, even went so far that he during Mikael Ohlsson's introduction speech at Blåsippan in Älmhult brought up Anders Dahlvig's alleged tiredness four times. In the end the slightly rejected Dahlvig asked Grosskopf in front of the entire gathering: 'Do I really look that tired, Göran?'

The other remarkable thing is that Mikael Ohlsson was restored as a favourite by Ingvar. He was a completely unexpected successor to Dahlvig since Ingvar extremely seldom, if ever, changes his mind about people once they have been sent into exile. Why? To me the answer is rather obvious. First and foremost there was no realistic rival candidate. Ingvar realises that a chief executive who knows what he is doing will be essential once the sons take over.

But it is actually exactly in the strength of Mikael's competence where the problems in the future will arise. Once Ohlsson and his group leadership will start to steer IKEA into the future, he will discover that the pleasant and Ingvar-like image of Peter Kamprad has a dark flipside. Because Mikael is not like his predecessors put there to develop IKEA, but appointed to do what the INGKA-board – read the Kamprad brothers – has decided it wants to see happen. To the letter. What was previously broad outlines from INGKA and Ingvar which were carried through with tact in the organization, will in the future be directives over every small detail. The dilemma for Mikael, with his integrity, is that if he opposes and tries to do what he thinks is best for IKEA he will lose his job. And if he applies all the flexibility and readiness to compromise he can, he violates his own personality.

# The rise and fall of IKEA UK

Most people know that a visit to an IKEA store can be a truly unpleasant experience. But however disagreeable a Saturday at IKEA may be with sold-out stock, crowds and queues for everything from checkouts to hot dogs, it is nothing compared to the bizarre exploitation and ill-treatment of customers by the IKEA group from the middle of the nineties and onwards in Great Britain.

It may sound somewhat extreme to accuse a company of exploiting its customers. The fact is that this is the most appropriate word I can find for it. Let me start at the beginning in order to describe how Great Britain became the golden goose of IKEA. The company established itself relatively late in Britain, in 1987, in comparison to almost all economically important nations in Europe. The first store was in Warrington outside Manchester, after which followed another four stores in the Midlands, Newcastle and London. A substantially larger store was built in the London council of Brent Park, an area known for its social problems and high criminality (the store is nowadays called Wembley on the company homepage). Next to the store, the UK managing director at the time Birger Lund erected an ugly discolored building with far too many floors which was to house the British head office for a number of years. Nine years later, in 1995, IKEA still had five stores in a country which counted well over 50 million inhabitants and was one of the largest economies in the world. In other words, the company and its brand led a dormant existence there.

But the Swedish home furnishing company eventually grew in importance with the British public. In the company's particular niche of Scandinavian-designed furniture at low prices, competition was, compared to many other IKEA-markets, largely nonexistent. At the beginning of the nineties the IKEA brand reached a critical mass as far as the degree of recognition was concerned and turnover took off at the five stores. Also internally within IKEA, not least with its owner Ingvar Kamprad, the enormous potential of the UK market became obvious. IKEA had become the in-thing in Britain and IKEA UK an established part of the group.

Under the leadership of Birger Lund, IKEA UK was not a very impressive selling machine. Birger was an able financial controller, and later became manager for the Kamprad brothers' own multimillion group IKANO with banking as an important activity. However not only did he, as a manager, lack the deep commercial knowledge that IKEA needed in Britain, at the time the entire group lacked a coherent commercial concept. Most things did therefore not work out well in IKEA stores. In the British stores things were even worse. The room interiors faced the wrong way against the customer flow, price labels were in the wrong place, if items had a price label at all, bestsellers were displayed to their disadvantage and important products were constantly running out. These were blunders that within IKEA Germany, the shining star within the group at the time, were considered as breach of duty with a subsequent written warning or even dismissal, but they seemed not to stand in the way of promotion on the other side of the English channel.

It was hardly surprising when Birger Lund was promoted sideways and upwards to manager of IKEA Sweden by IKEA's pompous Northern Europe manager Bengt Larsson. Bengt's previous financial controller, Ingvar's former assistant and the future Chief Executive Anders Dahlvig became UK manager.

During the years with Dahlvig at the helm, IKEA UK Ltd went from a backward position both, financially as well as commercially, to the top of the IKEA group. Dahlvig had rare qualities of leadership and breadth of knowledge. He instilled confidence in his British co-workers who during the previous years had been deprived of their self-esteem by conceited Swedish managers speaking English much like the Swedish chef in the Muppet show. Dahlvig took advantage of the IKEA-fever that at the time was spreading across England, by making the most of the marketing so that the stores were filled with customers, and by drastically elevating the commercial standards to make as much money from them as possible.

New stores were built in Leeds (mentioned later in the book), Thurrock and Nottingham whilst the old ones, by now rather run down metal boxes, were rebuilt and refurbished. However, during the same period of this wave of success at IKEA UK, the first British law on retail outlets saw the light of day. The main purpose of this legislation was to protect shops in the inner cities against competition from the enormous shopping precincts which were mushrooming outside the town centres. The result was that IKEA, being a large foreign company with enormous stores outside the town centres as part of its strategy, would rarely be granted permission to construct new centres.

IKEA UK rapidly shot up in the sales statistics and suddenly the UK divsion had the biggest growth rate within the group. It was an outstanding success. The crowds of visitors grew dramatically year on year in a way that the group had never experienced anywhere else in the world. But it was millions of new and old IKEA-enthusiasts who were forced to share with each other the same miserable experience as before, in the same handful of stores. Each year the pressure on the stores, on the co-workers and the logistical resources increased to cater for a flow of customers that never ran dry.

Naturally there were plenty of advantages with the enormous growth of IKEA in Great Britain. First and foremost the turnover increased. Within a few years the market went from being one of the IKEA-world's more mediocre selling machines to a position amongst the third or fourth most successful, on a par with Germany and North America, in monetary terms. Obviously it is not enough to just have enormous crowds of customers in order to increase sales. Equally important is to put up the prices as much as the wallets of the customers allow. But that is not one of IKEAs core strategies. It was Dahlvig who introduced this unusual pricing strategy in the UK, nonetheless. After all IKEA had always stood by the motto 'beautiful furniture at affordable prices'. Having had previous experience as a successful controller he decided that since there was no competition at all IKEA could demand any price they wanted in the British market. This was his interpretation of the comprehensive pricing strategy of the group: 'IKEA prices should always be ten per cent lower than comparable products by competitors'. All of a sudden IKEA found itself in a market without competition on comparable products and it quickly lost all self-control. Soon enough IKEA UK had the highest sales price of the entire world's subsidiaries apart from IKEA USA (whose high price are pushed up by exceptionally high marketing costs rather than policy), an embarrassing pricing strategy the company has maintained to this day as far as I can judge from prices in Europe.

I will never forget how my co-workers from the IKEA business area Storage, Media and Dining and I tried to get the British management to abide by the global pricing strategy of the group within our department only to be rebuffed year after year. An unfamiliar arrogant attitude that only profits counted while our competitors actually had higher prices had crept into IKEA UK. When we went to London, for example, in order to check the ugly face of this policy became clear at the first attempt, at B&Q in Thurrock, a few hundred metres from the IKEA store in the same shopping area. Several other storage shelves were 20-30 per cent cheaper than IKEA's BILLY and IVAR. Within IKEA company culture this was, and is, an absolute mortal sin. Naturally the IKEA UK MD Göran Nilsson knew that this was the case. And soon the management and company culture of IKEA UK was about to descend into chaos.

One might have thought that an expanding company such as IKEA UK would become a bit less tight-fisted as far as its operational budget was concerned. Extreme pressure on sales demanded plenty of staff as well as a few other extraordinary measures in order to be able to handle the chaos in the stores. Not so, however. Ingvar let the IKEA group's executives know that the newly found power house within the IKEA family should not only have the highest rate of increase on its sales, they were also expected to have even higher pricing levels than before. The result was that IKEA UK was quickly granted the ungrateful task of covering financially for its less successful sister-companies around the world. At this time it was really only IKEA Germany which financed the brand's progress worldwide. Germany had carried this burden since the eighties, which is why Britain was welcomed as another cash cow.

During these years up until 2000, IKEA's British subsidiary showed a profit which in percentage points surpassed the cost level of many sister-companies. Swedish legislation regarding company secrets unfortunately prohibits me from quoting the exact figures, but let me give a fictitious example by comparison. Say, the Hennings company runs ten textile stores and in all has a turnover of one billion kroner per year (£90/$140 million). The turnover of one billion corresponds to 100 per cent. The company's profits after having paid the purchase of all goods and materials are, say, 50 per cent. From the remaining 50 per cent it must cover all the costs of running the company and make a sufficient profit. The total cost of running Hennings corresponds to 40 per cent of turnover. Thus Hennings makes a profit 10 per cent (turnover less purchases less running costs), which is a fine result for any company. Now imagine a case, as with IKEA UK Ltd, where profits are actually higher than the cost of running the entire company! Very few retailers like that exist anywhere in the Western world.

Obviously such profit levels cannot be healthy for a subsidiary in the long run, as it amounts to ruthless exploitation of the customer. Only someone who shopped or worked in the British stores at this time can really understand the immense pressure both customers and co-workers were subjected to when far too many people crowded into a far too small space day in day out. As a customer you could frequently go neither forward nor backward in the store aisles, but were forced further into the interior of the building like penned cattle. This was a common state of affairs in the Wallau store in Germany when I first started working for IKEA. But there it happened one or two days a week. In the case of the UK the crush soon became unbearable throughout the week, and in many stores during all opening hours. This was a totally unique situation within the IKEA-world. Nowhere else – neither before nor after – has the customer experience been so unbearable, for such a long period, as in the British stores.

Just as unique was the fact that the crowds and the confusion became worse by the day, week and year. As soon as we thought that the limit of what was bearable had been reached we ended up in an even worse chaos. A shocking example was Brent Park in London where it was not physically possible to expand and catch up with demand irrespective of whether the authorities allowed store expansion or not. Soon enough each British store faced this reality.

With the quickly increasing volumes of items which were to be pushed through each unit in order to satisfy the customers a limit was reached. In other words IKEA discovered that there was an absolute limit to how many pallets with IKEA-products you could actually store and sell in a single store. Without new licences to establish new units or to expand, this physical limit consisted of the four walls of the store in the form of storage and sales areas. Confronted with this fact there was only one thing to do, cut the number of items on sale. The starting point was the range – the number of different items on offer to the customer – which was considerably more limited than with any comparable competitor. The London stores first cut their range at a rapid pace, then the rest of the British stores followed suit. This was done in such a dramatic manner that small stores in the Swedish and Norwegian provinces – which as far as turnover and number of customers were only a fraction of the British giants – soon offered a far larger range to their customers.

Anders Dahlvig was promoted to deputy Europe manager at the beginning of this process by the new Europe manager Bengt Larsson, hence Dahlvig's direct responsibility for what was about to unfold in IKEA UK Ltd was limited. The new MD was Göran Nilsson, who in many ways followed the lead of his chairman of the board Bengt. This duo, must, together with the chief executive Anders Moberg, but above all Ingvar Kamprad himself, be considered ultimately responsible for the exploitation of the British co-workers, customers and stores.

Faced by a country where new planning permission was, on the whole, impossible to obtain, and definitely not to the degree that the pace of growth required, IKEA's management, under Ingvar's supervision, nonetheless put all their efforts into one thing: planning permission. Despite the fact that all previous efforts with the local authorities had failed, Larsson and Nilsson carried on with a belligerence that defied reason. Over a period of 7-8 years IKEA only obtained the odd planning permit every other year. At the same time the company was growing by 15-25 per cent each year, and the pressure became enormous.

A group of stores that were full to bursting point ought to reasonably have asked themselves if the strategy for planning permissions was sustainable. They were hardly getting any permits. The situation was so serious that not even a hypothetical rate of establishing 2-3 new UK stores annually would have alleviated IKEA's growing pains. One obvious alternative would have been to divert the flow of customers from the stores into mail order, or rather internet selling. The IKEA brand was red hot in the country. Publicity and catalogues were pumped out at an ever increasing rate. It seemed that the British people could not get enough of the company's products. Attempts to steer the customers away from the stores to other forms of outlets should have been the only feasible way to reduce the pressure on customers in the stores. Even a less successful home page with sales of parts or the entire IKEA range would have become an immediate success. As far as I am aware (I left IKEA UK in 1996) a number of attempts at convincing the company to get going with web based sales were made around the millennium period, but Ingvar put a stop to all efforts in that direction. IKEA's dictator prevailed.

Ingvar's resistance to internet sales seems strange. Ingvar and his co-workers wanted to, at all costs, keep IKEA UK as cash cow for an expansion which was superior to everything within the group. At some point fairly soon the stores in Britain would reach boiling point, the logistical flow would collapse, customers would turn their backs on the company and the wave of success would peter out.

Obviously the brilliant and omniscient Ingvar, as well as the Chief Executive and management, must have known what was going on in the British stores. In detail. Anything else would be unthinkable within IKEA where the Chief Executive was required to constantly be one step ahead of Ingvar in his feeling for and control over the company s domain. But no one chose not to act.

I don't think that the resistance to a solution on Ingvar's part came from greed. If that were the case he would have been pleased about the English super profits year in and year out. That would be against his nature. Ingvar would never show any joy over profits and definitely not over super profits. With his focused expression and his lack of participation at board meetings he showed that he was by no means displeased. This brilliant business man could never be pleased. IKEA is his baby and all parts of IKEA are just as dear to him. But one part had to be put back in order for another to be able to grow in the future. His decisions were completely rational from his own point of view and were, essentially, two fold.

Profit is a fundamental necessity for IKEA to survive and grow, in line with its company culture. It may sound obvious, but the unique thing here is that profit should never be allowed to become a goal in itself, only a means to develop further. With bad profits in most other subsidiaries during this period, and a Germany which had achieved such high market shares that the company had reached a zenith in that market, it was time for a new cash cow. This naturally became IKEA UK Ltd.

Ever since the company opened its first store in the Swedish village of Älmhult, a tiny, completely unknown place to everyone apart from the villagers themselves, cars had been the key to the success of the company. A long time before other retailers, stores on cheap land which could only be reached by car became a prerequisite for success. By the turn of the millennium IKEA had well over one hundred stores which could actually only be reached by car. Whether the store was in France or Norway, a car was a requirement in order to reach the store. To open a new sales channel like internet sales, is not something Ingvar Kamprad would ever have seriously considered. As I discuss later in the book, he maintained that web-based selling as a phenomenon, irrespective of country, would threaten the attraction of the stores in the long run. Customers would, according to Ingvar, simply order from the sitting room sofa rather than bothering to visit a store. If the customers were able to pick the best out of what IKEA offers, the surplus sales (all those extra items that you do not really need but you still put in your trolley) would not happen.

There are bound to be many important, experts who, with years of experience behind them, would argue against his point of view. But at IKEA there is ultimately only one person who decides: the founder Ingvar Kamprad. One of the biggest problems in the group is that each and every person he meets within IKEA, and elsewhere, is a yes-man. On the whole, extremely able professionals, but ultimately his puppets. I was, after all, no different when I worked with him. You can discuss business for hours with Ingvar, but definitely not the principles of IKEA's business. They were sacred. As far as I am aware only one person has seriously told Ingvar off and survived and that is Bertil Torekull who wrote the book about IKEA. On the other hand Torekull was not employed by IKEA. Therefore for someone to in earnest take a stand and defend the UK stores in the board room and argue passionately for internet sales against the expressed approval of the old man, is completely unthinkable. Someone doing so would have been without a job before he even got to the last page of his power point presentation.

At the beginning of 2000, competition caught up with IKEA in the UK market both regarding price as well as design. The IKEA niche of Scandanavian-designed furniture, at high quality and low prices, started to become more and more narrow. This is, in reality, not so remarkable. Every economics student reads microeconomics and learns about supply and demand. In short the theory says that if one player in a market charges substantially high prices because he is alone, new players will be attracted by the surplus profits a high price formation allows. IKEA UK had the highest sales prices amongst more or less all IKEA countries during this period. We have also seen that this subsidiary maintained surplus profits which exceeded any comparison both within as well as outside the company.

Consequently it soon enough became just as crowded in the marketplace as in the IKEA stores. Customers chose at an accelerated speed to not accept unpleasant crowds and crazy prices which were easily beaten by the competitors. The fallout for IKEA UK was serious. Suddenly the growth in sales halted and was turned into lost market shares. Setback followed setback as dropping sales figures were quickly followed by demands for cost-cutting from the group's management. The golden boy of the IKEA group had within a period of nearly one year been put back in the corner of shame from whence it had come a decade earlier and had become IKEA's problem child in the worst sense of the word.

Ironically, IKEA UK in the end got both all the stores it needed as well as the internet sales the circumstances required. Since 2006 a large part of the range is sold via the net (if only for the moment) in England and Wales. The 18 stores which IKEA UK now covers England, Wales, Scotland and Northern Island. But it seems a paradox that this much-needed expansion, in order to ease the pressure on the existing stores and to make the customer experience more pleasant, came several years after IKEA UK's enormous growth in turnover and customers.

# Afterword

Notwithstanding that in this book I have brought up criticism, in some parts very severe criticism, I look back on twenty exciting years with IKEA with pleasure. Ingvar Kamprad is without a doubt the most fantastic and inspirational person I have ever had the advantage of having worked with. I think of Ingvar and all the colleagues and all the fun we have had together with warmth. One part of my heart will always be in IKEA. But today, looking back, I also realize what I have missed during all these years. Dialogue. An honest, open and critical dialogue about IKEA. The dialogue that really ought to be taking place both inside and outside IKEA, but that unfortunately has been completely absent behind the blue and yellow walls. Earlier we simply talked about loyalty. Nowadays words like alignment are used more often. The meaning is the same. Certain things are not to be questioned, not discussed by anyone outside a small chosen group of trusted people, mainly the IKEA-board INGKA Holding, Ingvar himself and his sons who to an increasing extent rule in detail over the group.

I maintain that this dialogue is fundamental. Because very few outsiders know hardly anything about IKEA and because probably nobody has not even a fragment of a comprehensive picture, no journalist has ever been able to penetrate the IKEA-wall. IKEA is one of the world's strongest brands. IKEA counts 150,000 co-workers. Including the suppliers and subcontractors 500,000-1,000,000 people depend on IKEA for their survival. Most of them in countries completely void of social safety nets. Still the surrounding world only gets to know a few nicely put together press releases, the odd interview with a chief executive and some seemingly intimate chat with Ingvar in a late summer field in Småland. Why?

The media and the public know rather well what Volvo does and what H&M gets up to, since both companies are listed on the stock exchange. But IKEA remains a mystery. Who benefits from this reserve? That IKEA being a non-listed family-run company has a legal right to remain silent and to act in secret does not mean that they have the moral right to do so. It is rather the other way around. With the size of the company comes a responsibility which must mean more openness and discussions about important issues. That is IKEA's responsibility towards society without which it would never have grown so big. My hope with this book is to initiate a more open dialogue about IKEA. Both inside as well as outside the blue and yellow walls of the company.

The same thing applies to Ingvar Kamprad who is literally a living legend. But in order to do him justice you also have to see his failings. And by that I mean seeing through the façade of alcoholism and dyslexia which he so skilfully hides behind. It will never be possible to understand neither the founder nor his creation unless you at the same time discover what a richly faceted human being Ingvar Kamprad is.

I end this book as I started it. These are my reflections of Ingvar and his lifework IKEA, my truths.

# The Future of Ikea after Ingvar's Death

An interview with Johan Stenebo

*Q: Who is in charge?*

'His sons were not brought up and guided by their father in any sort of way where they could hand over control to anyone outside the family. Their father was quite distrustful of anyone who wasn't a member of the family.'

While Anders Dahlvig, one of Kamprad's trusted lieutenants, is now the chairman of the holding company InterIkea, Stenebo says he is still ultimately answerable to the family. 'Anders Dahlberg is chairman but he can be fired at any time. He's not a puppet, but he's very much under the control of the sons. The Ikea chief executives that have followed Ingvar have been either former assistants or heads of Ikea Sweden, the product design subsidiary, in which Ingvar was most interested.'

*Mathias Kamprad, the most sociable and ebullient of the three, lives in London.*

'Mathias is the strongman I would say, of the three brothers [Mathias, Peter and Jonas]. I think Mathias has succeeded his father and is now at the helm of Ikea. He's not on the board of directors – nor was his father – but he's now running Ikea.'

'Mattias is outgoing, but he's hard to read. He's supposed to be the more gifted of the three sons,' Stenebo said. Mathias sits on the supervisory board of InterIkea, Ikano Group, and is also on the supervisory board of the Interogo Foundation, the enterprise foundation based in Liechtenstein which ultimately controls InterIkea.

'I don't think the sons will ever let go of their control. The unwieldy network of companies was just a way for Ingvar to seemingly separate himself from his wealth. But, whoever controls the foundation controls Ikea.'

*Peter, the eldest, was the brother Ingvar Kamprad initially hoped would replace him. He trained as an economist at a prestigious business school in Lausanne and worked in executive roles inside Ikea for decades, become finance director of the Belgian business. He is now chairman of the supervisory board of Ikano Group, which runs a bank, insurance company, and property company, and also owns Ikea stores in Singapore, Malaysia and Thailand. He lives in Belgium with his wife Laila.*

'Peter is more like an auditor, he's very controlled and into the nitty-gritty. He's very much about detail,' Stenebo said. 'When I worked for Peter, he had a very hard time getting his priorities straight, seeing what was a good thing to do at any moment in time.'

*Jonas, 51, trained as a furniture design in Switzerland, is the least visible of the brothers. In 2013 was reported to live in a house in Kensal Green, London, designed by the Swedish architect Gunnar Orefelt. He also sits on the supervisory board of Ikano Group.*

'Jonas is a quiet man,' Stenebo said. 'He keeps a low profile.'

Q: *What will the sons do?*

'Ingvar boasted that he had been planning for his death since the 1970s, and he handed over his holdings and board positions in the company back in 2013, leaving a relatively small amount of money for his sons and adoptive daughter from his first marriage to inherit on his death.'

'The issue for the sons is unlikely how to change the company's complex holding structure, or a battle over their inheritance. On paper, InterIkea and IkeaGroup are two different entities. But they are the same, the family sits on both. This structure was meant to render ownership opaque. Ikea shouldn't be transparent from a financial point of view – to avoid taxation.'

'The difference, compared with Ingvar, like with everyone else, is that he was a genius and they're not, but in the past five years they've done a decent job as far as I can see.'

'The big challenge however is not tax evasion, the big challenge for Ikea is how to handle e-commerce, that's much more complicated. The problem is that a lot of younger Ikea managers start as bureaucrats. What they are missing is an innovative outlook. If there ever were a time when Ikea needs Ingvar's genius it is now.'

Ingram Content Group UK Ltd.
Milton Keynes UK
UKHW022209190323
418794UK00006B/181

9 781783 341726